ł_

HISTORY OF THE
A. M. E. ZION CHURCH

Part I

1796 - 1872

By

DAVID HENRY BRADLEY, SR.

WIPF & STOCK · Eugene, Oregon

Wipf and Stock Publishers
199 W 8th Ave, Suite 3
Eugene, OR 97401

A History of the A.M.E. Zion Church, Part 1
1796-1872
By Bradley, David Henry, Sr.
Copyright©1956 by Bradley, David Henry, Sr.
ISBN 13: 978-1-5326-8854-6
Publication date 4/12/2019
Previously published by United Methodist Publishing, 1956

To my mother,
CORA ALICE BRADLEY
who shaped my first thought
To the Memory of
Job Mann
who, through the Job Mann Trust
opened the door for ministerial
training
To my Church
for opportunity of service

ACKNOWLEDGEMENTS

The author wishes to acknowledge the invaluable and substantial aid given to him during the writing of this work by Dr. James W. Eichelberger and the Christian Education Department for it was through this Department that the *History of the A.M.E. Zion Church* was undertaken ten years ago. Appreciation is also extended to the late Bishop James Clair Taylor who, through the pages of the *A.M.E. Zion Quarterly Review,* published the first draft of the book.

Our appreciation is given to the Senior Bishop of the Church, Bishop William Jacob Walls, who gave invaluable assistance in securing material on outstanding members of the church who contributed to the anti-slavery movement; to Bishop William A. Stewart for his continual prodding that the book be published; to Bishops Spottswood, Shaw and Jones for their work leading towards publication and to the first named for his extreme kindness where his district was concerned and to Bishop H. T. Medford.

The author likewise wishes to thank the two chairmen of the Board, Bishops Brown and Slade, for their sympathetic interest during the trying period of publication.

The Board of Bishops of the denomination has likewise given valuable encouragement and in many instances gave aid in seeing to its publication. Especially do we thank our own Episcopal District, who, under Bishop W. C. Brown, actively sponsored the book in its pre-publication stage.

The long list of ministers who gave encouragement to the project cannot be given here but to each and every one of them we acknowledge our debt of gratitude.

Our appreciation is likewise extended to the office staff of the Christian Education Department, Miss Elizabeth Madore of Bedford, and Mrs. Harriette Bradley, all who evinced more than ordinary patience in readying the manuscript for review and the publisher.

To the Reader

You will perhaps wonder at the many spellings we have used in designating the same person. In other instances you will note peculiar spelling of ordinary words. The author has carefully noted these differences, has attempted to correct them. In some, however, we have felt that the one or even three writers to whom we have referred knew more about the name than we. For example: there are at least two methods used in spelling Galbreath or Galbraith. Just how the individual wrote it we do not know so both modes are utilized.

In other instances common words have been *misspelled* according to 1955 standards. If the material is a quote we have attempted faithfully to reproduce it.

THE AUTHOR

Preface

THERE IS small doubt that a full history of the African Methodist Episcopal Zion Church in America will ever be told for sealed eternally are the lips of her early leaders, who, in many cases, were not gifted in writing, or, because of circumstances, were unable to open their thoughts and deeds to posterity. Perhaps many of them may have deemed their work so ordinary that that which they did or desired to accomplish was merely a milestone to be reached and passed for loftier aims. At any rate, we here in 1955 have but the barest outline of their thinkings and, scattered throughout this story are missing pages and, in instances, fragments of others.

But this we know, they dreamed large dreams and dared to attain them. Their drumming feet by day and night echoed more than casual ideologies for they brought to Methodism and the Protestant world of America an early battle of human rights and privileges. They showed amazing desire to widen the horizon of individual living beyond freedom of body to freedom of will and expression. Where once this struggle was insignificant within the Church, the African Chapel insisted that a liberal interpretation of the Christ Way demanded democracy wherever men met for prayer and hymn.

Twenty-five years before the 5,000 Stillwellites followed their namesake, William, from the Methodist fold, challenging its ministry on these rights and privileges of laymen and women, leaders of this African Church set out to gain for themselves and their descendants these very ideals. Strangely enough, the Methodist leadership who brought about the Stillwell secession, tolerantly acquiesced to the requests of their "African brethren," in 1796. Perhaps still harder to understand is the fact that this Chapel *followed* their minister, William Stillwell, from the Mother Church but refused any part of the new denomination.

Thirty-two years later the young denomination was forced to reaffirm these rights and privileges and in so doing, tried and expelled a Superintendent who dared to ignore its lay people in annual and quarterly conference.

Again, when organic union became a theme involving first the A.M.E. Church and, later, Mother Methodism, the Church preferred

7

to dismiss the thought of one great Methodism than lay aside this vital principle.

Within the Church itself were strange decisions—to label its chief leadership—*superintendent* rather than *bishop* when all other Methodist bodies, in the main, were using the episcopal form;—to elect these superintendents for a four-year term rather than for life, while her sisters and mother again followed the episcopal pattern. Not until 1868 did she drop the old title of *superintendent* and not until 1880 were her bishops elected for life.

It cannot be said that the African Chapel was an experiment for too purposeful was its establishment and every act. No road was too pioneering, no thought too liberal for these were freedmen, seeking spiritual freedom.

DAVID H. BRADLEY

CONTENTS

CHAPTER I

Mother Methodism, at Home and Abroad

TO ONE privileged to look back over decades of human effort, or as in the case of the eighteenth century, the lack of such enterprise, satisfaction can be gleaned in the ability to see there the whole pattern of life as well as the outcome of these periods of stress and strain. Oftentimes there exists, at first, a term of vigorous, revolutionary effort, which in turn brings its own time of personal satisfaction, dangerous and crippling, and in the end decadence. When this happens it usually depends on a few far-seeing personalities to rescue the situation, not only by promotion of radical and bitterly contested ideas and movements, but by their very efforts to call to arms the placid minds of their contemporaries.

Such was the case when the Methodist movement came to England. One writer declares that England in the eighteenth century was "one vast and political waste; the mere hunting ground of corrupt and dissolute aristocracy and a brutalized commonality. Its literature, with some noble exceptions, stands neglected on the shelves. Its poetry has lost all power to rekindle us; its science is exploded; its taste condemned; its ecclesiastical arrangements flung to the winds; its religious ideas outgrown and in rapid process of a complete and, perhaps, hardly deserved extinction." [1]

While this accusation leveled at the times may appear to be overly harsh, the writer was justified in his evaluation of the period. In all fairness it should be stated, as he does, that conditions along all lines were not so hopeless that some good could not be seen. In literature it was the age of Defoe, Addison, Steele, Swift, Pope and Berkley, and later, Johnson, Goldsmith, Gray, Gibbon, Burke, Burns and Cowper. [2] In science, Sir Isaac Newton (1642-1727) was busily engaged in laying the foundation of modern physics, theories which remained almost unquestioned until the twentieth century. [3]

---

[1] John Fletcher Hurst, *The History of Methodism* (New York, 1902), in seven vols. Vol. I, pp. 17, 18.
[2] Hurst, *loc. cit.*
   G. M. Trevelyan, *English Social History* (New York, 1942), pp. 347, 397.
[3] *Ibid.*, p. 257.

The bad taste left in England's mouth from the Puritan era no doubt contributed to the ground work of the Methodist movement.[4] The political experiment of Cromwell and others, ending not only in utter failure and disgust, brought about that which one writer has termed, "the wildest outbreak of moral revolt that England has ever witnessed."[5] One cannot understand clearly the pattern of the times, realizing on the one hand that two literary works of the period never lost their popularity (Bunyan's *Pilgrim's Progress* and Milton's *Paradise Lost*),[6] while, at the same time the writer of this latter work with his pleas for civil and religious freedom, for freedom of social life, and freedom of press was the most hated man in England at the time of the Restoration. His book was ordered burned by Parliament and for several years his life was worth very little in all the English countryside.

Perhaps the memories of the Puritans did prick English conscience somewhat for during the reign of Queen Anne, a "Goodhearted woman of no great ability"[7] but deeply devoted to the Church of England, three great movements got underway. Societies were formed for the "Reformation of Manners," for "Promoting Christian Knowledge" and for the "Propagation of the Gospel in Foreign Parts."[8] Many Charity Schools were established, poor clergymen were aided financially and churches were built all over the realm.[9] Interest was at a new high and this enthusiasm touched even the House of Parliament which was persuaded to vote for a college in Bermuda.[10] More and more people began to read *The Vicar of Wakefield* by Goldsmith, a story of a country minister. Gray's "Elegy Written in a Country Churchyard" aided in this glorification of the parish church and its work. It is significant, too, that Joseph Addison's hymn "The Spacious Firmament on High" came out of this period of apparently sluggish moral and spiritual attitudes.

Hurst, in his *History of Methodism*, lists several reasons for this

---

[4] John Richard Green, *A Short History of the English People* (New York, 1900) in 3 vols. Vol. II, p. 320.
[5] Hurst, *op. cit.*, p. 34.
[6] Samuel Rawson Gardner, *The First Two Stuarts and the Puritan Revolution* (New York, 1891), p. 201.
[7] Henry Cabot Lodge, ed., *The History of Nations* (New York, 1936), in 25 vols. Vol. II, p. 453.
[8] George M. Trevelyan, *England Under Queen Anne* (New York, 1930), pp. 65, 68, 69.
[9] *Ibid.*, pp. 20, 65.
[10] Hurst, *op. cit.*, Vol. I, p. 19.

moral and spiritual decay.[11] Bitter controversies, he declares, were rife. To a vast majority of readers of the period too often the fact that the government of the seventeenth century had fallen to a new low ebb is overlooked. This had its effect even after the Georges were consigned to Mother Earth. The uncertainty as to what type of state religion the nation would have was not settled until the regime was closed. Commercial prosperity brought its influence to bear also, with its new intepretation on human behavior and its narrowing of the conception of responsibility. The opening of new fields of conquest, such as the American, the beginnings of the slave trade, all tended to lessen religious scruples.

In the midst of these conditions the church found itself with precious few aggressive leaders. One writer declared that "England had never been *thoroughly* evangelized (anyway)'; it had been ecclesiasticized, instead." [12] Moreover, "The very Christianity they (Italian missionaries sent out by Gregory the Great) brought from Rome was to a sad extent a mongrel compromise with paganism." [13]

From the standpoint of the State there was very little incentive to right behavior since the age of the Georges had ushered in gross immorality from the kingship to the lowly workingman. Instead of speaking out against these evils the pulpit too often was used to flatter the very individual who was most flagrant with his violations of moral codes. More than one ecclesiastical office was tainted with money and a few there were who paid attention to common bribery.[14]

Gambling, that old curse of man, adultery and every other form of sexual vice flourished without restraint.[15] Those who took the church or religion seriously were ridiculed.[16] Bishop Butler declared that "It is come, I know not how, to be taken for granted by many persons that Christianity is not so much a subject of inquiry; but that it is now at length discovered to be fictitious, and accordingly they treat it as if in the present age this were an agreed point among all people of discernment; and nothing remained but to set it up as a principal subject of mirth and ridicule, as it were, by way of reprisals for having so long interrupted the pleasures of the world." [17]

[11] Hurst, *op. cit.*, Vol. I, p. 22.
[12] *Ibid.*, p. 23.
[13] *Ibid.*, p. 22.
[14] *Ibid.*, p. 24.
[15] *Ibid.*, p. 25.
[16] *Ibid.*, p. 34.
[17] *Ibid.*, p. 32.

Few segments of English society escaped the influences towards deterioration. Cockfighting, bull and bear baiting, obscene plays along with an almost total lack of recreative reading were signs of the times. With the arrival of gin in 1684 a new threat could be noted. By 1724 the masses were taking on the new fad of drinking. Signs of ginshops offered people enough to make them "drunk for a penny, dead drunk for twopence, and a straw to lie upon." [18] It was a conceded fact that this gin drinking contributed to an alarming condition, a situation which saw the death rate surpass the birth rate.[19] The sordidness of the period is well depicted in Hogarth's contrast of Gin Lane and Beer Street in the "Beggar's Opera."

Green in his *History of the English People*, declares that "life among men of fashion vibrated between frivolity and excess." One of the comedies of the time tells the courtier that "he must dress well, dance well, fence well, have a talent for love-letters, an agreeable voice, be amorous and discreet—but not too constant." [20] Instance after instance of the adherence to this pattern can be noted. On one occasion the Duke of Buckingham fought a duel in which the husband of the Lady of Shrewsbury was killed simply for the purpose of consummating the Lady's seduction. The strange twist to the particular story is that the Countess, disguised as a page, held the Duke's horse while the murdering was being done.[21]

There is little doubt that many fairly decent Englishmen stood by while things went to extremes merely to see re-established many of the customs outlawed by the Puritans. Still others were unwilling to accept the rash approach to religion that Puritanism brought and demanded in this period of reaction, a sane and reasonable approach to spiritual life.

In all too many cases the clergy itself was *fiddling while Rome burned*. George Herbert wrote in his work on *A Priest to the Temple* "some live in universities, some in noble houses, some in Parishes residing on their cures." Those who were to be found in the university were there as members of the clergy simply because fellowships were to be desired and most of them obtainable only with the obliga-

---

[18] Hurst, *loc. cit.*, Vol. I, p. 24.
[19] Trevelyan, *loc. cit.*, p. 341.
[20] Green, *loc. cit.*, Vol. II, p. 320.
[21] *Ibid.*, p. 321.

tion that the holders enter into Holy Orders in the Church of England.[22] Mowat in his *England in the Eighteenth Century* states that "the clergy were not careless, but they were not zealous." [23] The second class noted by Herbert, *the chaplains in the noble houses*, were those who failed to secure fellowships. Like the former group they were more interested in an easy life than that involved in active parish service.

It must be admitted that this second class faced difficulties in attaining to any type of leadership. One can easily see how necessary it was for a chaplain in any household to refrain from resented criticism. As has been stated, many of the nobles and political heads of the country lived in wild abandon and their spiritual advisers had to conform to this way of life. From the group it appears that only one individual can claim our attention today and that is Jonathan Swift, and Swift was more of a secretary and librarian than a domestic chaplain.[24] From his pen came two notable works: the *Tale of a Tub* and the *Battle of the Books*.

It is not strange that the Great Revival began in a parish rectory. Most of the active clergy, those in the villages, towns and cities in charge of churches, were well thought of by the middle class and poor people. This is easily demonstrated in the writings of the time, some of which have been mentioned before, Fielding's *Parson Adams*, Goldsmith's *Vicar of Wakefield* and *The Deserted Village* and *The Diary of a Country Parson* by James Woodforde. It is said that Goldsmith might have been partial in that his Vicar was no doubt his own brother Henry, who was the parish priest at Kilkenny, Ireland.[25] A full description can be noted in his *Deserted Village* as well.

While these priests were in the main good men from many angles, yet as one writer notes, "there was perhaps no great spiritual earnestness about the Reverend James Woodforde, and he certainly would never have frightened any of his parishioners away from church by the intensity with which he conducted the services." Nevertheless, no one could declare that the country was godless for people did attend church and did take communion.

One weak point of the setup, no doubt, was to be found in the

---

[22] R. B. Mowat, *England in the Eighteenth Century* (New York, 1932), p. 39.
[23] *Ibid.*
[24] Mowat, *loc. cit.*, p. 41.
[25] Mowat, *loc. cit.*, p. 42.

fact that the rulers of the church came mainly from the first and second classes of the clergy and not from those who were nearest the people. They may have had the church at heart but they were not aggressive and what progress was achieved in the period came as the result of the activity of the evangelical movement, and, later, the Wesleyan influence. The evangelical movement was one which appears to have been recurring in the church for many decades. Its main thesis was an attempt to return to the original simplicity of the Church as it was in the time of Christ.

During the eighteenth century this group was led by William Law, who wrote several works, chief among them being *A Serious Call to a Devout and Holy Life,* which Wesley is said to have read. Selina Hastings, Countess of Huntingdon, was the great patron of this group, oftentimes protecting them from the bishops by appointing them her chaplain.[26] For several years she conducted a college at Trevecca in North Wales for ministers or prospective ministers. Aiding the movement by his friendship, while remaining within the Church, was August Toplady, the writer of the hymn "Rock of Ages."

In the midst of these conditions some well thinking men moved to place the church, at least, on the right track. Deism had undermined faith to the extent that outspoken people were eager to banish the idea of God in the world. The Bible, these people declared, was not a revelation, and there was no truth in the word incarnate. In order to refute these claims and re-establish Christianity, Bishop Butler published his famous *Analogy,* and a little later, Bishop Warburton's *Divine Legation of Moses* was issued. Hurst declares that while these works served a great purpose it remained for Methodism to apply the principles of Christ "to the heart and life of the whole people."

One might ask concerning the Free Churches of the Nation just what had happened to them and what were they doing concerning the decay. It appears that not less than two million nonconformists were in England around 1702. The largest of these groups were the Presbyterians with the Independents (Congregationalists) and Baptists having the next largest numbers. To analyze their attitudes here would take too much space, so it may be well to use one state-

---

[26] Mowat, *loc. cit.*

ment of a prominent writer in describing their positions. Stoughton says that "with certain exceptions a spirit of indifference respecting the masses of the people infected the respectable congregations of the Protestant meeting houses." Defoe, as late as 1712, considered "Dissenters' interests to be in a declining state."

In the midst of these conditions the Wesleys came on the scene. Three of the nineteen children of Samuel Wesley claim our attention. They are: Samuel, born in 1690; John, in 1703; and Charles, in 1708. For our purposes, the study of the early lives of these three boys can be passed over, a period of twenty-five years, for it was with the organization of the Holy Club at Oxford that Methodism really began.

Hurst paints a beautiful picture of the first meeting of this group. He states that it was in November, 1729, that four college students met to form what was to be known as the Holy Club. John Wesley was twenty-six at the time, while Charles, his brother, was twenty-two. The other members of the group were William Morgan and Robert Kirkham. It appears that others joined the group later.

Prior to the organization of the Holy Club there is little doubt that John Wesley had taken a serious slant on life and had attempted to influence his brother, Charles. Charles rebelled at this new interest in holiness and as one writer has put it, "objected to becoming a saint all at once." Charles changed his attitude, however, and really was responsible for this first meeting of the Holy Club.

There was nothing radical about the actions of this little group. They merely decided to follow closely the rules of the University and adopt certain plans for right living. As a result, however, they were styled *Methodists* by a young man at the college.

The Holy Club continued to be an influence among young men of the University in spite of the derision it incurred. The group studied the Bible as its first work but held on to the ideas of spiritual and humanitarian changes. Other members were added, among them being John Clayton, Benjamin Ingham, John Gambold, James Harvey and Thomas Broughton. The group remained together until, one by one, they entered the active ministry. However, the two years of its life left not only a profound effect on the University but planted the seeds of Methodism.

In 1735, John and Charles Wesley, fired with the missionary zeal, left England with the design of preaching to the Indians in the then sparsely settled colony of Georgia in America. Here, ordinary success met the young missionary, John Wesley, and after an unpleasant experience with a young woman who later married a Mr. Williamson, Wesley left Georgia to return to England.

There is little doubt that Georgia had its effect on John Wesley. It may have paved the way for the famous experience when his heart was "strangely warmed." For Methodists, the date will be long remembered: May 24, 1738.

In the rise of Methodism, John Wesley himself has listed four stages of development. The first is Biblical, or that period having to do with the Holy Club at Oxford. The second is brotherly; the third, doctrinal; and the fourth, organic. The last stage began on Monday, May 1, 1739. The days intervening between John Wesley's conversion and the date of the birth of a separate organization are both dramatic and fascinating. In them the trend of this great leader's preaching led to the closing of the Established Church to this handful of devout men who went about crying for the repentance of the people.

For fear that many may misinterpret the intention of Wesley, may we state that at no time did the founder of Methodism contemplate separation from the Mother Church. He distinctly felt that the calling of his group, himself, Whitfield and others, was to purify the church, not to destroy it. It is a current belief that Wesley, in organizing Methodism, was definitely unwilling to consider this a new denomination. After his death, the drift away from the Mother Church became a fact.

For five years, John Wesley and other leaders of the movement traveled throughout England. In that time, forty-five preachers, three or four of them clergymen of the Established Church, gathered around him. In that time the church became a church without a name. Sacraments were observed, fellowship and church government practiced, pastors were in evidence, but the belief of the head that no new denomination was intended was ever paramount.

In 1744, the first "conference" of Methodism was held in London. For five days, beginning with the 25th of August, the Fathers of the movement discussed doctrines, beliefs and attitudes, Present were the two Wesleys and four other clergymen, John Hodges, Henry Piers, Samuel Taylor and John Meriton. Meeting with this group were four lay *assistants*, Thomas Richards, Thomas Maxfield, John

18

Bennet, and John Downes. Hurst states of this last group, only John Downes remained with the Church throughout his life.

This first conference of Methodism considered three things: what to teach, how to teach and how to regulate doctrine, discipline, and practice. For two days they talked about "Such vital doctrines as the Fall, the Work of Christ, Justification, Regeneration, Sanctification." Hurst says that the answer to the question, "How to Teach" was fourfold: to invite, to convince, to offer Christ, and to build up. Preachers were instructed to do this in every sermon.

Regarding the Established Church, it was agreed to obey the Bishops "in all things indifferent." They were convinced that the new group at no time would leave the Mother Church unless forced out and all would work against the things which might bring this about.

In spite of the opposition to the movement it was decided in this first conference to continue the salvation of souls, to plant organizations wherever possible, governed by a policy of going "little and little farther from London, Bristol, St. Ives, Newcastle, or any other society."

During the sessions, Lady Huntingdon invited the conference to her home in Downing Street and there Wesley preached his famous sermon, "What hath God Wrought." Later, this home was to become a bulwark of Methodism under Whitfield.

CHAPTER II

The Founding of the Methodist Society in New York

IN ONE of the early *Disciplines*[1] the following statement of the founding of the Methodist Church in America is to be noted:

> During the space of thirty years past, certain persons, members of the Society emigrated from England and Ireland—settled in various parts of this country. In the latter end of the year 1776, Philip Embury, a local preacher from Ireland, began to preach in the city of New York and formed a society of his own countrymen and the citizens; and in the same year, Thomas Webb preached in a hired room near the barracks. About the same time, Robert Strawbridge, a local preacher from Ireland, settled in Frederick County in the state of Maryland, and preaching there, formed some societies. The first Methodist Church in New York was built in 1768. "Richard Boardman and Joseph Pilmoor came to New York, who were the first regular preachers on the continent. In the latter end of 1771 Francis Asbury and Richard Wright of the same order came over. "We humbly believe that God's design in raising up Methodism in America was to reform the continent and spread scripture holiness over these lands.

In the John Street Church, New York City, hangs the portraits of two of these early founders of American Methodism. That of Philip Embury (listed pastor—1768-1770) and his wife, Margaret. The paintings were made by John Barnes in 1773 and later came into the possession of John Street as a gift from the late Reverend Howard Ingham of Baltimore, who, in turn received them from his father, William A. Ingham.[2]

Philip Embury was born in 1728 at Ballingrane, the son of parents who had fled the Palatinate around 1709 when Louis XIV invaded Germany. At the instance of Queen Anne of England these German refugees settled in County Limerick, Ireland.[3] It was here that John Wesley preached such stirring messages (1750-1752) that many of these people became members of the Methodist Chapels.[4] Philip Embury, in his diary, tells of his conversion in the following way:

---

[1] The *Discipline* of the Methodist Church (Philadelphia, 1792), edited by Thomas Coke and Francis Asbury.
[2] Robert H. Dolliver, *The Story of the Mother Church of American Methodism* (October, 1945), p. 12.
[3] *Ibid.*
[4] *Ibid.*

"On Christmas Day, being Monday, ye 25th of December, in the year 1752, the Lord shone into my soul by a glimpse of his redeeming love, being an earnest of my redemption in Christ Jesus to whom be glory for ever and ever. Amen"—Philip Embury[5]

According to belief it was not long after this conversion that Philip Embury was licensed to preach and aided in the establishment of the Methodist Chapel at Ballingrane.

When the Conference in Limerick was held in 1758 he was recommended for the itinerancy, but before he could be assigned to active service he was married to Margaret Switzer in the Rathkeal Church, November 27, 1759.[6]

Then as now, one of the constant irritations of life was the matter of taxation. While, in many instances the older people chose to endure this affliction rather than migrate, the younger people looking for ways and means of making progress, decided to leave the country.[7] So it was that in 1760 Philip Embury and his young wife, Margaret, embarked on the good ship Perry, arriving in New York, August 10, 1760. The passage, which took about sixty-three days, was just three days less than the time consumed on the crossing of the Mayflower. With Embury and his wife were thirty-five other Methodists.[8]

While the source of the following facts is not known, it is concluded that in December, 1760 the first child was born to the Emburys and named Catherine Elizabeth.[9] There appeared to have been no effort made at this time to form a new church for it is recorded that Philip Embury, Paul and Barbara Heck communed at the Trinity Lutheran Church, Broadway and Rector Streets where the Reverend Albert Weygand was pastor, on Christmas Day.[10]

When the time came to baptize Catherine Elizabeth, she was presented in the same Lutheran Church (January 9, 1761), and in the following November, Jacobina Elizabeth, daughter of Paul and Barbara Heck, was born and baptized in the same church.

Meanwhile, Philip Embury was not only following his trade of a carpenter [11] but was also interested in the teaching profession as well.

[5] *The Diary of Philip Embury.*
[6] Dolliver, *loc. cit.*
[7] Hurst, *loc. cit.*, IV, p. 4.
[8] Dolliver, *loc. cit.*, p. 13.
[9] *Ibid.*
[10] *Ibid.*
[11] Hurst, *loc. cit.*, IV, p. 3.

In April 1761, the following advertisement appeared in Weyman's German Weekly in the *New York Gazette:*

PHIL. EMBURY, SCHOOL-MASTER

Gives Notice, that on the first day of May next, he intends to teach Reading, Writing and Arithmetick, in English, in the New School-House now building in Little Queen Street, next door to the Lutheran Ministers: and as he has been informed, that several gentlemen were willing to favor him with their Children, he gives farther Notice, that if a sufficient number of scholars should attend his school, he would teach in company with John Embury, (who teaches several Branches belonging to Trade and Business) that Children might be carefully attended as he faithfully desires the Good of the Publick. He now teaches at Mr. Samuel Fosters, in Carman's Street.

Still another individual with whom we should treat in this brief chapter on American Methodism is Barbara Heck. Above, we have noted that she and her husband had been closely identified with the Emburys, no doubt coming over in the same ship and attending the same Lutheran Church as is noted in the baptism of their daughter, Jacobina Elizabeth.[12] Barbara Heck, likewise, was born in Ballingrane, County Limerick, Ireland, perhaps in 1734. Her father was Sebastian von Ruckle (or Ruttle). Dr. Dolliver states that the house in which she was born (built in 1710) still stands as one of the early shrines of American Methodism. Her descendants remain in possession of the property. In the yard can be seen the old pear tree under which "John Wesley preached, and where Barbara as a young lady of 18, was converted." [13]

In the historic John Street Methodist Church visitors can still see and hear, preserved *alive* an old timepiece inscribed, "Be ye also ready, for in such an hour as ye think not the Son of man cometh." [14] The placing of this old clock in the first Chapel of Methodism closed an epoch in Christian history seldom surpassed in the annals of time. Interested minds groping for the light of human progress would find it necessary to go back several years to discover just what force or forces set in motion the ticking of this old colonial relic.

Hurst in his *History of Methodism* states that little is known of the new group (two of whom we have mentioned above) except for the

[12] Old records as recorded in the *Story of the Mother Church of American Methodism, loc. cit.,* p. 13.
[13] *Ibid.,* p. 13.
[14] Dolliver, *loc. cit.,* p. 33.

fact that they experienced some difficulty in setting up their indus-trial colony (as they had come over, mainly to establish the flax, hemp and linen industry), because they could not find a suitable tract of land.[15]

At this time several churches had been established in New York City, among them being several Dutch organizations where most of the aristocracy worshiped.[16] The fashionable English speaking people attended the Church of England, while mention is made of a struggling Baptist Church and a Moravian group. As a result of this religious setup few of the new German settlers attended church.[17] At first this condition was not so noticeable but with the increase in the number of these German-Irish Methodists the condition grew worse.[18]

One evening Dame Barbara Heck walked into her kitchen to find a card game in progress. She became so indignant that she gathered the cards into her apron and shook them into the open fire.[19] Then, evidently, shaken with anger, she consulted Philip Embury, who was a relative.[20] Embury, at first, listed the obstacles to his holding preaching services since he had no congregation and no church; but Barbara Heck urged him to hold services in his own house and preach to his own family.[21]

While it appears it is not certain just how many individuals at-tended the first *services* of these devout Methodists, six are listed as being present: Philip Embury, who preached; Mrs. Embury, his wife; Barbara Heck and her husband, Paul; a John Lawrence and a Negro servant, Betty.[22] This little group gradually increased until the house was overcrowded and the congregation had to move a few doors down the street.[23] Others soon joined the number, among them being Jonathan Morrell, Mary Parks and her mother, Mrs. Devereaux, Billy Littlewood, keeper of the poorhouse, James Hodge, Addison Low and John Buckley.[24]

Soon after the removal to the upper room from Embury's house a

[15] Hurst, *loc. cit.*
[16] Hurst, *loc. cit.*, IV, pp. 1, 3.
[17] *Ibid.*, p. 3.
[18] *Ibid.*, p. 6.
[19] Hurst, *loc. cit.*, p. 6.
[20] *Ibid.*
[21] *Ibid.*
[22] Dolliver, *loc. cit.*, p. 14.
[23] Jesse Lee, *History of the Methodists* (Baltimore, 1810), p. 14.
[24] Dolliver, *loc. cit.*, p. 14.

new impetus was given the movement when Thomas Webb joined the congregation and began assisting Embury with the preaching. Because of the novelty of seeing a British officer (army) preaching in a Methodist Chapel the new quarters were soon outgrown and another move was made necessary,[25] this time to the "Old Rigging Loft" on that which is now William Street, between John and Fulton. This building was about 18x60 feet so that it was not long when this too became too small.

Up to this time the Methodist movement in America was not considered a rival denomination to any of the established churches.[26] It was not long, however, before the friendliness of other groups cooled somewhat. Meacham brings this out in his work when he states that the new building "had to have a fire place and chimney to get around the law." In a letter to John Wesley dated New York, April 11, 1768, it was further stated that "ministers have cursed us in the name of the Lord." Until the development of this animosity, however, the new group was able to secure gifts from several churchmen in the city as well as from other leading citizens for the building of the first chapel.

In 1768, the plot of ground located on John Street was leased, being purchased two years later. On this ground the first chapel was built.[27] The obstacles which confronted the group were great for the members were poor as well as few in numbers and not a few individuals opposed them.[28] Among those who aided with their meager funds were two individuals called Rachel and Margaret. It is reasonable to believe that these were Negro servants who had been attending the Methodist meetings.[29] Their contributions were nine and seven shillings.[30]

The new Wesley Chapel was 42x60 feet and could probably seat, at first four hundred and fifty or five hundred persons.[31] Lee, in his *Early History* states that the building could seat one thousand two

---

[25] Lee, *op. cit.*, p. 24.
[26] *The Journal of Francis Asbury*, in 3 vols., I (New York), Meacham, p. 267.
[27] *Ibid.*
[28] *Ibid.*, p. 268.
  The colonial law stated that "none but the established service could be performed in what was commonly called a church." Places of worship belonging to dissenters were to have some appendage about them which should cause them to be classed as ordinary dwellings.
[29] From "*The Old Book of Record of the John Street Society.*"
[30] *Ibid.*
[31] Dolliver, *loc. cit.*, p. 23 ff.

24

hundred or one thousand four hundred people.[32] This, perhaps, was the case after the building of the galleries. Methodist historians, time after time, have stated that goodly portions, oftentimes fully half of the Methodist converts were Negroes.[33] With the knowledge that the initial purpose of the Methodist Church in England and America was not to establish a separate church, with the bringing to light the fact that the early work of both Philip Embury and Thomas Webb showed deep sympathy towards those who no doubt were not welcomed in the established churches, one can be led to believe that not only did the Methodist Church allow Negroes to attend their meetings but they welcomed them. Perhaps this work among the unfortunates of New York, both white and colored, allowed the movement the respite it needed to get underway before the *storm*. In the same year their chapel was dedicated, however, a letter to John Wesley spoke of the ministers of New York cursing the group "in the name of the Lord." [34]

A great amount of this hostility would have been levied on any organization other than the Established Church for there were laws which prevented the dissenter groups from enjoying the privileges of the recognized denominations.

Opposition of other groups of Protestants no doubt caused the new Methodist group to "throw aside the shackles of prejudice and hereditary customs." [35] They appeared to care little about the results for they were ridiculed and hated anyway. Meacham declares that the other denominations "were dreading the influence of their incontrovertible doctrines." He further states that "it required all the art of parents to keep their unprejudiced children from what they deem is spiritual contagion." [36] Pamphlets were published against them and discourses were delivered but the movement went on.[37]

[32] Lee, *loc. cit.*, p. 25.
[33] Meacham, *loc. cit.*, pp. 272-274.
[34] *The Journal of John Wesley.*
[35] Meacham, *loc. cit.*, p. 267.
[36] *Ibid.*, p. 267.
[37] *Ibid.*, p. 268.

CHAPTER III

Beginnings of Organized Religion Among Negroes

THERE ARE no records available of what the Negro actually did or thought religiously prior to 1619. We have every reason to believe that he did give thought to the spiritual things of life. His religious background emphasized his belief in spirits and the practice of "Black Art." Every Negro slave entering the colonies in this and succeeding years was indoctrinated in the native interpretations of good versus evil spirits. No death in so far as the slave or Negro was concerned was due to natural causes. If a man died by drowning the water spirit triumphed; if he succumbed to disease, those individual spirits conquered. In other words, no Negro had personal control of his own destinies.

It appears that one of the reasons for the rapid growth of the Negroes' interest in Christianity stemmed from this revolutionary idea of individual privilege in determining destiny. The native religion and superstition made no pretense of defining man's relationship to man. It was, in truth, a vertical religion rather than the horizontal that Jesus preached. The revolutionary idea proved such an interesting new world to these Africans and descendants of Africans, that one of the earliest Negro poetesses could exclaim . . .

> Twas mercy brought me from my Pagan land,
> Taught my benighted soul to understand
> That there's a God and there's a Saviour too
> Once I redemption neither sought nor knew.

One can run across the statement in his reading from time to time that Negroes were used as slaves because of their ability to endure slavery and a friend once declared that this ability is one of the chief reasons why the Negro race should be considered great. Other than the accounts of the Jewish people, no other group has had the power and fortitude to bear up under slavery. However, there was another reason why the Negro became the pawn in the then known Catholic world. Only non-Christians could be enslaved and so the attention of Portuguese and Dutch and English merchantmen were turned to the Africans.

One of the hidden pages of history and one which has not been carefully explained by historians, is that dealing with the struggle to recognize the Negro as a human being. More than the wars and the struggle for empire and riches, this establishment of human principle opens the first phase of our racial development. Like all great movements which have profound effect it went unnoticed to a great extent and lies even today hidden by swift moving events of a more spectacular nature.

In so many ways it appears that the Negro has never appreciated the bitter struggles which have gone on in his defense. It is true that he suffered and this suffering is borne out in his spirituals, but the world has never been without its courageous leadership and even when the massive weight of evidence seemed to be able to turn any tide, voices were raised and men suffered much to be Christian. There is a little book printed in 1680 by a man whose name was Godwyn, *The Negroes Advocate*. While his missionary work was not carried on in America, it had a profound effect on Negro religion in the colonies. Godwyn believed that a Negro was just as important in God's sight as anyone else and practiced this belief. Baptism even more than anything else was the door to the church and once having been baptized any individual had the rights and privileges pertaining thereto. So when Godwyn baptized Negroes he ran into tremendous opposition.

One woman declared that he might as well baptize puppies as Negroes. He got by baptizing Mulattoes because it was a peculiar belief that a little bit of white blood made one more human. In his little treatise, Godwyn summed up the opposition's arguments under three headings: "He could not be a Christian because he was black." Of course there is still a white heaven. "A slave could not be Christian because he was in bondage and slavery had the great art of transforming men into beasts." And finally he could not be a Christian because of his "stupidity." Enemies of the Godwyn theory even went to the Bible to prove their contentions. The Negroes were descendants of Cain and that was the reason they were so brutal. It is not known how this particular group got around another contention but it was declared that the Negro was not human at all. Godwyn answered these critics by declaring that every man before God had an equal right in religion and that the Negroes were men. This being the case, to deprive them of Christianity was the highest injustice. Of course some of his critics declared that the dancing of the Negroes showed that they were not susceptible to Christianity. Godwyn answered this by saying that dancing was a part of divine worship, so he was not a Methodist.

There was another angle to this controversy over the Negro's religion. So long as he stayed away from divine services he was saved from eternal damnation; but if he were baptized he was in danger of hell fire. Of course there was an economic side to the whole problem. Jesus' doctrine of the horizontal interpretations of religion and the universal brotherhood of man did prick some consciences so it became easier to have heathen slaves than Christianized Negroes.

DuBois states, incidentally, that witchcraft persisted among the Negroes simply because the masters offered nothing better.

It appears that many historical writers of the race can be justly accused of making statements that are easily refuted. One noted race writer declares that the colonists were not especially interested in the Negro. It is hard to write off the action of Peter Williams in coming to the John Street Methodist Board of Trustees and the subsequent events as disinterest. Any student of the period will become quite aware of the seriousness of the act—first as a precedent-setting act and second as a determining factor in the futurism of the Old John Street Church.

It is hard to explain away the fact that thousands of slaves were freed at the close of the seventeenth century and the opening of the eighteenth century. Records are available concerning one group forming the nucleus of the Negro population inhabiting central Pennsylvania—giving birth to such Zion Churches as Wesley in Pittsburgh, Harrisburg, York, Williamsport, and Bedford. Of interest too are actual documents of manumission still to be found. One cannot easily explain away the action of churches in expelling slave-owning preachers because the church decreed this action necessary.

In our study of the Civil War, its causes and the incidents attendant, we, as Methodists, should never forget that the pronouncements of the church and the writings of her ministry were in many estimations as much responsible for the freeing of the slaves as Harriet Beecher Stowe's *Uncle Tom's Cabin*, the work of the abolitionists, the act of Abraham Lincoln.

On one occasion a petition was dispatched to the House of Parliament against slavery. Of the 352,040 recorded names 229,426 were

Methodists. We cannot forget Freeborn Garretson, and the Ecclesiastical laws of 1780 and 1784 prohibiting the acceptance of slaveholding clergy and laymen.

Contrary to belief, even before the battle concerning the Negro's capabilities was joined—his salavation was not wholly neglected. When, on February 16, 1623, the names "Anthony, Negro; Isabell, Negro; William, their child, baptized" were recorded in the "List of names of those living in Virginia, Elizabeth City Co." the authority relating the account exclaimed that this was a Red Letter Day for the Negro for it was the beginning of his stewardship in spiritual things. A rather small beginning but when Zion was celebrating her centennial at the close of the 1890's almost 300,000 Negroes belonged to churches in that state.

One John Gaween, a slave owned by a William Evans, had a habit of calling on a girl owned by Lt. Tobert Sheppard on a neighboring plantation. In 1641 he became a father and decided that he didn't want his child to be a slave. It appears that his master was sympathetic and allowed him to raise hogs on shares. With this money he purchased the child and arranged that he should be educated as a Christian.

The annals are filled with incidents like that. In 1645 two Negro children were given to a Francis Pott of Northampton County, Virginia, that they might be reared in the fear of God and the knowledge of Jesus Christ. In 1655 someone gave to a Mihill Gowan, a free Negro, a male child "born of Negro Rosa and baptized William, September 2, 1655."

It is recorded that Negroes were welcomed in the Quaker meetings in Virginia as early as 1667. And, even earlier, September 17, 1630, a white man by the name of Hugh Davis was publicly whipped before Negroes because of immorality involving a slave. One wishes that pattern were repeated today instead of the incessant persecution of Negroes.

Even Virginia was willing to admit in 1670 that only servants not being Christians could be enslaved for life.

By this time both sides of the ocean were writing on the subject of the Negro's religion. In 1700 one Commissary Blair in communicating with the Archbishop of Canterbury suggested that one important matter was the "Christian education of our Negro and Indian children."

The following year, June 16, 1701, the Society for the Propagation of the Gospel in Foreign Parts, was set up in England. This organization had a three-fold purpose: to supply the want of religious instruction and privileges in America among the established churches; the conversion of the Indians and the conversion of the Negroes. Most of its work was carried on in New York and South Carolina.

In reading through some old accounts, reference was made to the diary of Colonel James Gordon who wrote in 1738 that he had gone to church and that Sunday two hundred and twenty-nine whites, one hundred and seventy-two blacks, fifteen Quakers and two Anabaptists communed. One wonders what was the color of the Quakers and Anabaptists. They weren't black, of that we can be sure. An unfortunate incident mars the old gentleman's diary Christmas Day, 1759, for he records: "Some of our Negroes got drunk, that has given me some uneasiness." Either the weather was bad or folks didn't feel like going to church on September 11, 1763, for he notes one hundred and fourteen whites and eight-five blacks communing. Christmas 1763, one hundred and thirty blacks and whites communed. He made no distinction here. On July 15, 1769, he read a sermon to the Negroes.

Philip Vickers Fithian, who was a school teacher in 1773-74, lets us realize that times don't change much. He writes: "Dispersed a large crowd of Negroes and two of the Carter boys found dancing in my school room."

Easter Sunday they redeemed themselves, however, for everybody went to church, but on Easter Monday not a Negro could be found, he lamented, because they were all at the cock fights.

Another writer intimated that the Negro, no matter what happened during the week, always brightened upon Saturday.

The work of Christianizing the slave was carried on by most of the denominations in the colonies. The Moravians and United Brethren from Pennsylvania used to make expeditions into the South preaching to the Negroes but weren't welcomed because the slave owners did not care for strangers to preach to slaves. This, no doubt, accounts for the willingness to allow the Negro preacher a little more freedom.

The work of the Quakers, the attitude of John Fox and the efforts of John Wooman can be expressed in the Annual Meeting of Friends' statement of 1759, "that all Friends do treat them with humanity."

30

Down in the Methodist Historical Society here in New York hangs a picture depicting the consecration of Bishop Asbury. One of the spectators is a Negro named Black Harry, constant companion of the Bishop. Ablest of the early Negro preachers, he was preceded by a host of white ministers who took seriously their work among Negroes. Along with Bishop Asbury were two other prelates who lent moral support to the movement, Bishop Gibson and Bishop Porteus. The first successful worker among the slaves and freed men was a Reverend Samuel Thomas who labored in the Goose Creek Parish of South Carolina. He began his work around 1695 and ten years later had at least twenty Africans, as they were commonly called, in his congregation. By 1705, it is said that he had around one thousand slaves under instruction. One writer states that in "some of the congregations, Negroes constituted one half of the communicants."

In 1723, a Reverend Guy baptized a Negro man and woman and twenty years later the interest in the advancement of the Negro had reached such a stage that a group opened a special school in Charleston, South Carolina, for the race. This venture was closed in 1763, but it at least demonstrated the possibilities.

Work in North Carolina began about 1712, when a Reverend Ranford of Chowan baptized three Negroes and boasted of the fact that in one year he had baptized twenty slave and freed men. In the same year, the Reverend G. Ross wrote a letter of commendation to a Mr. Yates in Chester, Pennsylvania, for his interest in the training of Negroes. Mr. Ross records that he himself had baptized twelve Africans.

The visitors to the Sesqui-Centennial celebration heard from time to time of Zion churches in neighboring communities. It is not by chance that two of our oldest organizations, that at Newburgh and New Rochelle, have been respected churches for a number of years. Work among Negroes began in New Rochelle in 1737, in Newburgh, somewhat earlier and in Albany in 1714.

This evangelistic enterprise was fostered chiefly by three denominations, the Methodists, the Baptists and the Scotch Irish Presbyterians. It is frequently stated that Virginia was lost to Methodism simply because the Methodist church was unwilling to ordain the Negro. There is another reason which one can list, however. The declarations of the Methodist General Conferences against slavery, one writer states, "sounded more threatening than anything that a

31

local group might state" so these pronouncements created more animosity toward this church than for any other church.

There was something in the peculiar attitude of Methodists too, which seemed to bear out the contention that these people who emphasized the "heart strangely warmed" process, created more unrest among slaves. Time after time in listing run-away slaves the owner declared that he was a Methodist who did a little preaching.

In Baltimore, Thomas Jones ran away from his master in 1793. He was a Methodist preacher of sorts. In Maryland too, Jacob, a slave, a Methodist and a preacher, departed for parts unknown, in 1800. In still another case, Richard, a man who preached occasionally to the slaves, disappeared. He, too, was a Methodist, and down in Newbern, North Carolina, Simboe, a Methodist preacher departed without saying goodby.

Some of these preachers of various denominations either remained on in slavery or obtained their freedom legally and were well known for their work. We have already mentioned Black Harry, Bishop Asbury's servant, who could, according to an account of Bishop Coke (who hailed from Accomac County, Eastern Shore, Virginia), (written in 1784) preach as well as the Bishop (Asbury). On one occasion the crowd was so great that many people could not get in the church. Unable to see the speaker they went away exclaiming about the wonderful message they had heard. Then someone told them that it was not the Bishop who preached but his servant. Bishop Asbury's fame went abroad for it was said that if the servant could speak like that, what must the master be.

Incidentally there are several stories told about Black Harry. It appears that Richard Allen undertook to teach him how to read and write. Black Harry soon discovered that the more he understood about this art the less effective was his preaching. So he gave up trying to become literate. Another interpretation given to the loss of his tremendous preaching ability was that he fell from grace and even though he repented he never was able to preach so well again.

Bishop Asbury states in his Journal that Black Harry got the "big head," so much so that it interfered with his outlook on things. As a result the good Bishop sent him to do missionary work in Western New Jersey.

Other noted early Negro ministers who we will just name were: George Lisle and Andrew Bryan in Georgia and South Carolina;

Uncle Jack, who labored around 1792; Henry Evans, John Stewart of Virginia; Lemuel Haynes, James Varick, Abraham Thompson, Miller and Rush who came later; and June Scott.

Two other preachers of note we should mention, however, Richard Allen, the founder of the A. M. E. Church, and Absolom Jones, the founder of the oldest Negro Episcopal Church. Both were Methodists originally but withdrew to form the Free African Society because of prejudice in the other church. On one occasion it is said that they were literally pulled off their knees by the officers of the church. The Society was founded in 1787 and disbanded in 1792. Bethel Church appears to have dedicated their first church building in 1794, receiving thereafter regular ministers from the mother church. Richard Allen was ordained a deacon by Bishop Asbury in 1799.

Absolom Jones with his group purchased land and erected a church in 1794. He was ordained a deacon in 1795, by Bishop William White and ordained to the priesthood in 1804.

The first Negro Baptist Church, according to Carter G. Woodson, was organized in 1773, at Silver Bluff, across from Augusta, Georgia. Other churches followed: in Petersburg in 1776; Williamsburg, Virginia, in 1785; Savannah, the same year; Philadelphia, in 1809; and a year prior to this in New York, 1808. This church is now known as Abyssinian Baptist Church.

CHAPTER IV

The Methodist Church and Slavery

IT IS not hard to establish the fact that the Methodist Church was one of the great factors in the incidents and movements leading up to the Civil War and the eventual emancipation of the Negro. Volumes have been written on the attitude of this particular church towards slavery. De vinne, in his work, *The Methodist Episcopal Church and Slavery*, states this premise most clearly in the beginning of his book:

> In this historical survey, I purpose to prove that the Methodist Episcopal Church was founded on a non slave-holding basis—that it never was the intention of her founders that slavery should have been continued in her communion."

The writer goes on to declare that slavery was wrong because it was contrary to the laws of God as well as those of man. In addition, it was an unnatural state. It was hurtful to society and every man controlled by his conscience rejected it. "Pure religion could not exist with it for it nullified marriage and the Sabbath by repelling slave testimony. As well, it raised a screen in the church to cover every abomination."

De vinne further declared that a great revival sprang up among the Negroes, carrying over from 1780 to 1800 and the Methodist Church was a great instrument in this awakening. While Bishop Asbury was voicing his prayer for the enslaved "sable sons of Africa" Negroes were crowding the Methodist meeting houses and chapels accepting Christ as their Saviour. "Under one sermon, as we have seen, twenty-three slaves were known to have been set free," one writer states, showing that the effect of the great revival was visited on slave and owner alike. Bishop Asbury, visiting Annamessex, Maryland in 1788 saw fit to write "most of our members in these parts have freed their slaves." The statistics of freed slaves in the state of Maryland alone, is interesting:

Year	Population	Free colored
1790	103,036	8,043
1800	105,638	19,538
1810	111,562	33,027
1820	107,398	37,730

The tradition of Methodism must have aided the band of crusaders in this great task of keeping the church as pure of that *taint* as possible. Certainly the Methodist ministry was well aware of the pronouncement of John Wesley on the subject. His *Thoughts on Slavery* were published around 1774 and were known to many of his *reading* ministers. In part, he declared:

> and this equally concerns every gentleman that has an estate in our American plantations; yea, all slave holders of whatever rank and degree; seeing men—buyers are exactly on a level with men-stealers:— Now, it is your money that pays the merchant and thru him, the captains and the African butchers. You, therefore, are guilty, yea principally guilty, of all these frauds, robberies and murders.

Yes, the Methodist minister read these words and attacked the problem. On one occasion Dr. Coke was preaching in a barn and found a time to refer to the evils of slavery. A small number of the congregation withdrew with the intention of attacking the minister. One lady offered 50 pounds if he were given one hundred lashes. He was saved by a magistrate.[1] On another occasion, Joseph Everett, who began his preaching career in 1781, left a house where he was staying because of the presence of slaves in the household.

It may be well to note the work of the Methodist Church in a small section of the country in order to more clearly understand the problems which confronted the group in New York. For this purpose we must begin our study with the building of the Chapel (later John Street).

So effective was the work among the Negro element that by 1769, one year after building the Chapel, a letter was written to John Wesley (November 4, 1769) in which the following was stated: "The number of blacks that attend the preaching affects me."[2] The letter goes on to state "One of them came to tell me that she could neither eat nor sleep because her master would not suffer her to come to hear the Word. She wept exceedingly, saying, 'I told my master I would do more work than I used to do, if he would let me come, nay, I would do anything in my power to be a good servant.'"

A year later a Mr. Pilmoor wrote Wesley on May fifth, declaring that God is no respecter of persons. "Even some of the poor, despised children of Ham are striving to wash their robes and make them

---

[1] De vinne, *The Methodist Episcopal Church in Slavery* (New York, 1857), p. 72.
[2] *The Journal of Rev. Francis Asbury*, in 3 vols. (New York, 1821).

white in the Blood of the Lamb." Bishop Asbury likewise was impressed by the desire of the Negroes of New York to be *saved* for he mentions in his Journal "the poor blacks who attended the services."

The movement of conversion among Negroes was going on not only in New York City but in outlying districts as well. When Thomas Webb preached in Jamaica, Long Island, twelve whites and twelve blacks were converted.[3] In 1770 a letter was written to John Wesley dated April 24 by Joseph Pilmoor in which he stated that he had had one thousand seven hundred hearers and that the number of blacks that attend the preaching "affects me very much."[3]

In 1771 Bishop Asbury wrote in his Journal "and to see the poor Negroes so affected is pleasing; to see their sable countenances in our solemn assemblies and to hear them sing with cheerful melody their Redeemer's praise, affected me much and made me ready to say, of a truth I preceive that God is no respecter of persons."[4] Later, the following year, the Negro situation came up again when he stated, "We dined with Mr. R who cannot keep Negroes for conscience sake, and this was the topic of our conversation." And still later, "O when will liberty be extended to the sable sons of Africa?"[5]

De vinne declares that early Methodist members were so poor that slave ownership was no problem.[6] This may account for their keen interest in the extension of Christianity to this group, but even this item appears to have been an obstacle rather than an aid to evangelization of the Negroes. In the Christmas Conference held in Baltimore, Maryland in 1784, the policy of Methodism was defined in the answer to the 42nd Question: "What method can we take to extirpate slavery? We view it contrary to the Golden Rule of God on which hangs all the law and the prophets—and the inalienable rights of mankind as well as the principles of the revolution—so many souls that are capable of the image of God."[7] The Conference insisted upon the "full and entire emancipation of every slave in the possession of the members of the Church and that such an instrument should be legally executed and recorded."[8] If individual members did not wish to comply they could quietly withdraw, but those with-

---

[3] Asbury, *loc. cit.*, I. p. 26 (New York).
[4] Asbury, *loc. cit.*, I, p. 26.
[5] *Ibid.*
[6] De vinne, *loc. cit.*, p. 16.
[7] *Ibid.*
[8] *Ibid.*

drawing should be excluded from the Lord's Supper. Hereafter, no slaveholder should be admitted to the communion.

Thus, early, the Methodist Church took a stand against slavery while the issue waged furiously in other churches. Time proved that this stand was to be a hard principle to maintain as is shown in the records of succeeding General Conferences. The sympathy shown in the action of the General Conference held in Charleston, South Carolina when it was voted to establish "Sunday schools for poor children both white and black," [9] was little in evidence just ten years later when the General Conference met in Baltimore. In the minutes of that session [10] a motion by the Rev. Mr. Ormond to take up the slavery question was voted down. The ban against ministers being slave owners still held, however. The best which could be done to extend this authority to all members was the appointment of a Committee to prepare "an affectionate address to the Methodist Societies in the United States" stating the evils of the spirit of slavery and the necessity of doing away with that evil. The results of this committee action were to be submitted to the annual conferences and if agreed to by the Bishops, should become law.[11]

Before the situation reached this stage of affairs, however, the new group declared that the "Gospel was for all, whether bond or free." Many Christians of the time supposed, actually, that baptism imparted an "Impersonation of Christ" so slavery was inconsistent with the dignity of the Christian.[12] The Gospel was to go to all, whether bond or free. There was one law for the home born and the stranger.[13] The belief began to grow that the Negro must either remain without benefits of Christianity or "he must be admitted to emancipation." [14]

In the defense of holding Christian Negroes in slavery some colonial legislatures ventured to decree that baptism and slavery were not inconsistent. The Crown lawyers, Yorke and Talbot, concurred in this interpretation.[15] In time the question was referred to the Church of England, and Gordon, Bishop of London, pronounced *ex cathedra* that "the embracing of the gospel did not make the least

---

[9] De vinne, *loc. cit.*, p. 72.
[10] *Minutes of the General Conference*, May 16, 1800, p. 40.
[11] *Ibid.*, p. 41.
[12] De vinne, *loc. cit.*, p. 9.
[13] *Ibid.*
[14] *Ibid.*
[15] *Ibid.*, p. 10.

alteration in the civil property." [16] As a result a new interpretation had to be found for Biblical reference to the question.

While the problem was being discussed by other churches to its full, the Methodist bodies went serenely on with their program of evangelizing the Negro. By 1790 the Charleston Conference mentioned above was ready to pass the resolution which stated that it was planned "to establish Sunday school, for poor children, both white and black."

The fact that Bishop Asbury was able to use his servant, "Black Harry" as a preaching substitute in major areas of the church denoted the country-wide acceptance of these Methodist views on the Negro. In the Asbury Journal under date of Sunday, April 13, the following is noted: "Preached at the Chapel (evidently Forest Chapel in Maryland). Afterward, Harry, a black man, spoke on the "barren fig tree." This circumstance was new and the white people looked on with attention.[17]

In the General Conference held in 1796, it was declared that slavery was an evil and Methodist clergy were requested to use caution in admitting persons to official station in the church. Those being thus elevated should be required to emancipate slaves either immediately or gradually. It was further agreed that the yearly conference should take additional steps at regulating slavery. However, no slaveholder should be admitted to the church until the minister had spoken to him freely and frankly. Every member who sold a slave should be excluded from the society. The Conference declared that any member purchasing a slave was to take the matter up with the Quarterly Conference which should decide how long the slave should work before being freed. Documents to this effect should be drawn up and signed by the owner. Every male child should be freed at twenty-five years and every female at twenty-one. In concluding this extraordinary action the preachers and laymen were asked to study the matter of Negro slavery until the next General Conference.

Changes were developing, however. Lines along the slavery question were being sharply drawn and the new denomination was to see rough times ahead. Bishop Asbury began complaining that

---

[16] *Ibid.*
[17] *The Character and Career of Francis Asbury* (New York, 1872), by Rev. Edwin L. Janes, p. 156.

"Harry seems to be unwilling to go with me. I fear his speaking so much to white people in the city has been, or will be, injurious. He has been flattered, and may be ruined." [18]

There is little doubt that the church was affected by the controversies and certainly after the death of Bishop Asbury the statements of the church were not so rigidly adhered to. Somehow, if the new denomination was to bring in other white members it could not continue to be even 40 per cent Negro. In this Dr. Joy, Historian of the Methodist Church, agrees.

Bishop Robert Paine, in his book, *The Life and Times of William M'Kendree,* states that "Two subjects gave trouble" in the Tennessee Conference, which was in session October first, 1813, slavery, and the war. He asserts that the Conference was "stringent" in its application of the rules against the buying and selling of slaves. He declares that several local preachers had been arrested and tried, but in most cases the Quarterly Conference had refused to punish them. In one case, however, the Quarterly Conference had suspended the individual. An appeal was made to the Annual Conference and the case was considered by that body. The defense declared that a great deal of harm was being done because of this intermeddling with the legal and private rights, and it was the concensus of opinion of some that "they could not and would not conform to their views of the rule." Bishop Asbury sat in the session saying nothing but Bishop M'Kendree reminded him that "he ought to keep the rule or change it." The rule was upheld.[19]

Thus from 1796 on, the Methodist Church found this question of slavery more and more vexing. In the Conference of 1800 three motions were voted down. The first excluded all slaveholders from membership; the second attempted to free all slave children after the Fourth of July; the third stated that all slaves were to be given an instrument of emancipation within one year of the date "hereof," the Quarterly Conference to decide the time "the slave shall serve," "if the laws of the state do not expressly prohibit their emancipation." A fourth motion was carried. We have stated this above concerning the special committee appointed by the conference.[20]

[18] *Ibid.,* p. 160.
[19] *Life and Times of William M'Kendree* in 2 vols., I (Nashville, 1874), by Bishop Robert Paine.
[20] De vinne, *loc. cit.,* p. 41.

By 1820, when the General Conference met in Baltimore, a sufficient number of Methodists were so wary that it was voted to leave the matter of slavery "no longer in the hands of the annual conference." [21] It might be stated that in the 1804 Conference, feeling had been so bitter that Freeborn Garrettson had suggested that the matter of slavery should be left to the three Bishops in order that the Northern and Southern attitudes "might be satisfied."

This change of heart, no doubt, was occasioned by the first real division in American Methodism. From 1776-1787 the conference had been held in the slaveholding states. This was logical for in that period out of 14,000 members, only 2,000 lived in that which was known as free territory. De vinne states that in "1779, mainly because of the 'ordinances' more Southern preachers, amounting to more than one half of the entire body, seceded, holding a separate conference at Fluvanna, Virginia. The original body was held by Bishop Asbury at Kent County, Delaware." [22] This division continued for the seventh and eighth conferences, in 1779, 1780. The two bodies met together in 1784.

It might be well to close this chapter by giving some idea of the number of white and black members in the church in this period. Turning to an early statistical report of the time, the following is noted: In 1786 there were (contrary to De vinne's figures) 16,791 white members and 890 Negro. The following year there were 19,300 whites listed to 3,780 colored, an increase of 212% for the Negro group. In still another year the Negro group had gone up 69%, to 6,422, while the white membership totaled 26,242.

In 1790, 37,016 white people were noted as being members along with 11,682 Negroes, a 77% increase of Negroes. In 1793 the growth of Negro members slowed up considerably when only a 34% increase is noted; however, white membership increased by 3% to 38,413. At this time fully one third to one half or more than 40% of the total Methodist membership in America was Negro.

The one item pertinent to any history of Zion Methodism is the number of Negro members in the John Street Church. It is safe to say that from the reference made in various writings of the early church leaders these individuals must have been considerable. If

---

[21] Paine, *loc. cit.*, p. 396.
[22] De vinne, *loc. cit.*, pp. 12, 13.

the tendency increased as time went on, even to the percentages noted, the John Street Church must have had a problem when it came to the matter of caring for so large a number. By the time of the organic separation in 1820, Seaman records that the New York Methodism boasted 2,440 white members, 88 Negro members, with 690 being listed as members of Zion and Asbury, both colored organizations.

CHAPTER V

Early Beginnings of the African Chapel

THE MATTER of slavery was a subject for controversy and action in every local congregation. Bishop Asbury recognized the importance of the subject in his accounts of the reception of Black Harry. The John Street Church was certainly concerned with the controversy. It appears that favorable action must have been recorded by this chapel for it was considered a haven for slaves who wished aid in changing their status.

Rev. John B. Wakley in his *Lost Chapters* states that Peter Williams was not the first sexton of Wesley Chapel in New York which leads one to believe that perhaps the benevolence of the Board of Trustees of the Chapel was well known to Negroes of the city.[1] However, it is with Peter Williams that we are most concerned.

A slave by the name of Peter Williams approached the officers of the John Street Church requesting them to purchase his freedom and allow him to repay them as he was able. There is every reason to believe that Peter was accustomed to work for the Church as occasion demanded, for payments to him are noted in May, 1776, and April of the same year as well.[2] It may be that the slave was *loaned* to the congregation from time to time.[3]

Peter was a short, stout man, who later in life became bald and wore a wig. He was born in New York, and for a time lived with a family in Beekman Street. Contrary to custom, when slaves took the name of their owners, Peter's family name was Williams, his father's name being George and his mother, Diana. It is said that at least one of the parents was of pure African stock. His dwelling place, as perhaps his birthplace, was a section of the building given over to the cows and other animals. It is stated that he often declared, "I was born in as humble a place as my Master."[4] He had

---

[1] Rev. J. B. Wakley, *Lost Chapters*, recovered from *Early American Methodism* (New York, 1858), p. 539.
[2] *Ibid.*, p. 460.
[3] *Ibid.*
[4] Wakley, *loc. cit.*, p. 487.

two brothers and seven sisters, none of whom became Methodists. Peter was probably converted in the old *rigging loft* in the days of Embury and Webb.[5]

Peter married Mary Durham, a native of St. Christopher's, West Indies. She was two years older than her husband, "beautiful and full of good sense and distinguished for her consistent piety." [6] She had been brought to America by the Durham family and somehow found her way to the Methodist Chapel where she met her future husband.

While it is hard to trace Peter Williams' early history, it appears that he later became the property of James Aymar, who was a tobacco merchant. In Aymar's shop Peter learned the tobacco business which was to stand him in good stead later.[7] When the War of Independence broke out, Aymar, who was a Tory, was forced to flee and Peter finally ended up by working for the father of a Dr. Milledollar.[8] It may have been in this period that he approached the officials of John Street Church about his freedom.

As has been mentioned above, Peter evidently had been in the habit of working for John Street Church at intervals so his coming to the officers for aid was logical from the dual standpoint of church attitude towards slavery and the fact that he was a member and well known to them from membership and work.

The church officers decided to *buy* Peter and allow him to repay them as he was able. The first payment recorded was a gold watch. One can wonder just where a slave could secure a gold watch but we have the assurance that the officers of the Church were well satisfied with the payment. Conjecture would have it that Peter either had performed some service of merit or, since the burial of members was in the hands of the sexton (who served as undertaker) someone could have willed it to him. There is little doubt that the purchase of his freedom was a long uphill journey and would have been an almost idle dream were it not for the fact that the Church paid him a stipulated sum for his services and from this amount payments were made. The accounts from the Old John Street records are interesting:

---

[5] *Ibid.*
[6] *Ibid.*
[7] *Ibid.*
[8] *Ibid.*

1783, June 10, Paid Mr. Aymar for his negro Peter.........£4000
1783, May 27, Credit a watch received from Peter............£ 500
1783, July 12, Received of black Peter at sundry times.........£ 400
1783, Dec. 1, By Peter Williams in part, his
      indebtedness to this society ....£ 400
1784, Feb. 28, By cash from Peter Williams ....£ 340
1784, May 1, By cash from Peter Williams toward his debt......£ 340
1784, June 26, Peter, toward his debt ....£ 280
1784, October 3, By Black Peter ....£ 200
1784, Dec. 18, from Peter Paid ....£ 340
1785, November 4, By cash received of Peter Williams
      in full of all demands on the— ....£ 570

Later, Peter set himself up in the business of a tobacconist and succeeded so well that he was able to purchase his own home on Liberty Street.[9] Since Peter was not able to read or write and his wife could do little, his son, Peter, Jr., kept the accounts of the business.[10] This son was licensed to preach in the Protestant Episcopal Church on Center Street (St. Philip's) presumably around 1820.[11]

Peter and Mary (some appeared to have called her Mollie) lived in the Methodist parsonage for seven years. Here they took loving care of the single preachers who pastored the congregations of the New York area. The Church paid Mary for her services as well as paying her husband. It is unfortunate that more cannot be told of this relationship of sexton and ministers for it appears that here lies the real truth of the establishment of Zion Church in New York.

One writer states that "Brother Williams would, on special occasions when a number of preachers were in the City, invite a company of ministers and their wives to dine or take tea at his humble dwelling." [12] If this is true, and we have no reason to doubt the statement, Peter Williams was in close enough touch with the ministry of John Street Church to know of all problems which the congregation faced. He was known as one deeply interested in the welfare of his people, so much so that he became a trustee of Zion Church or Chapel, or, as it was called, "The African Chapel." In spite of this he kept his membership in John Street Church.

It is not hard to establish the idea that Peter Williams was one of the most respected Negroes in New York. We know that his

---

[9] Wakley, loc. cit., p. 487.
[10] Ibid., pp. 442-443.
[11] Ibid., p. 487.
[12] Wakley, loc. cit., p. 487.

opinion was listened to by the ministry of the Church. Any problem pertaining to the Negro membership would have been brought to him. Nevertheless, for another reason too, all Zionites should remember this ex-slave. From the beginning he played a major part in the formation of Zion Chapel and, consequently, our denomination. We can, with assurance, credit him with a great part in the establishment of the first Negro Methodist Church in America. It was he, too, who was accorded the honor of laying the cornerstone of Zion in 1801, when the building was being erected on the corner of Church and Leonard Streets.

John Jamison Moore, an early Bishop of the African M.E. Zion Church, states that the great reason for the separation from the mother church was the rapid increase in the Negro membership.[13] Rush, another Superintendent of the Church, states that a meeting was held in 1796 with Bishop Asbury at which time the matter of the Negro membership was discussed.[14] The members of this committee who talked with Bishop Asbury were: Francis Jacobs, William Brown, Peter Williams, Abraham Thompson and June Scott. After discussion with the Bishop the Negro members were given permission to meet in the "interval of the regular preaching hours of our white brethren." [15] The arrangements for the services brought its problems for Rush states that the Negro members were to conduct their services in "the best manner they could." [16] This seems to infer that Bishop Asbury recognized the fact that the ruling elder and his assistant (s) were carrying a great load as it was. Rush lists, along with the Committee who talked with Bishop Asbury, the following: Samuel Pontier, Thomas Miller, James Varick and William Hamilton. Others he could not recall.

According to Bishop Rush, several problems faced those interested in the Negro of New York City. The John Street congregation had licensed Negroes to preach, but beyond that nothing was done. Seaman states that by 1800 there were only three colored preachers and one exhorter in New York. Evidently, these were Abraham Thompson, June Scott and Thomas Miller.[17] The fact that these ministers

---

[13] *History of the A.M.E. Zion Church*, by John Jamison Moore (York, Pa., 1884), p. 15.
[14] Christopher Rush, *A Short Account of the Rise and Progress of the African Methodist Episcopal Church in America* (New York, 1843), p. 10.
[15] *Ibid.* (1866), p. 9.
[16] Rush, *loc. cit.* (1866), p. 9.
[17] *Ibid.*, p. 10.

could not perform all the services required and therefore Negro members were deprived of some of the most sacred rites of the church, could have brought about deep thought on the part of the Negro leadership. A basic cause for dissatisfaction, however, must have been the restrictions under which the Negroes were conducting their worship. Bishop Hood lays great stress on the twenty-fifth question asked at the Conference of 1780:

> Ought not the assistant (Mr. Asbury) to meet the colored people himself, and appoint as helpers in his absence proper white persons, and not suffer them to stay so late and meet by themselves?
> Answer: Yes.

It appears that this regulation was a slap at Elder Asbury as well as being obnoxious to the colored brethren.

An outstanding item in this all-important meeting in 1796 is that James Varick does not appear to have been closely identified with the early formation of the church. It is very difficult to arrive at a solution to this matter for Rush appears to have had a light opinion of Varick. Flood, in his *History of the Bishops*, states that Varick was born in 1795. When one realizes that he would have been seventeen or eighteen years old when he was licensed to preach and only twenty-five when the church was established as a denomination in 1820, this date appears to have been too late. An earlier date listed for the birth of Varick would make him too old for the election as Rush states it in connection with Abraham Thompson. The question then arises concerning his being a minister at the time of this first meeting.

To establish clearly the reason for the request made to Bishop Asbury, let us return to Rush's *History*. Bishop Rush makes the statement that the seats among the white brethren were limited. While the Minutes of the New York Conference have not as yet been located, statements of other writers of the period bring out the fact that in 1802 there were 726 white members evidently at John Street and in New York City 211 colored. In 1803 there were 248 Negro members and 268 the following year. In 1810 there were 490 Negro members and in 1812, 540. The following year there were 627, while in 1819 this number had dropped to fifty, presumably because of the fact that Zion and Asbury were now recognized as a separate charge. [18] It was in 1818 that the first minister was appointed to the Negro churches, a Rev. W. Phoebus.

It appears that one can safely note that the increase in the number of Negro members was providing a problem for John Street Church. It may have been that, taken as a whole, the white and Negro membership crowded her facilities and certainly burdened her ministry. Surely the ministry knew this, and perhaps talked the matter over with the Negro leaders in the community. The first efforts to adjust this condition were carried out in such a way as not to interfere with the regular preaching services at John Street. In fact, Rush states that even after the African Chapel was established they refrained from holding any meeting during the regular worship periods at John Street.[19] Prayer meetings were held Sunday afternoons and "also a Wednesday night service." [20]

The Reverend B. F. Wheeler in his book *The Varick Family* makes some pertinent statements concerning the founding of the A.M.E. Zion Church when he declares that the "Methodists did not persecute colored people but simply denied them certain privileges." [21] They were certainly more generous than any other denomination and even after the withdrawal of the Zion Church still permitted the Negro ministry an important part in their evangelistic work. It appears that their efforts to restrain the functions of these ministers aided in the loss of Virginia to Negro Methodism.

The American Revolution left its distinct mark on the church in that in this period slavery crept into the church "without the knowledge of Asbury and Wesley." This change was aided by the first split in American Methodism. Above we have stated that the Southern wing had withdrawn because of the "ordinances," continuing the separation until 1784. It appears that this sharply drawing of lines affected even the most liberal of churches.

Previously, we have stated that Bishop Moore had listed reasons for the increase of tension between the Negro and white groups. While one had to do with the increase in the Negro membership, the second concerned the refusal to allow Negro ministers to join the

[18] *Annals of the New York Conference*, p. 209.
NOTE: Benj. F. Wheeler in his booklet *The Varick Family*, states that Bishop Varick married Aurelia Jones when "around 48 years of age." The date given is 1798. To this union were born four children.
[19] Rush, *loc. cit.* (1866), p. 9.
[20] *Ibid.*, p. 10.
[21] Benjamin F. Wheeler, *The Varick Family* (Mobile, 1906), p. 7.

conference as itinerants.[22] Thus, both the lay member and preacher were committed to a change in these conditions. The meeting with Rev. Asbury resulted.

With the initial step taken to form a new church, the problem of finding a place of worship presented itself. The larger committee, consisting of those who talked with Rev. Asbury and those mentioned later from Rush's *History* formed the charter group of the new Chapel. After much searching, a cabinet maker's shop, the property of William Miller, was chosen as the first meeting place of the Chapel.[23] This first location of the Zion Church was on Cross Street between Mulberry and Orange. In reality the shop was an old stable which had been converted to a cabinet maker's use.[24]

Rush states that the shop was fitted with seats, a pulpit and a gallery. Here, prayer meetings were held each Sunday afternoon, and, in the interval of divine worship at John Street Church, preaching and exhorting meetings.[25] Just what nights were utilized is not known but Rush mentions Sunday afternoons, Wednesday nights, and later, Fridays.[26]

The preachers serving the new organization appear to have been Abraham Thompson, June Scott and Thomas Miller with William Miller serving as exhorter.[27] Mention is made of visiting preachers from Philadelphia also,[28] as well as Negro preachers from other places.[29]

It was in 1796 that the first meetings were held in the cabinet maker's shop. Three years later, the Negro membership of John Street Church had grown to such proportions that the idea was advanced concerning the erection of a house of worship. The matter of seating space in John Street Church was again a factor. By this time, the Chapel had grown in importance. The members, seeing success crown their initial efforts, began to discuss a more permanent setup. Abraham Thompson and June Scott were active in expressing their viewpoints and it may have been through this pressure that a meeting was called in which it was finally decided that the

---

[22] John Jamison Moore, *loc. cit.*, p. 15.
[23] Rush, *loc. cit.*, p. 10.
[24] *Ibid.*
[25] *Ibid.*
[26] *Ibid.*
[27] Rush, *loc. cit.*, p. 10.
[28] *Ibid.*
[29] *Ibid.*

time was ripe to proceed with the plans for a regularly organized chapel.[30]

From Rush's account, it appears that the group decided to appeal to all who might be interested in the venture, not limiting participation to those then in the venture. Rush states in part: "For this purpose they called a meeting of some of the most respectable and intelligent religious colored men of the city, in order to consult upon the best method to proceed in this great undertaking for colored people of the City of New York." [31]

Later plans lead one to believe that this appeal went beyond the matter of religious worship to that of future educational desires. The meeting was held in the cabinet maker's shop on Cross Street, and while Rush realizes that he could not recall all who attended (no minutes having been preserved), he does mention George E. Moore, Thomas Sipkins, David Bias, George White, Thomas Cook, John Teesman and George Collins.[32]

No hint has come down to us that those attending this meeting did not see the wisdom of a chapel in which Negroes might worship. It is not quite clear as to their over-all intentions, however. This writer cannot seem to discover whether the members and friends had in mind a new denomination or merely proceeded with the idea that they mainly wanted their own meeting house. The group agreed that the form of government should be Methodist. Rush places it this way: "They concluded that the church should be under the Methodist government." [33] Later, he states: "When our White brethren, the Ministers of the Methodist Episcopal Church, found that we were determined upon becoming a separate body, or society, they appointed the Rev. John McClaskey, at their General Conference, who was one of the stationed Elders for the Methodist Episcopal Church in the City of New York, to make arrangements and effect some articles of agreement with us for our government, in order that the spiritual part of the government might be under the direction of the General Conference of the Methodist Episcopal Church from time to time, and so keep the two churches or societies in union with each other." [34]

---

[30] *Ibid.*
[31] *Ibid.*
[32] *Ibid.*, p. 11.
[33] Rush, *loc. cit.*, p. 11.
[34] *Ibid.*, p. 13.

The name selected for the new organization is merely listed by the early historian without any explanation. It was common practice for Negro groups to use the name "African" and it is supposed that this was true in this instance. It appears that the group wanted the distinguishing word in order that the name might denote a non-white group. For more than twenty years the name *African Chapel* appears in reference after reference to the new group. (It was common practice, likewise, to list many of the Methodist churches in the area as *chapels,* so the word *African* referred to the Negro church.) The name *Zion* appears to have been used as over against *St. George's Chapel,* or later, *Asbury.* The Methodist Episcopal was the given name of the denomination.

Rush states that the Methodist ministry seeing that the group was determined to establish itself brought the matter before the General Conference meeting in 1800.[35] A Rev. John McClaskey, one of the *Elders* stationed in New York City, was appointed to work out an agreement with the new organization. The relationship between Mr. McClaskey and the African Chapel appeared to be very friendly and there was no unwillingness in working with him. Under his guidance the trustees of the new chapel drew up two legal documents, one pertaining to incorporation under the laws of the State of New York and the other an agreement with the Methodist Church. Those trustees as elected who worked with the minister were: Francis Jacobs, William Brown, Thomas Miller, Peter Williams, Thomas Sipkins, William Hamilton and George Collins.

We list herein the Charter and agreement which the Trustees and Mr. McClaskey drew up:

CHARTER OF THE AFRICAN CHURCH

In pursuance of an Act, entitled an Act to enable all the religious denominations of this state to appoint Trustees who shall be a body corporate, for the purpose of taking care of the temporalities of their respective congregations and for other purposes therein mentioned, passed the sixth day of April, 1784, public notice was given in the African Methodist Episcopal Church (Called Zion Church) of the City of New York, in the State of New York, as the aforesaid law directs; and we, the subscribers, being nominated and appointed, agreeably to the aforesaid Act, Inspectors of an election held in our place of meeting, the eighth day of September, 1800, do report and declare the following persons duly elected by a plurality of voices, to serve as Trustees for

---

[35] Rush, *loc. cit.,* p. 13.

the said Church, viz: Francis Jacobs, George Collins, Thomas Sipkins, George E. Moore, George White, David Bias, Peter Williams, Thomas Cook and William Brown, which said persons, so elected, and their successors in office, shall forever be styled and denominated the Trustees of the Corporation of the African Methodist Episcopal Church in the City of New York.

Given under our hands and seals, this fifth day of February, one thousand eight hundred and one.

HIS

PETER   X   WILLIAMS

MARK

FRANCIS JACOBS

STATE OF NEW YORK, ss:

On this sixteenth day of February, 1801, before me personally came Peter Williams and Francis Jacobs, to me known to be persons within described, and who executed the within conveyance, who duly acknowledged the same—and there being no material erasures or interlineations therein, I do allow it to be recorded.

(Signed) JAMES M. HUGHES, *Master in Chancery.*

Recorded in the office of the Clerk of the City and County of New York, in Lib. No. 1 of Record of Incorporation of Religious Denominations, page 28, this ninth day of March, 1801.

Examined by

(Signed) ROBERT BENSON, *Clerk*

ARTICLES OF AGREEMENT

Made the sixth day of April, 1801, between the Rev. John McClaskey, in behalf of the General Conference of the Methodist Church in the United States of America, of the one part, and the Trustees of the African Methodist Episcopal Church in the City of New York, of the other part, showeth, for themselves and their successors in office:

ARTICLE I

It is provided and declared that the style and title of this Corporation shall be "The African Methodist Episcopal Church of the City of New York, in the State of New York," and shall consist of Francis Jacobs, George Collins, Thomas Sipkins, George E. Moore, George White, David Bias, Peter Williams, Thomas Cook and William Brown, Trustees and Members of Zion Church, and their successors duly qualified, elected and appointed according to law (for the purposes and with the powers and privileges hereinafter granted and specified), of the Church called Zion Church, and of all and every such other church or churches as do now, or hereafter shall become the property of the Corporation.

ARTICLE II

The Corporation aforesaid and their successors forever, do, and shall have and hold the said building called Zion Church, and all other churches which are now or shall become the property of the Corpora-

51

tion, in trust, for the religious use of the Ministers and Preachers of the Methodist Episcopal Church, who are in connection with the General Conference, of the said church, and likewise for our African brethren and the descendants of the African race, as hereafter specified, and also for ministers and teachers of our African brethren, duly licensed or ordained according to the form of discipline.

Article III

It is provided and declared that the rents, issues, profits and interests of the real and personal estate of and belonging to the said Church and Trustees and their successors shall, from time to time, be applied and laid out for repairing and maintaining their said Zion Church, and all and any other place or places of public worship, lot or lots of ground, burial grounds, or buildings which now do, or at any time hereafter may or shall belong to the said Church or Trustees, as shall, from time to time, be thought proper and expedient by the Trustees for the time being; and if the funds and revenues be sufficient, the Trustees may and shall be permitted, in their own discretion, to allow a reasonable and proportionable part for the support of the Ministers.

Article IV

It is provided and declared that the said Trustees and their successors shall not, by deed or otherwise, grant, alien, convey, or otherwise dispose of any part or parcel of the estate, real or personal, in the said Corporation vested or to be vested, or in any other way to mortgage or pledge the said real estate for the payment of any debts by them contracted to any person or persons whatever, unless such grant, alienation and conveyance be made by and with the consent of two-thirds of the regular male members of the said church, of at least twenty-one years of age, and one year's standing.

Article V

It is provided and declared that none but Africans or their descendants shall be chosen as Trustees of the said African Episcopal Zion Church, and such other church or churches as may or shall hereafter become the property of this Corporation, and none shall be eligible to the office of a Trustee but such as are received and acknowledged to be members of the said church by the elder of the Methodist Episcopal Church in the City of New York, who shall be appointed by the Conference of the said church, to the charge of the Methodist Society in the said city.

Article VI

All elections for Trustees for the aforesaid Zion Church shall be by ballot of the male members, in close communion with them, or as many of them as attend, after being duly warned thereto; and no one shall have a right to vote for Trustees until he has been a member standing in full connection, one year at least; and no person shall be chosen a Trustee of said Corporation until the said person shall have been a member in full connection and standing, at least two years. And no person shall be admitted into close connection with their classes or be enrolled on their books but Africans and descendants of the African race.

ARTICLE VII

It is provided and declared that the Trustees aforesaid and their successors forever are and shall be empowered to have, and shall have, the entire direction and disposal of the temporal revenue of the aforesaid African Zion Church, and, after paying the ground rent of the said church, are to apply the remainder for the benefit of the said church, as a majority of the aforesaid Trustees and their successors shall, from time to time, direct. And the aforesaid Trustees and their successors forever shall have the disposal and management of the temporal concerns of the aforesaid African Methodist Episcopal Church, subject, nevertheless, to the provisions, and under the regulations made and provided in the fourth article of this instrument.

ARTICLE VIII

It is declared that the Trustees and members of the African Methodist Episcopal Church do acquiesce and accord with the rules of the Methodist Episcopal Church for their church government and discipline, and with their creed and articles of faith, and that they and their successors will continue forever in union with the Methodist Episcopal Church in the City of New York, subject to the government of the present Bishops and their successors, in all their ecclesiastical affairs and transactions, except in the temporal right and property of the aforesaid Zion Church, which is to be governed as herein directed, as long as the said articles and creeds of the said church remain unchanged.

ARTICLE IX

It is declared that the elder of the Methodist Episcopal Church, for the time being, in the City of New York, appointed as aforementioned, shall have the direction and management of the spiritual concerns of the said Zion Church, or any other church or churches which may or shall be built hereafter by the Corporation aforesaid, or by any other means become their property, agreeably to the form of discipline of the said Methodist Episcopal Church, *Provided,* always, that the said elder shall receive no person into the African Society but such as are previously recommended by a Trustee or Trustees of the said African Zion Church. And upon complaint being made to the said African Church, or to the elder, of any of its members having walked disorderly, they shall be dealt with according to the form of discipline; *provided,* always, that their triers be members of their own church, and that the member, if condemned in the first trial, have an appeal to the Trustees, local preachers, exhorters and class leaders of the aforesaid Zion Church. And it is further declared that no person who may come recommended to the elder from other societies as a member of the Methodist Episcopal Church, shall be admitted or considered as a member of the African Church if he refuse to have his name registered in the books of the said Zion Church, after notice having been given him.

ARTICLE X

It is agreed and declared that the elder of the Methodist Episcopal Church in the City of New York, appointed as aforesaid, shall, from time to time, forever hereafter, nominate the preacher who shall officiate in said African Methodist Episcopal Church, and any, and all, other church or churches, which shall hereafter become the property of the Corporation, and shall attend to the said church or churches himself, to administer the ordinances of Baptism and the Lord's Supper, as often as he, the said Elder, can make it convenient. And the said Elder for the time being, shall license to exhort and preach any one or more of the brethren who are, or shall be, members of the said church, and shall appear, to the satisfaction of the said Elder, to be adequate to the task, and to have grace and gifts proper to appear in public: *Provided,* always that such persons are previously recommended to him by a majority of the Trustees, local preachers, exhorters, and class leaders, of the aforesaid church. And if either of the said African brethren shall graduate into holy orders, it shall be done in such manner and way as the General Conference has directed. And it is provided and agreed that the said Elder may claim for himself and his white brethren, and shall have and possess, a right to preach once on every Sunday, and once during the course of the week (and no more, when there is a sufficient number of African Preachers), in any or all the houses set apart and built, or to be set apart and built, by the aforesaid Trustees, or their successors, of the said African Zion Church, in the city and suburbs of New York.

ARTICLE XI

It is provided and declared that no powers and authorities hereby given to the aforementioned Trustees shall be understood, taken, or construed, in any wise to prohibit or prevent the Elder, for the time being, duly authorized and appointed as aforesaid, the religious use, benefit and enjoyment of the church known by the name of Zion Church, or of any other church or churches which, at any time hereafter, may be purchased or built by the said Corporation, or in any other way become their property in the City of New York or the suburbs thereof, but that the same shall be, and forever after continue to be, had, used, and enjoyed by the said Elder for the time being, as heretofore, and by no other person whatever, of another denomination, unless by the particular license and consent of the Elder for the time being, with the concurrence of two-thirds of the Trustees, for the time being, anything to the contrary in these articles notwithstanding.

(Signed)

FRANCIS JACOBS,	GEORGE COLLINS,
HIS	HIS
THOMAS X SIPKINS,	PETER X WILLIAMS,
MARK	MARK
GEORGE E. MOORE,	THOMAS COOK,
HIS	HIS
GEORGE X WHITE,	WILLIAM X BROWN,
MARK	MARK
	DAVID BIAS.

54

One of the objects of any history is to preserve for posterity all known facts or links associated with the subject at hand. Somewhere the late Bishop E. D. W. Jones began a manuscript on the History of the Church which has never been published. Evidently many of the facts he intended to utilize are to be found in his *Comprehensive Catechism*. It is from this source that we take the following additional items on Peter Williams.

Jones reiterates the belief that Peter Williams was a member of the Methodist Church prior to the erection of the John Street Church, securing these facts from Wakley. He further quotes Wakley: "Peter felt a deep interest for the welfare of his own color. He knew religion had made him all he was on earth and all he hoped to be in heaven. He did all he could to elevate his race. Peter thought a House of Worship expressly for the people of his own color might be exceedingly beneficial. He aided in circulating a subscription and raised money to build the church at the corner of Leonard and Church Streets, which is called *Zion Church*. It was built in 1801. This was the first church edifice built expressly for the people of color in New York. Mr. Williams laid with his own hands the cornerstone of this building and was one of the original trustees. . . ."

From the recently published book *As You Pass By* by Kenneth Holcomb Dunshee (Hastings House, 1952) the following statement appears concerning Mollie Williams:

One of the famous *volunteers* of the earlier days was an old Negro woman named Molly, a slave of John Aymar, one of the last of the old Knickerbockers of New York. Aymar was himself a famous figure in New York in those days. A trim old gentleman he continued to wear the style of dress common among the wealthier old aristocrats—a long-tailed coat, knee breeches, silver shoe-buckles and the inevitable queue.

The boys of the company used to call Molly "Volunteer No. 11." She considered herself a very important member and often was seen running at the sound of an alarm in her calico dress and checkered apron, a clean bandanna handkerchief neatly folded over her breast, and another wound about her head. Once during a blinding snowstorm there was a fire in William Street, and it was hard work to draw the engine; but the first to take hold of the drag-rope that day was Molly, pulling away for dear life. This may have been the only time she took hold of the rope, but afterward, when asked what engine she belonged to, she always replied, "I belongs to ole 'Leven; I allers runs wid dat old bull-gine." Later, one of the 11's boys wrote, "You could not look at Molly without being impressed by her really honest face—it was a beaming lighthouse of good-nature." [36]

From another account in this same work the following appears:

Peter Williams, a former slave of Benjamin Aymar, tobacco merchant, was bought by the trustees of the church for forty pounds sterling and was installed as first sexton. Peter married the substantial and happy Molly (another Aymar ex-slave), whose heart was closely attached to "Moll's Boys" and that "Ole 'Leben engine" in Hanover Square. Peter earned his freedom after "keeping" the chapel with his wife, Molly, for many years. They were much respected citizens and attracted to Wesley Chapel a devoted group of their own people, who later formed the first colored Methodist congregation in New York. Emulating his ex-master, Peter Williams, already an expert cigarmaker went into the tobacco business, and became an early "American success story." He used a considerable part of the fortune he amassed, as well as his time and energy, in making possible the building in 1801, of the first Methodist Church for Negroes in New York. The former slave laid the cornerstone of this the Zion African Methodist Episcopal Church, located at Leonard and Church Streets, on July 30, 1800.

Union Engine Company No. 18, whose first engine house was in Water Street, near Fulton, in 1787, moved to quarters "on the Hill at John Street, near Pearl" in 1796. They were known as the "shadbellies" in those early days but later preferred to be called "Drybones." Try as they might, they could not win the affections of Molly Williams away from "her" Engine 11, even after she moved to John Street.

When yellow fever struck New York in 1822, John Street was in the center of its most virulent devastation. People dropped on the streets like flies and everyone who could fled to Greenwich Village or anywhere else free from the contamination. Living in John Street at that time was an old colored woman named Chloe, who sold flowers and did odd jobs. She was a great favorite of the lawyers in the vicinity, whose offices she often cleaned. As the John Street folks prepared to leave, Chloe obstinately refused all who offered to take her with them. After the plague had run its course and the residents returned to their homes and shops, they found that Chloe had remained for a very definite purpose. There she was in her small quarters surrounded by all the dogs, cats, goats and birds which had been abandoned. She had faithfully tended and fed them.

Everyone was so touched and gratified that enough money was quickly collected to have Chloe's portrait painted, surrounded by the pets whose lives she saved. The artist chosen was no less than William Dunlap, historian, actor, artist and local celebrity, who wrote the "History of the American Theatre," as well as the tremendous work, "History of the Arts and Design in America." The finished painting

---

[36] Kenneth Holcomb Dunshee, *As You Pass By* (Hastings House, 1952), p. 53.

must have delighted everyone because an engraving was made from it so that prints could be distributed to the folks who had contributed toward the painting. It is strange that the original painting, as well as all of the engravings, has disappeared but as long as the memory still lives, who knows but that some day Chloe and her pets will come to light again.[37]

[37] Dunshee, *loc. cit.*, pp. 106, 107.

CHAPTER VI

Establishing a Permanent Organization

IN THE corporation document it was stated that all property was to be owned and controlled by the Board of Trustees of the African Methodist Episcopal Church. This not only took care of any property of the Chapel but any other property secured by that organization or any of its branches.

The significance of this statement is realized when one notes that the Board of Trustees of John Street Church owned and controlled all Methodist property in the city. The fact that it made no effort to secure to itself the property of the Negro group is significant. The fact of control by this one board brought about one controversy over the carpeting of the platform at John Street. A great many of the other Methodist groups in the city were bitter. They declared that two churches, one, John Street, were getting the lion's share of improvements and, anyway, no church should have a carpeted platform.

The agreement with the Methodist Church contained two items of note: one, that the Methodist Episcopal Church should appoint ministers to the group. The other stated that the Board of Trustees of the Chapel, as it was able, should contribute to the support of the minister.

On this last point the first difference in the Chapel hinged.[1] Abraham Thompson and June Scott, two of the three Negro ministers in the city at the time of the formation of the Chapel (the other being Thomas Miller; William Miller was an exhorter), felt that Negro ministers should receive some compensation for their services as well as the elder who would receive all available funds under the new agreement. They, therefore, suggested that the Chapel should sever all relations with John Street and establish themselves as a denomination. Rush appears to overlook the injustice which was being done the Negro ministry and states that they were more interested in money than the spiritual welfare of the people.

A white man by the name of John Edwards who had been ex-

---

[1] Rush, *loc. cit.*, p. 27.

pelled from the Quaker Society took advantage of the dissatisfaction. There is little doubt that the three felt that if the Negro ministry withdrew that most of the members would follow. Edwards was a scale beam worker and Rush states, at times "he acted as if he did not enjoy his right mind." However, Edwards professed his call to preach and purchased a lot on Green Street. Here he succeeded in erecting a church with two wings, one housing the church and the other for the use of the ministry who might join the group.[2]

Abraham Thompson allegedly joined the movement to secure free rent in the building.[3] June Scott also transferred his membership to this new venture which took the name of "The Union Society." When the African Chapel heard of the move it took steps to expel the men. As a result, Thompson came back pleading ignorance of what he was doing. June Scott remained with the group until it was abandoned because of financial difficulties. He subsequently joined another church.

In the Agreement of 1801 (April) other items pertinent to the Zion Church history are to be noted. For example, buildings which might be constructed were to be used only by ministers and preachers of the Methodist Episcopal Church and the African people or the descendants of Africans. The final article of note had to do with the trustees. The agreement stated that only trustees of African blood could act for the corporation.

Two years before the agreement with the Methodist Episcopal Church, the Board of Trustees named earlier had moved to secure a more permanent place of worship. The old cabinet maker's shop had been outgrown and it became imperative to do something about the matter. So, in 1799, the Board authorized Thomas Miller to secure a lot. They had raised the sum of eighty dollars by subscription, gleaned from the "citizens of New York." [4] This sum was deposited with the Treasurer, Thomas Miller. Miller followed the directions of the Board, securing a plot of ground twenty-five by seventy-five or one hundred feet on Orange Street between Cross and Chatham. He had the deed drawn up in his own name, so the Trustees, upon the suggestion of the elder, decided not to build on the property.[5] It might be said, in all fairness, that Miller, recog-

[2] Rush (1866), *loc. cit.*, p. 27.
[3] Rush, *loc. cit.*, p. 11.
[4] Rush, *loc. cit.*, p. 11.
[5] Rush (1843), *loc. cit.*

nizing that he was not only severely criticized for his act but was looked down upon by the people of the community, relented, and after searching around for a buyer and finding one, requested the board to sell the lot in the legal manner.[6] The chairman of the board, Francis Jacobs, and another trustee, William Brown, the former "being a very intelligent man and of good repute," undertook the task of securing suitable property and finally found two acceptable lots on Church Street at the corner of Leonard. Rush corrected an error in his first book when he writes "each twenty-five feet front and seventy-five feet deep."[7]

Advised by Rev. McClaskey, the board proceeded to raise money for the erection of the first church building. Subscription books were issued and contributions were secured from all who would give. Rush states that this was the first time the Negro people of the city had been asked to support a venture. In September or October, 1800, the frame building was complete. It had an over-all length of 45 feet with a width of 35 feet.[8]

The lots secured by Jacobs and Brown were not bought but leased for twenty-one years, the agreement being dated July 21, 1800.[9] A clause was inserted in the document stating that if the trustees so desired they might purchase the property prior to the expiration of the lease. This was later done.[10] Three other names not heretofore noted appeared on this paper, George White, George Moore and Thomas Cook.[11]

The following year the active Board of Trustees decided to buy another lot which was found available next to the two already leased. Purchased April 8 for $750.00, this lot was likewise twenty-five by seventy-five feet and fronted on Church Street.[12]

Not being content with having the vacant lot, the Board searched until they found an "old house" for which they paid a small sum. This structure was moved to the new site, repaired and placed in use as a dwelling.

By this time the original church structure, built in October, 1800, was proving too small for the congregation. The Board was

---

[6] Rush (1843), *loc. cit.*
[7] Rush, *loc. cit.* (1866), p. 12.
[8] *Ibid.,* p. 12.
[9] Rush, *loc. cit.* (1866), p. 24.
[10] Rush, *loc. cit.* (1843), p. 25.
[11] *Ibid.* (1866), p. 24.
[12] *Ibid.*

again faced with a problem of expansion so decided to increase the seating capacity by extending the church by "fifteen or twenty" feet. The unoccupied portions of the lots were being used at the time for burial purposes. In order to relieve the crowded conditions of the churchyard, the Board resorted to vaults which were opened, from time to time, to receive new bodies. This condition continued until the governing body of the city forbade this procedure because of the yellow fever epidemic.

On application, the Board was granted permission to use a section of that which was known as "Pottersfield," evidently a section now known as the *Village*. This was fenced in and used each summer when it was unlawful to open the vaults. Later, the *Village* section was improved by the city and the Board was forced to find another burial ground. By this time they were able to purchase seven lots in that which was known as Yorkville. The inference of Rush is that more than these seven lots were purchased, however. [13]

The Rev. John McClaskey having been assigned elsewhere, the elder in charge of the African Chapel, Rev. John Wilson, went ahead with the progressive program of the group. A significant notation made by Rush intimates that the appointments to the Chapel were made by the General Conference of the Methodist Episcopal Church. Whether, at this time, the yearly conference was considered a General Conference is not clear. Its work appears to have been that of both sessions, in fact. As with the Reverend McClaskey, the Chapel seemed to have fond affection for the elder who surely had their interests at heart. Rush places great stress on his aid in the raising of funds with which the work was carried on. It was he who suggested that the colored people should be approached for subscriptions and that the membership should be called upon for regular and systematic giving.[14]

The Elder in charge of the Chapel was no doubt a very busy minister. His schedule called for his preaching in the Zion Church every Sunday afternoon and on Wednesday night of every week, except, as Rush puts it, "on the days of the administration of the Lord's Supper, then his appointment was on Sunday morning, and was agreed upon to be the second Sunday of every month, because the first Sunday in the month was the time for administering the

---

[13] Rush, *loc. cit.*, p. 25.
[14] Rush, *loc. cit.*, p. 26.

Sacrament in his own church." [15] The Negro preachers preached on Sunday mornings and Friday nights.

For a matter of ten years affairs at Zion Church continued on an even tenor when in 1813 one of the leaders of Zion, Thomas Sipkins, who had been a trustee and who had been expelled "therefrom for being somewhat headstrong and rather ungovernable" set about to establish another Negro Methodist Church in New York. He found a piece of property for sale on Elizabeth Street. On this land a church was erected and several individuals joined the group, among them being William Miller, an ordained deacon of Zion Church.[16]

The Asbury group evidently set out to be an independent organization but finally applied to Rev. Phineas Cook, now in charge of Zion, for consideration. Rev. Cook called the trustees of Zion about the matter. When these men were consulted, a Rev. Thomas Ware, an elder, met with the group also. The discussion was held in the home of William Brown, who was the treasurer of Zion. Brown, at the time, lived on Nassau Street, one door from the corner of that which is now Fulton. After much thought, the trustees of Zion consented to the establishment of Asbury Church.[17]

While we can say little of the relationship of these churches to the New York Conference, yet records were kept of Negro members as far back as 1801 when Seaman in his *Annals* states that in New York City there were 685 white members and 150 colored. These 150 members evidently belonged to the Chapel.

The establishment of the separate charge consisting of Zion and Asbury took place in 1818, the Rev. W. Phoebus being the chief minister in the city at the time. In 1819, a Rev. William Stillwell, nephew of Samuel Stillwell, was appointed to supervise the work of the two churches. Statistics of the Troy Annual Conference (New York Conference meeting in Troy) bear out this separation in that 2,339 white members were noted to only fifty colored. At that time, Zion and Asbury had a combined membership of 791.

By 1818 several new faces appeared on the Board of Trustees of Zion Church. Those listed now included William Brown, John Dias, Thomas Jenkins, Charles Tredwell, Tobias Hawkins, Philip

---

[15] *Ibid.*
[16] Rush, *loc. cit.*, pp. 28 ff.
[17] *Ibid.*, p. 30.

Searing, Epiphany Davis, Isaac Benson and George Collins. These men shouldered the task of caring for the needs of the congregation as they began talking about another house of worship since the one they then occupied had become overcrowded and was in bad repair.

Evidently the long anticipated dream of the people was to be realized in the proposed new church for not only did they plan for an adequate church structure for worship purposes but they likewise considered the needs of the children of the neighborhood. They, therefore, laid plans for a schoolroom under the church.[18] On November 25, 1818, a committee was appointed to consider plans for the building and the obtaining of bids or estimates for construction.[19] On July 13, 1819, a contract was let to James Dubois and Thompson Price to construct a stone building fifty-five by seventy feet at a cost of $11,500.[20]

The new building was commenced July 16 but the money soon gave out and it was decided to petition the legislature for funds to continue since the church was to take care of the educational needs of the community as well as the spiritual.[21] The legislature deemed it best not to aid the enterprise and the project came to a standstill. The Board decided that the old structure, around which the new one was being built, should be torn down, so this was done, leaving the congregation without a church home and the new building so incomplete that it could not be used.

There is little doubt that the controversy which was being waged in the Methodist Churches over property control at this time had its effects on money-raising projects, and this, coupled with the evident inexperience of Rev. Stillwell, the minister, left the little congregation in a bad plight.

With the destruction of the old church in May, 1820, the Board was compelled to rent a Riding Circus in "Broadway between Hester (now Howard) and Grand Streets, in which we held meetings."[22] Worship services were limited here, however, for it appears that they had the use of this hall only on Sunday mornings and afternoons. If Sunday evening services were held they had to resort to

---

[18] Rush, *loc. cit.*, p. 30.
[19] *Ibid.*
[20] *Ibid.*
[21] *Ibid.*
[22] Rush, *loc. cit.*, p. 30.

another house on Rose Street, "between Pearl and Duane Streets." [23] This building was styled the *Rose Street Academy*. Weekday services were held here as well.

Because of the wisdom of Rev. John Wilson, in leading the people to purchase the original property, they were now able to mortgage it for $3,000. For this it was necessary to secure the permission of the Master in Chancery. The money was obtained from Mr. James Bogert and on June 5, 1820, the work on the new structure got underway again.[24] By October 3, when the Board met in its regular session (all being present except Thomas Jenkins), Rush states that "the building still progressed; the floor being laid but the seats were not fixed," [25] the roof having been shingled by September. The dedication of the new structure had taken place during the summer. An interesting comment was made by Rush when he tells of this dedication. During the services it began to rain but those who were provided with umbrellas merely raised them, no one leaving until the services were concluded.

Two interesting dates need to be recorded concerning this new structure. On August 20, 1820, the Sacrament of the Lord's Supper was administered for the first time "within the walls of the new church, by William M. Stillwell." And, on November 2 "they began to fix up the seats." [26] The financial report given November 2 likewise is interesting. We, therefore, record it as Rush has written:

November 2nd, 1820, being the first Thursday of the month, the Leaders' meeting and Quarterly Conference of Zion Church were held together, by the advice of the Elder in charge, at the residence of William Brown in Leonard Street, and there were a large number of the official brethren at this meeting. The Secretary of the Leaders' meeting (George Collins) reported the amount of money received during the three years last past, ending the third of October last viz., $4,654 62½ and $3,000 borrowed, making $7,654 62½ and the expenditures, for the same time, $7,238 78, leaving a balance on hand of $415 91½, which, he said, had been since paid to the builders, viz., cash $5,542 78, and that the old house sold to the carpenter, and stone sold to the mason, together with some money which the builders said they had collected, for the Church, he supposed, would amount to about $300, which would make $5,842 78.[27]

[23] *Ibid.*
[24] *Ibid.*, p. 47.
[25] *Ibid.*, p. 49.
[27] Rush, *loc. cit.*, pp. 50, 51.

The data listed below is found in the *Minutes of the Common Council of the City of New York 1784-1831.*

Vol. II, p. 452. In Common Council held on Monday, the 25th day of June, 1798:

A Representative of the Trustees of the African School in this City was read and referred to the Committee on the Subject of Schools and it was ordered that an advance of $250 out of the monies granted by the Legislature for the encouragement of Schools to be made to the Trustees for the use of the said School and that Mr. Mayor issue his warr (nt) on the Treasurer for payment thereof account.

Vol. III, p. 564. (519) In Common Council, July 10, 1804:

Returns were received from the following churches of the monies given to them for the use of Schools agreeably to law wit, the German Lutheran Church, the Methodist Episcopal Church, the Scotch Presbyterian Church and the African Church.

Vol. IV, p. 389. (354) In Common Council, March 30, 1807:

SECTION II

The memorial of George Collins and others, Trustees of the African Church, complaining of their worship's being disturbed on Sundays by Boys and unruly Persons and requesting that a watchman may be stationed at said Church during their hours of public worship was referred to the Watch-Committee with instructions to have a watchman stationed there accordingly.

Vol. IV, p. 682. (430) In Common Council, December 28, 1807:

A Communication was received from the Committee appointed by the Africans and descendants of Africans in this City "to make arrangements for celebrating the period which puts a stop to commerce of the human species" returning their acknowledgments to the Corporation for the grant of officers to preserve good order on the occasion, and soliciting the members to accept tickets of admission to the oration which is to be delivered by the African descendant at the African Church in Church Street corner of Leonard on Friday the 1st day of Jan. next 10 o'clock.

Vol. V, p. 59. (245) In Common Council, March 21, 1808:

A memorial of the African Zion Methodist Episcopal Church praying a grant of that portion of Potter's Field which has been assigned to them for a burial place, to be exonerated from any assessment for regulating a street adjoining said ground understood to be called First Street, amounting to about Twenty-eight Dollars.

Whereupon Ordered that a warrant to be issued in favour of the Collector for the amount of said assessment.

Vol. V, p. 74. (259) In Common Council, March 28, 1808:

The Clerk presented the following communication. The Clerk has the honor to represent that at the last meeting of the Common Council on hearing the Petition of the Trustees of the African Zion Methodist Episcopal Church, a warrant was ordered in favor of the Collector for $27 to exonerate said Society from an assessment for the regulation of First Street.

On investigation it appears that the lot occupied as a burial ground on which (276) said assessment is levied, belongs to some African Society, and Mr. Dunstan, Collector informs the Clerk that means are provided to discharge same as some mistake therefore has arisen in respect to the merits of the Petition, it may be proper, perhaps, for the Board to rescind their order and to permit the Petitioners to withdraw their petition.

Which is respectfully Submitted,

JOHN PINTARD

Vol. V, p. 272. (159) In Common Council, September 26, 1808:

A memorial of the Trustees of the African Methodist Church complaining of riots before their place of worship and against Duncan McDonald, a watchman, for abuse of his duty, was referred to the Market Committee.

Vol. V, p. 278. (166) In Common Council, October 2, 1808:

The subject of fixing a watch box and stationing a watchman at the African Church was referred to the Watch Committee.

Vol. IX, p. 40. (232) In Common Council, March 10, 1817:

A Petition of Sundry members of the African Episcopal Church complaining of riotous conduct at Mr. Broad's Church in Rose Street was referred to the Committee on Police.

Vol. IV, p. 256 (130) In Common Council, August 4, 1806:

A Petition of the African Church was referred to the Alderman and Assistant of the Fifth Ward and the Comptroller.

Vol. VIII, p. 729. (152) In Common Council, April 18, 1814:

A Memorial from Sundry Inhabitants complaining of the riotous conduct of boys assembling on Sundays at the African Church, corner of Leonard and Church Streets and of the extreme late hours of the night to which the exercises in said Church are continued, was read and referred to the Police Magistrates.

Vol. IX, p. 111. (351) In Common Council, April 21, 1817.

The Comptroller on the Petition of William Miller presented the following report which was agreed to:

The Comptroller Respectfully Reports on the Petition of William Miller and claims exemption of Assessment to the amount of Fifteen hundred Dollars on a house and Lot of Ground No. 36 Mulberry Street in the Sixth Ward which is rated at Eighteen hundred Dollars on account of his being a Minister of the Asbury African Church. The facts stated by the Petitioner appears to be correct and satisfactory. Testimony has been exhibited of his exemption in the sum stated agreeable to the 28th Section of the "Act for the Assessment and Collection of Taxes" Passed April 5th. 1813. It is therefore Respectfully (359):

Recommended that the Collector of the aforesaid ward should be directed to make the necessary deduction and return the amount with the list of Errors.

G. N. BLEECKER, *Comptr.*

Vol. IX, p, 372. (74) In Common Council, December 1, 1817:

A Petition of the Trustees of the African Zion Church to be released from the payment of an assessment for Canal Street, was read and referred to the Committee of Charity to report.

Vol. IX, p. 387. (95) In Common Council, December 8, 1817:

The Committee on Charity on the Petition of the Trustees of the African Church in Church Street Reported as follows: That the Petitioners are not entitled in Law to be released from the payment of the assessment laid and support of places of worship as highly beneficial not only to the morals, but to the industry of the lower classes of the Community and considering also that people of Color Composing the Society are poor and already embarrassed in their church affairs, Your Committee recommend that the Board (107) relieve them from payment of this assessment.

(Signed) STEPHEN ALLEN
JOHN B. COLES
SAMUEL STEVENS
ELDAD HOLMES
ARTHUR BURTIS

WHICH REPORT WAS APPROVED

Vol. XII, pp. 485-86. (84) In Common Council, July 22, 1822:

The same committee to whom had been referred the Petition of William Sebureman, reported as follows:

The Committee on the Fire Department to whom was referred the memorial of William Sebureman to be renumerated to the sum of ninety Dollars and Thirty two Cents the amount of costs accruing from a persecution instituted against him for sending an unruly and disorderly person to the Watch house although he was compelled to do so in the execution of his office as Fire Warden while at the fire which consumed the African Church on the 20th of December last

RESPECTFULLY REPORT

that they have made enquiries relative to the facts and circumstances set forth in said memorial and find them in substance correct.

67

That while said memoralist was executing the duties of Fire warden and after using every other means was compelled by the disorderly conduct of Herman Martin to call (119) upon a watchman to take him to the Watch House. The said memoralist was afterwards prosecuted for false impr (is) onment and a judgement obtained against him for ninety five dollars and Thirty two Cents, which your Committee deem oppressive and unjust and that said memoralist is entitled to the protection of your Honorable Body while executing his office and ought to be remunerated to the amount of said Judgement. Your Committee therefore recommend the following resolution:

Resolved that the Comptroller is directed to pay to the said William Schuerman the sum of Ninety Five Dollars and Thirty Two Cents.

(Signed) DAVID SEAMAN
JAMES HALL

Vol. XV, p. 330. (179) In Common Council, April 10, 1826:

A Petition from the Trustees of the African Church corner of Church and Leonard Streets praying the Corporation to grant them Engine House 31 was read and referred to the Committee on the Fire Department.

Vol. XV, p. 430. (339) In Common Council, May 22, 1826:

The Committee on the Fire Department to whom was referred the Petition of the Trustees of the African Church corner of Church and Leonard Street praying the Corporation to grant them Engine House No. 31 presented the following report in favor:

The Committee on the Fire Department to whom was referred the petition of the African Church corner of Church and Leonard Streets praying the Corporation to grant them Engine House 31 Respectfully Report that they have enquired into the facts stated in their Petition and inform the Board that Engine House No 31 has been located on the Church Ground for the term of 20 years last Past during which no Ground rent has been required and as the House is of small value, it being a frame building and not large enough to make it convenient for the Company attached (377) to said Engine your Committee are of the opinion that the Prayer of the Petitioners is not unreasonable and ought to be granted they therefore offer the following Resolution:
Resolved that the Prayer of the Petitioners be granted.

Resolved that the Superintendent of Repairs Cause a house to be built on the ground belonging to the New York Sugar Refining Company in Leonard Street under the Direction of the Committee on the Fire Department.

JOHN AGNEW
SAMUEL GILFORD, JR.

which was approved and the Resolution adopted.

While the writer makes no effort to specifically trace the history of the Mother Church beyond the point of actual formation of the denomination, yet it is felt that bits of this history will be of genuine interest to Zionites everywhere.

By careful analysis it will be noted that several years were consumed in the erection of the second Mother Church. In fact, the decision to leave the Mother Methodist Church found the structure still incomplete. Just when the work was finally accomplished we have been unable to ascertain. However, we do know that the structure was well built and ample for the needs of the congregation until its destruction by fire in 1839.

Rush gives a good description of the actual size of the building and the plans for its construction. It was located across the street from the old Italian Opera House (later the National Theatre) which likewise faced Leonard and Church Streets. A block away, on Franklin Street, was the Eglise Du St. Esprit and farther north was the Dutch Reformed Church. Engine Company 31 was to the rear of Zion Church. References to this Engine Company No. 31 are found in Common Council Minutes of May, 1826. Those who may be interested in the exact location of this church should know that most of the land on which the old church stood is now a part of the widened street.

The writer has been somewhat puzzled over Common Council Minutes of July 22, 1822, where reference is made to the destruction of the African Church. If this statement concerns Zion Church then the building destroyed in 1839 had to be the third structure instead of the second. However, it does not appear logical that two years after the building of the church it was destroyed by fire. An account of the 1839 fire is herein listed. Kenneth Holcomb Dunshee in his book *As You Pass By* has this interesting account of the Zion African Methodist Episcopal Church:

> "Where there is danger there you will find Hope" was just a way of saying, when the fiery demon threatened, that there you would find the boys of Hope Engine Company No. 31. This lively group of "firesparks," organized in 1805, was assigned a small house on the southwest corner of Church and Leonard Streets, in a section of the city once called "Frogtown." Whether this appellation came from the amphibious croakers of the not-too-distant Lispenard Meadows to the north or from the presence of the Eglise Du St. Esprit, center of worship for the French colony of the city, on the Franklin Street corner, now can be only guessed at. Nearby stood the Dutch Reformed Church, the Italian Opera and the Zion African Methodist Episcopal Church. When the latter was enlarged in 1820 to occupy the corner Hope's house was

69

moved to a space at the rear of the church. After 1834 the company was located in Chapel Street (West Broadway) near Beach.

It was on a quiet Monday afternoon late in September (1839) that huge columns of smoke rolling over the city gave the sign that a big fire was in the making. The word soon spread that the National Theatre (The Italian Opera House) was burning. A general alarm brought engines racing from all parts of the city. Thousands of curious spectators followed. Soon the entire vicinity was one of almost indescribable confusion.

The theatre burned so fiercely that the flames quickly spread to the adjoining French Church and leaped Leonard Street to ignite Zion Church. Both the Dutch Reformed Church and school and many houses were caught in the spreading flames. Throughout, the firemen worked in a steady, calm manner and they showed great heroism in a number of rescues and in the saving of much property. The despair-stricken French; the despondent Negroes; chattering half-clad women; actors; horn-toting musicians; excited citizens—all combined in this drama of fire.

The contents snatched from the various buildings and hastily tossed into the street presented a scene of ludicrous contrasts. Stage properties and church furniture, bibles, prayerbooks and hymnals; tomes of Shakespeare, and the librettos of operas were strangely mixed with the gaudy contents of a number of the indefinitely described houses in this curious neighborhood.

When the fire was brought under control the theatre was a total ruin. James Wallack lost uninsured property valued at twenty-five thousand dollars. Empty walls remained of the Dutch Reformed Church, which was insured for ten thousand dollars. The French Church and contents were severely damaged and numerous other buildings and dwellings partially destroyed. Only the Zion African Methodist Episcopal Church was fully insured.[28]

---

[28] Dunshee, *loc. cit.*, pp. 201, 202.

CHAPTER VII

The Zion Church and Stillwell Secession

THE AFFAIRS of Zion and Asbury could not long remain serene. The groups seemed content to increase their numbers within the city itself, extending little beyond the environs of that community to Long Island and Brooklyn. Dissatisfaction was not confined to the John Street congregation later events proved. In Philadelphia, Reverend Allen (later, the first Bishop of the African Methodist Episcopal Church) had established a church separate from that of the mother church.

It is necessary to turn aside for a brief period to examine the relations of the white conferences to these two movements. Careful analysis will bring the conclusion that Bethel Church faced a situation much more conducive to progress than did Zion. The writer concludes this because of the attitude of the parent organizations towards the Negro churches. Theodore L. Flood and John W. Hamilton, editors of the work *Lives of Methodist Bishops* (New York, 1882), record the following resolution of the Philadelphia Conference:

> The Philadelphia Conference do advise and recommend that one of our bishops do attend and preside in the African Conference appointed to sit in New York, as an African Methodist Conference, under the patronage of our bishops and conference agreeable to the proper plan (if the New York Conference agree with us) to wit: 1, One of our members always to preside in said conference or in case no bishop be present, then such white elders as the bishop may appoint, are to preside. 2, Our bishops to ordain their deacons and elders, such as shall be elected by their own Conference and approved by the Bishop, and educated for the office.[1]

Thus, it appears clear that the Philadelphia area was willing to compromise the matter but the New York Conference rejected the overture.

Relations between the two churches, Zion in New York and Bethel in Philadelphia, became strained when William Lambert, a one-time member of Zion, withdrew to join Asbury. Feeling that

---

[1] *Lives of Methodist Bishops*, ed. by Theodore L. Flood and John W. Hamilton (New York, 1882), p. 678.

he had a call to preach, he appealed to William Miller, head of Asbury, who, not wanting to grant his request, recommended him to Rev. Allen (later Bishop). Lambert received a commission from Bishop Allen as a missionary and returned to New York to organize a Bethel Church. This, both Zion and Asbury Churches resented. They showed this resentment by denying Lambert the pulpit and Zion went so far as to forbid Zion ministers to have anything to do with that which was styled the "Allen movement." [2] In this resolution Rush is emphatic in stating that all the Zion ministers as well as William Miller of Asbury agreed. He writes "believing that Bishop Allen had acted very unkind towards the Church, by sending an Elder into this city, with the intention to establish a third society of the African Methodists, thereby taking advantage of our present necessity, they met together and resolved not to preach for them, nor to allow them to preach for us." [3]

The only one who seemed to have been exempted from this agreement was George White, "a member and ordained Deacon of our Church." [4] Earlier, White had given aid to Lambert in securing the Mott Street schoolhouse and fitting it for church purposes. Rush hints that White was in touch with Bishop Allen, informing him of the turbulent state of affairs, especially as it pertained to the building project.[5]

Bethel Church was dedicated on Sunday, July 23, 1820, and not long after the dedication, Bishop Allen paid a visit to New York, sanctioning all which had been done. The ministers of Asbury and Zion had a change of heart at his arrival and freely attended the meetings held in Bethel. Rush states that some of them "sat in their altar and one of them (James Varick) opened meeting for the Bishop on the second or third Sunday night of the existence of that Society." [6]

The week before Varick led the opening worship in Bethel Church, the great storm broke which ended in the separation of Zion and Asbury from the Mother Church. On July 16, Elder William Stillwell, who had been in charge of the two churches since 1818, attended services in the Rose Street Academy and just before the conclusion of the worship period informed the Trustee Board and

[2] Rush, *loc. cit.*, p. 32.
[3] *Ibid.*, p. 33.
[4] *Ibid.*, p. 32.
[5] *Ibid.*, p. 33.
[6] Rush, *loc. cit.*, p. 34.

Leaders (as well as those who happened to be present) "that he and several hundred of his (white) brethren had that day withdrawn from the Methodist Episcopal Church, in consequence of some resolutions of their preachers in Conference." [6]

William Stillwell was the nephew of Samuel Stillwell, one of the class leaders and a trustee of John Street Church. As class leader, Samuel Stillwell was, significantly, the leader of Peter Williams, a trustee of Zion. Rev. William Stillwell was admitted to the New York Conference in 1814 and served several churches up the "North River." He was then appointed minister of Zion and Asbury Churches in New York City. Dr. Joy, historian of the Methodist Church, states that General "Vinegar Joe" Stillwell of China-Burma-India fame is a descendant of this first regular minister of Zion Church.

Fortunately for Zion Church, the major part of her financial worries were behind her, when the storm broke. At the zenith of the Stillwell movement, the *Circus* was closed to the use of the church and they were without a home. Rush voices the consternation of the members when he recalls that the walls of the new church were only half up and the "circus was closed to use." The trustees got busy and laid boards over the floor beams so that services could be held. Fortunately, it was warm weather so they could do without a roof unless it rained. As recounted above, the first service was held July 30, 1820, with the Rev. William Stillwell preaching. At the afternoon services, Abraham Thompson preached and James Varick closed the meeting. At the third service, conducted at an early evening hour, 6:30, John Dungy preached, thereby closing the day's activities before "candle-light." The congregation continued to hold its other services at the Rose Street Academy.

There are many reasons given for the Stillwell movement. We list several at this time. The lay people had the feeling that the church was solely in the hands of the clergy, their main contention being that it was the clergy who formed or drew up the discipline without the advice or consent of the lay members. In this way they were able to seize control of church government. Their second grievance was the fact that there was no lay representation in the annual conference. Probably because of this control the next complaint arose, that of the gradual increase in ministerial power. The group further contended that the presiding elder system was useless and out of date. The New York churches added another to this list, their dissatisfaction with the temporal affairs of the church.[7]

It appears, as stated before, that one board of trustees served for all Methodist Episcopal churches in the city, other than Zion and Asbury.[8] Over this organization of several members presided an elder or chief pastor. The temporal affairs of all these city churches were naturally handled by one board.[9] At the time there were six groups organized as Methodist Episcopal chapels or churches. As early as Asbury's time, dissatisfaction had been expressed as to the way money was handled [10] but nothing was done about it. By this time, however, the groups were lining up with those in the upper part of the city on one side and the two in the lower section on the other. The clash came when the trustees decided to place carpet on the platform of the new John Street Church.[11] Fuel was added when the uptown membership realized that most of their money was being spent downtown. In the trustee elections which followed, some uptown men were elected and it looked as if the struggle might cease, but hardly had the one matter been taken care of when another, that of class collections, came in for consideration. Some of the class leaders insisted on paying their sums to the trustees while others followed the custom, paying to the ministers. On one occasion, the battle of words waged so that a class leader made unsuitable remarks about the *Discipline*. The minister retorted: "If you do not care for the *Discipline* you are not fit to be a class leader." [12] Since the ministers were paid out of the class money and quarterly collections one can easily see why the matter was so vital. For some reason these collections were falling off and the ministry was insufficiently paid. The Board of Trustees served notice on the ministry that it would follow the *Discipline* and make no further provisions for the ministry.[13]

When the news got to the New York Annual Conference it was decided to petition the legislature to so amend the laws governing the incorporation of religious societies that the State laws and those

---

[7] Samuel Stillwell, *Rise and Progress of the Methodist Society in the City of New York* (New York, 1821) , pp. 37, 38.
[8] Seaman, *loc. cit.*, p. 216 (*Annals of New York Methodism*, New York, 1882) .
[9] *Ibid.*
[10] *The Journal of Francis Asbury*, Friday, September 11, 1772.
[11] Seaman, *loc. cit.*
[12] *Ibid.*, p. 217.
[13] Stillwell, *loc. cit.*, p. 23.

of the church would not conflict. It appears that the petition was never presented but the ruling preacher began to interfere more and more so that four of the trustees resigned.[14] In the meantime, *select* meetings were being called ostensibly for the purpose of changing the laws of election of the Board as well as the nominating group.[15]

Temporal affairs were confusing to many members, some declaring that the new Board of Trustees, building too expensively, could not pay the interest on the church debt, being in arrears around $600. The debt at this time seemed to have been $30,000. Meanwhile, the organization was being sued, at the time a suit was pending in Chancery. Many others made the contentions stated above, that the clergy had drawn up the *Discipline* to suit its need and without consultation with the laymen. Time after time, individuals had attempted to secure representation in the annual conference but to no avail. Furthermore, "the presiding elder was worse than useless."

We can only guess as to why the Rev. William Stillwell agreed to withdraw, but his uncle, Samuel Stillwell, was in the thick of the John Street controversy, and our belief that he persuaded his nephew to lead the group going out of the church seems not too far-fetched. Samuel was a native of Jamaica, Long Island, born October 22, 1763. His paternal ancestor was a member of the Commission which tried and convicted King James I. Samuel came to New York in 1783 and became prominent in civic affairs, being an intimate friend of DeWitt Clinton. He was a surveyor by trade. He died in 1848.

When the dissatisfied group in the Methodist Churches finally withdrew, Rev. William Stillwell came to Zion Church and stated that he, along with many others, had decided to withdraw from the Methodist Episcopal Church. After the minister stated the reasons for withdrawing to the officers present, the trustees naturally became alarmed for "they recalled previous threats and unkind statements by the elders of the circuit."

Official word was received from the elder in charge of the New York churches that Stillwell was no longer in charge of the church and the members were asked what they were going to do. It appears

---

[14] *Ibid.*
[15] *Ibid.*

that the elder opened the door for conflict for the logical step in this case was the appointment of another preacher. There had been friction between the Negro and white preachers, however, in the matter of a local preachers' conference.[16] It appears that the Board was requested to meet with the presiding elder at the residence of Peter Williams in Liberty Street. The trustees attended the meeting along with Abraham Thompson, the "oldest preacher and deacon in the church." The presiding elder, Peter P. Sandford, was present along with Aaron Hunt, Joshua Soule and Thomas Mason. It was here that the blunt question was put to the Zion trustee board. They asked for time, agreeing to give answer shortly.

Meanwhile, the preachers of the Zion Church had called a meeting at the residence of James Varick in Orange Street, "in order to see what was best to be done." [17] After discussion, they decided to appoint Abraham Thompson, James Varick, John Dungy and George Collins to call on Doctor Phoebus, "an old Elder of the Methodist Episcopal Church (who was said to be neutral in the case of division), and William L. Stillwell, to gain further information on the subject, and to obtain from William L. Stillwell a copy of the resolution which had caused the schism in the white Methodist Church." "They also agreed to request a meeting of all official members of Zion Church, at the Rose Street Academy, the following Friday night, at which time they hoped to come to a final decision among the official brethren." [18]

Realizing the seriousness of the Stillwell movement, Bishop George began to hold meetings with the Negro officials. On Saturday, August 12, 1820, such a meeting was held at the residence of Morris Carter on Church Street. Attending this meeting were Tobias Hawkins, William Brown, Thomas Jenkins, Bishop George and the "white elders." After a two-hour conference the meeting adjourned apparently "with the best of friendship." Bishop George requested the Zion trustees to allow Joshua Soule the privilege of explaining to the church the true state of matters regarding the difference of opinion.

The meeting requested by the preachers on Friday, July 21, was held. Few new church groups have had to face the critical situa-

---

[16] Rush, loc. cit., p. 35.
[17] Ibid.
[18] Ibid., p. 36.

tion confronting the new organization with the limited training such as many of them had. There is little doubt that a few were anxious to bring about no break with the mother church. The preachers seemed to be in agreement for a separation. After discussion the following set of resolutions were agreed to and the meeting adjourned.

WHEREAS, A very grievous schism has taken place in the Methodist Episcopal Church in this city, in consequence of a resolution of the last General Conference, and that resolution acted upon by the annual Conference of the New York District, the substance of which is (as we are informed) that a memorial shall be drawn up, subscribers obtained by the preachers, and the same to be presented to the Legislature of the State of New York, at their next sitting, praying for a special Act of Incorporation, to suit the peculiarities of the Methodist discipline, so that the preachers may have more authority to exercise their functions in the church than they now have; and

Whereas, it is reported that, should the Legislature deem it expedient to grant the requests of the memorialists and enact the said special Act of Incorporation, it will very materially change the present manner of conducting the temporal concerns of the said church (as Trustees or Stewards to be appointed, according to the contemplated mode, will hold the property of the Society in trust for the preachers in Conference instead of, or more than for, the members of the Society) ; and whereas, in consequence of the aforementioned schism, a very different explanation is given relative to the contents of the said memorial, and fearing that the said report is true, and that our Church property will be involved in the same difficulties should the contemplated Act of Incorporation be obtained, having no desire to transfer our church property to the Methodist preachers in Conference; therefore we have resolved—

1. That we cannot fairly understand the intention of the said preachers, in praying the Legislature for a special Act of Incorporation, and having some reason to fear the above-mentioned report is correct, we are much dissatisfied and do highly disapprove of said memorial.

2. That in consequence of the dissatisfaction and doubt existing in our minds, relative to the intended special Act of Incorporation, and to the conduct of the preachers in Conference requiring such

an Act, we decline receiving any further services from them as respecting our church government.

3. That George Collins, Tobias Hawkins and William Brown be a committee appointed to inform the presiding Elder of the District, or the ruling Elder of the city of New York, of the above resolutions.

4. That we request William M. Stillwell to continue his services with us for the remainder of the year.

5. That we recommend the above to the members of our Society.

The words of Rush reveal more than any other words can the spirit of the African Chapel (called Zion) when the meeting ended that July night. Nothing was settled for another meeting was to be held and another vote taken.

> While the Trustees were thus struggling under three difficulties (which were the withdrawing from the white church, the efforts of Bishop Allen to take advantage of our necessity, and the uneasiness of some of our members) to keep matters together in the best way they could, they were informed that some of our preachers were inclined to join Bishop Allen's connexion and had called a meeting to consult about it. This so early an apparent change in the minds of the preachers, together with a notice that they had received from Enoch George, Bishop of the White Methodist Church, upon the case of our withdrawing from them, sickened the hearts of some (if not all) of the Trustees; but they took courage and went on, looking unto the great Head of the Church for His gracious aid.[19]

The preachers held another meeting at the residence of William Miller in Mulberry Street and again requested a meeting of all official members of the Church.[20] The meeting was held August 11, 1820. Two important questions were asked and settled at the meeting. They were: "Shall we join Bishop Allen?" The answer was, No.

The second question on the matter of secession was, "Shall we return to the white people?" The answer was, No. Thus the African Chapel became a new denomination, the African Methodist Episcopal Church in America. It was not until a much later date that the name Zion was added.

Horace M. Du Bose in his *Life of Joshua Soule,* edited by Bishop Warren A. Candler, states that Joshua Soule had declared to Bishop George that "serious and very unpleasant results await us in this

[19] Rush, *loc. cit.,* pp. 38, 39.
[20] *Ibid.,* p. 39.

city."[21] He had tried to prevent it in every way and, it is believed, his efforts did delay it.[22] His reasons given for his keen interest in Zion and Asbury were that the "Negro churches were burdened and weak."[23]

A letter written to Bishop McKendree September, 1820, is a fitting conclusion to this chapter:

> You will doubtless see Bishop George in Baltimore or its vicinity and receive from him a narrative of the disastrous events which have transpired in this station. Suffice it to say that several hundred have separated themselves from the fellowship of our church, established an independent congregation embodied under a system of government which secures a perfect equality of right and power to every member, male and female—properly speaking, an ecclesiastical democracy in the most extensive sense of the word.[24]

[21] *Life of Joshua Soule,* by Horace M. Du Bose, ed. by Bishop Warren A. Candler (Nashville, 1911) , p. 161.
[22] *Ibid.,* p. 160.
[23] *Ibid.,* p. 160.
[24] *Life of Joshua Soule,* by Horace M. Du Bose, ed. by Bishop Warren A. Candler (Nashville, 1911) , p. 161.

CHAPTER VIII

The Long Road to Independence and Destiny

WHEN THE members of the African Chapel (both male and female) met on Friday, August 11, 1820, to vote on their future course of action, little work was done on the forming of the new denomination. They knew, however, that which they wanted to accomplish and "after several brethren had given their opinions, it being late, the meeting was adjourned to the following Tuesday night." [1]

Thus the organization, really undertaken as early as the seventeen eighties (in the minutes of the Methodist Conference:

> *Question 25:* Ought not the Assistant (Mr. Asbury) meet with colored people himself and appoint as helpers in his absence, proper white persons and not suffer them to stay late and meet alone?
> *Answer:* Yes).

launched its independent career. The next day, Saturday, August 12th, as noted above, a meeting was held with Bishop George.[2] On the following Tuesday Rush states that the official members met as they had agreed, at the home of William Brown on Leonard Street.[3] Abraham Thompson was selected chairman while Charles Anderson was selected secretary. William Miller represented Asbury Church.

The matter of chief concern to the membership had to do with that of ordination.[4] Evidently this was the first business of importance, for, from the account we note that the word "considerable" appears in several accounts in speaking of the discussion at this meeting. It appears that Abraham Thompson and several others wished to request Bishop Allen to ordain an elder or elders for Zion.[5] By now the bitterness towards the white group was growing and the suggestion of others that Bishop Hobart of the Protestant (Episcopal) Church be approached met with opposition, an opposition

---

[1] Rush, *loc. cit.*, p. 39.
[2] *Ibid.*, p. 39.
[3] *Ibid.*, p. 40.
[4] *Ibid.*, p. 40.
[5] Rush, *loc. cit.*, p. 40.

headed by Thompson.[6] The group requesting that Bishop Hobart be approached won out, however, for a committee composed of William Miller, Thomas Jenkins and Lowther Bruce was assigned the task of approaching Bishop Hobart.[7] This, in spite of discension which was so great that the group, to test the statements of the minority, appointed a committee to see Bishop Allen on the matter first.[8] Tobias Hawkins, William Brown, Thomas Jenkins, George Collins, and Charles Treadwell from the Board of Trustees and four preachers, Abraham Thompson, William Miller, Christopher Rush and James Varick made up the committee.[9]

The meeting with the Bishop was entirely unsatisfactory to the majority of the group. The Zion representatives soon learned that Bishop Allen had "no intention to assist in ordination, unless we put ourselves under his charge." [10] Rush certainly grew more and more bitter over the matter and throughout his life he resented the sister church.

As agreed, Reverend William Stillwell continued to conduct the services and on August 20th the first Sacrament of the Lord's Supper was held in the new church, still not completed.[11]

Approximately two weeks after the memorable meeting at which time the two committees were selected to confer with Bishop Hobart and Bishop Allen on ordination for one or more of the Zion preachers, the group assembled to hear the results of the interviews.

Rush states that Abraham Thompson, now an old man, evidently found it hard to make his report. He led the fight against any appeal to any white ministers and suggested the friendship of Bishop Allen. His report of failure destroyed his faith in the Bishop.

William Miller reported that he had attempted to contact Bishop Hobart without success since that prelate was out of town. He had talked with a minister, the Reverend Thomas Lytel, the Presbyter of Christ Church ("in Ann (now Worth) Street."). Mr. Lytel appeared very cordial, promising to talk with Bishop Hobart upon his return and further stating that he saw no reason why any ordination would be such a task.[12] He, however, stated, that since the

---

[6] Ibid., p. 40.
[7] Ibid., p. 40.
[8] Ibid., p. 41.
[9] Ibid., p. 41.
[10] Ibid., p. 41.
[11] Ibid., p. 41.
[12] Rush, loc. cit., 46.

Reverend William Stillwell was an ordained elder in the newly formed church he saw no reason why he could not ordain the candidates.

So vital was the matter of ordinations that an unofficial group had made some contacts with Reverend Stillwell on the subject and that minister had agreed to aid.[13] The fact that Abraham Thompson "had now become more reconciled and stayed in his mind" brought the factions together and it was agreed that Reverend Stillwell should be officially asked to aid.[14]

It was not until September 13th that the elder, Reverend Stillwell, got around to the vexing problem. He called the official members together and informed them that he lacked the required number of elders to ordain the deacons of the new organizations, much as he regretted it.[15] However, he had occupied the time in reading up on the opinions of others and now felt that some action could be taken. He convinced the membership that students of ecclesiastical law felt that in times of necessity elders could be elected by the congregation. This being such a case he urged them to elect. Two were nominated at this September 13th meeting, Abraham Thompson and James Varick.[16] Accordingly they were recommended to the Church to be elected elders.

On Sunday afternoon, October 1st, 1820, the membership, "both male and female," remained after church and proceeded to elect Abraham Thompson, "by a large majority if not by the whole body" an elder. James Varick was likewise elected. It is significant to note that Rush refuses to state conclusively that Thompson was elected without opposition.[17]

Meanwhile, the Methodist Episcopal Church had not abandoned the Negro organizations. Bishop William McKendree expressed the desire to meet with some officials or official members of the Chapel.[18] The Bishop appeared sympathetic but being bound by the annual conference opinion he requested the group to wait until the New York Conference met.[19] The group stated that while they could not wait to elect elders they would wait for ordination.

---

[13] *Ibid.*, p. 46.
[14] *Ibid.*, p. 46.
[15] Rush, *loc. cit.*, p. 49.
[16] *Ibid.*, p. 49.
[17] *Ibid.*, pp. 50, 51.
[18] *Ibid.*, p. 45.
[19] *Ibid.*, p. 46.

Rush states that "Sunday, November 12th, 1820, being the second Sunday in the month and our communion day, James Varick, one of our elders-elect, for the time being, consecrated the elements for the Lord's Supper, and together with Abraham Thompson, the other elder-elect, administered the same to the members of the Church, and Levin Smith, our ordained deacon, assisted them." [20]

Meanwhile, new societies had been formed in New Haven and Philadelphia, the latter choosing to organize their own group rather than join Bishop Allen.[21] They, therefore, approached the *Zionites* in New York City on the formation of a denomination.[22] Incidentally, it appears that in the celebration of our sesqui-centennial the part played by the Philadelphia Church should not be overlooked. It was the insistence of this church which really brought into existence the new denomination.

The first of December, 1820, Abraham Thompson and William Miller were sent to Philadelphia by the Church while Christopher Rush went to New Haven, there to talk over the matter of union with Asbury and Zion.[23] While this matter will be taken up later, the significant item is the report of Abraham Thompson who, while in Philadelphia, had talked with one Ezekiel Cooper, an "old member of the connexion of our white brethren." [24] Cooper advised Thompson to have drawn up a letter stating the desires of the Church. He suggested that the letters be sent to the Wesleyan Church for concurrence and then that the letter be presented to the Methodist Yearly Conference meeting at Milford Delaware, in the Spring.[25]

The letter, addressed to both the Philadelphia and the New York Conferences of the Methodist Episcopal Church set forth the desires of the churches located in New York, Long Island, New Haven and Philadelphia, the Philadelphia Wesleyan Church having examined a copy when it was presented by Abraham Thompson and Smith.[26] The churches stated that it was well known that the conferences would not accept Negro ministers and they requested the right of establishing an annual conference presided over by Bishop McKendree or "any other." In fact, that which the Negro churches

---

[20] Rush, *loc. cit.*, p. 55.
[21] *Ibid.*, p. 49.
[22] *Ibid.*
[23] *Ibid.*
[24] *Ibid.*, p. 55.
[25] *Ibid.*
[26] *Ibid.*, p. 60.

HISTORY OF THE A. M. E. ZION CHURCH

suggested was a "Central Jurisdiction" one hundred years before it came into existence.

The Philadelphia Conference, always more liberal than their brothers in New York State, probably because of the lack of conflicts in their area, agreed with the Negro group when the letter was presented at Milford Delaware.[27] Both Rush and Flood mention the agreement.[28] For our purposes the account in Flood, the short version, will suffice. It states:

> The Philadelphia Conference do advise and recommend that one of our bishops do attend and preside in the African Conference appointed to sit in New York, as an African Methodist Conference, under the patronage of our Bishops and Conference, agreeable to the proper plan (if the New York Conference agree with us), to wit:
> 1. One of our members always to preside in said conference, or in case no bishop be present, then such white elders as the Bishop may appoint, are to preside.
> 2. Our Bishops to ordain their deacons and elders, such as shall be elected by their own conference and approved by the Bishop, and educated for the office.

The letter which occasioned the above and addressed to the two conferences was signed by James Varick and George Collins.[29] The memorial drawn up by the Philadelphia Conference of the Methodist Episcopal Church was signed by Ezekiel Cooper, Thomas Ware and Edward White as committee members and George Cox, Conference Secretary, and was dated Milford Delaware, April 19, 1821.

The letter written by the Negro Churches follows:

Respected Brethren:

We, the official members of the African Methodist Zion and Asbury Churches, in the city of New York, and of the Wesleyan Church, in the City of Philadelphia, on behalf of our brethren, members of the aforesaid Churches; likewise of a small society at New Haven, and some of our colored brethren on Long Island, beg the favor of addressing you on a subject, to us, of great importance, and, we presume, not a matter of indifference to you.

In the first place, suffer us to beg you will accept of our humble and sincere thanks for your kind services to us when in our infant state, trusting that the Great Head of the Church, the all-wise and gracious God, has, and will continue to reward you for your labors among us, having made you the instruments of bringing us from darkness to

---

[27] Rush, *loc. cit.*, p. 60.
[28] *Ibid.*, pp. 56-60.
[29] Rush, *loc. cit.*, pp. 56 ff.

light. And from the power of sin and Satan, to Him, the true and living God.

In the next place we proceed to say:—When the Methodist Society in the United States was small, the Africans enjoyed privileges among their white brethren in the same meeting-house, but as the whites increased very fast the Africans were pressed back; therefore, it was thought essentially necessary for them to have meetinghouses of their own, in those places where they could obtain them, in order to have more room to invite their colored brethren yet out of the ark of safety to come in; and it is well known that the Lord has greatly enlarged their number since that memorable time, by owning their endeavors in the conversion of many hundreds. Many preachers have been raised up among them, who have been very useful in a located state; but they have hitherto been confined; they have no opportunities to travel, being generally poor men, and having no provisions made for them to go forth and dispense the Word of Life to their brethren, their usefulness has been greatly hindered, and their colored brethren have been deprived of those blessings which Almighty God might have designed to grant through their instrumentality. And now, it seems, the time has come when something must be done for the prosperity of the ministry amongst our brethren; and how shall this be accomplished? for we have not the least expectation that African or colored preachers will be admitted to a seat and vote in the Conference of their white brethren, let them be how much soever qualified for the work of the ministry; nor do we desire to unite with our brother Richard Allen's connexion (for our brethren, the members of the Wesleyan Church in Philadelphia, withdrew from them to build their present house of worship, named as above) ; therefore, our brethren in the City of New York, after due consideration, have been led to conclude that, to form an itinerant plan, and establish a Conference for African Methodist preachers, under the patronage of the white Methodist Bishops and Conference, would be the means of accomplishing the desired end. Believing that such an establishment would tend greatly to the prosperity of the spiritual concerns of our colored brethren in general, and would be the means of great encouragement to our preachers, who are now in regular standing in connexion with the white Methodist Episcopal Church in the United States, and also to such as may be hereafter raised among us, who may be disposed to join the said Conference and enter on the traveling plan. And, in order to commence this great work, the two societies in the City of New York united and agreed that the title of the connexion shall be "The African Methodist Episcopal Church in America," and have selected a form of discipline from that of the mother (white) church, which, with a little alteration, we have adopted for the government of the said connexion, and to which we beg to offer you.

After the perusal of our selection and the consideration of our case, should our proceeedings meet your approbation, and you should be disposed to patronize the same, we will stand ready, and shall be glad to receive such advice and instruction as you may think proper to give us, through our father in the Lord, Bishop McKendree, or any other person the Conference may be pleased to appoint.

On the subject of ordination to Eldership (a privilege which our preachers have been long deprived of) permit us to say that we might have obtained it from other sources, but we preferred and determined to follow the advice of Bishop McKendree, given to our brethren in New York the last time he was with them, and wait until the meeting of your Annual Conference in this and the district of New York, in order to understand what encouragement we may look for from the mother church. But, in consequence of some uneasiness in the minds of some of our members in New York, occasioned by our brother Richard Allen's determination to establish a society of his connexion in that city, our brethren there have been under the necessity of solemnly electing three of their deacons to the office of Elders, and some of their preachers to the office of deacons, to act only in cases of necessity, and to show to our people that our preachers can be authorized to administer the sacrament of the Lord's Supper as well as those of brother Allen's connexion—that thereby they might keep the body together, and we believe it has had the desired effect, for very few have left the Societies there, notwithstanding the efforts made to induce them to leave us.

We expect that our first yearly Conference will be held in the City of New York, on the 14th day of June next, at which we hope to have the happiness of hearing that our Father in the Lord, Bishop Mc-Kendree, presided, and commenced his fatherly instructions in an African Methodist Conference, formed under the patronage of the Methodist Episcopal Church in the United States of America. With this hope we shall rest, waiting your answer; meanwhile praying that the great Shepherd and Bishop of souls and our most merciful Father will be pleased to bless and guide you in your deliberations on our case, so that your conclusions may be of such as shall be pleasing in his sight, and tend most to the prosperity of his kingdom amongst the Africans, and consequently prove an everlasting blessing to many precious souls.

N.B. Should the above address be sanctioned by your respected body, and you should be pleased to act upon it, we will thank you to transmit the same to the New-York Annual Conference, for their consideration, and should the time appointed for the sitting of the African Conference be inconvenient for the person who may be appointed to organize the same, we are willing that it should be altered to a few days sooner or later, provided you would be pleased to give us timely notice of said alteration. But should you be disposed not to favor the said address in any respect, you will please have the goodness to return it to the bearer.

Signed, in behalf of the official members of both Societies, at a meeting called especially for that purpose, March 23rd, 1821, in the City of New York.

JAMES VARICK, *President.*
GEORGE COLLINS, *Secretary.*[30]

[30] Rush, *loc. cit.,* pp. 56 ff.

The Zion and Asbury officials were satisfied that the vexing problem was finally solved and then came the communication from the New York Conference. This group still bitter over the revolt of the laymen (The Stillwellites) refused to do anything for the Negro group until they decided to accept the revised discipline of the Methodist Episcopal Church which aimed to curtail the power of the lay people. This, Zion and Asbury refused to do and in their refusal they were joined by the Long Island Churches, the Philadelphia organization and the New Haven group.

The disheartened group met in June 1821 and after considering the problem, decided upon a course of action as that laid down by the Philadelphia Conference. A resolution was passed suggesting that the Philadelphia plan be followed by the Methodist General Conference. On these terms Zion and Asbury agreed to return to the Church, but they again insisted on their own discipline. George Collins and Charles Anderson were selected to so inform an old friend of the group, Joshua Soule.

This matter drifted on for another two months or more, September 27, 1821, to be exact.[31] By this time the two chapels found themselves divided into three groups; the first suggested an unconditional return to the Mother Church. The second felt that the key to the question still rested with their minister, Reverend Stillwell, while a third group held the convention that carrying on as they were would bring its own solution. Many letters of advice were written on the subject according to Rush.

Since we have in part presented the reaction of the Philadelphia Conference and given in full the report which occasioned this reaction students of history may be interested in the reply of the New York Conference:

> The Committee to whom was referred the Memorial of the Africans in the City of New York and other places, together with the accompanying documents, after due consideration, report as follows:
>
> 1. The committee conceive that humanity and religion combine to influence us to do all in our power for the instruction and salvation of colored people. To have the pure word of life preached among them, and the discipline and ordinances of the Gospel faithfully administered, is of indispensable necessity, and requisite to their happiness and prosperity. It is believed that, in these respects, we have cause to charge ourselves with too little attention

---

[31] Rush, *loc. cit.*, p. 71.

to their spiritual interest, and, as though they were an inferior class of beings, they have too often been treated with unwarrantable neglect. It is to be feared that their loss of confidence in us, and the consequent measures which many of them have pursued, may, in a considerable degree, be traced to our neglect as the cause. But, painful as this consideration is, we cannot approve of the course which our colored brethren have taken, in separating themselves from us, and forming themselves under a distinct title, as an independent body. This course is more to be regretted because it places them in a position which the constitution of our church cannot cover. Your committee conceive that the primary object contemplated in the memorial and accompanying documents lies beyond the limits of the constitutional powers of an Annual Conference. To organize a Conference *subject to the order* and discipline of the Methodist Episcopal Church, is the prerogative of the General Conference alone. An Annual Conference, or Conferences therefore, cannot, organize even *such* a Conference, much less one acting under a distinct discipline and independent authority. In this view of the subject, your committee are of the opinion that the African Conference, specified in the memorial, cannot be constitutionally organized or adopted; that it would not be advisable for our Bishops, or any one appointed by them, officially to preside at said Conference, or to ordain any deacon or Elder elected by them. But, although we judge it inexpedient to prostrate the constitution and government of the Church to accommodate any case whatever, firmly believing the evil would ultimately over-balance any good which might be supposed to result from it, we consider the condition of the Africans such as to demand every prudent exertion within our power to recover them from their wandering, and preserve them in the confidence and communion of the Church. Your committee, therefore, recommend the adoption of the following resolutions:

Resolved, 1st—That if the African brethren, who have addressed the Conference by memorial, will agree to be subject to the government of the Methodist Episcopal Church, in common with their white brethren, in such case, under the present existing circumstances, it is expedient and advisable that such colored preachers as are regularly constituted, be appointed to labor among them and take the pastoral charge of them until the next General Conference.

Resolved, 2nd—That the colored brethren submitting themselves to the order and discipline of the Church, are entitled to the same rights and privileges, with respect to the election and ordination of local deacons and Elders, as the white societies, the same form of order and discipline applying to both.

Resolved, 3rd—That the organization of an African Annual Conference, on the same principles, and subject to the same order and government as other Conferences, may be effected by the General Conference, but cannot be by one or more Annual Conferences.

Resolved, 4th—That it is advisable a member or members of this

Conference be appointed by the Bishop to present the above resolutions to the African Brethren in New York, together with any explanations and instructions which may be thought proper, and to receive their answer. (Joshua Soule was appointed to present the foregoing report, and Thomas Mason accompanied him.) [32]

Even though the ordination controversy was of so vital a concern to the new denomination and the adverse decision of the New York Conference placed a definite damper on enthusiasm plans for the yearly conference went ahead anyway. Bishop George, who was asked to preside, stated that he would be busy and two other bishops were too ill to attend, but Bishop George did suggest that they continue with their plans.

Meanwhile, a committee had been at work on a discipline, the document which appeared to be the stumbling block in the reunification of the Negro and white groups. As early as September 1820 George Collins had suggested that such a set of rules would be necessary so a committee of five was selected: James Varick, George Collins, Charles Anderson, Christopher Rush and William Miller. This same meeting is significant for other reasons for it was at this session that the first dissatisfactions with the ministry were expressed.[33] Rush states that proper assistance had not been given to organizations which were springing up in the vicinity of New York. The ministry declared that they, being poor, had not the means of traveling. This problem, evidently, found a partial solution when the elder, Reverend Stillwell, returned to the church the money he had received during the year.[34] However, the damage had been done and evidently many organizations which should have joined Zion, went over to Bishop Allen.[35]

Meanwhile, Zion and Asbury had come to an agreement regarding union. Rush lists the articles in full (see appendix at the end of this chapter). The main points had to do with the desire for preservation of their individual organizations, right to their own property and poor money as well as supervision of all other funds.

The Discipline Committee met on September 4th at the home of William Miller in Mulberry Street, but Rush states that at this first meeting the group did not do much.[36] They did decide on the title

---

[32] Rush, *loc. cit.*, pp. 61 ff.
[33] *Ibid.*
[34] Rush, *loc. cit.*, p. 51.
[35] *Ibid.*, p. 50.
[36] *Ibid.*, p. 48.

and the name of the new denomination, "The Doctrines and Discipline of the African Methodist Episcopal Church in America." [37] This point is significant, for it establishes the thought that the Allen followers were not then known as the African Methodist Episcopal Church, for the leaders of the New York group would have objected to using the same name and title. Two other individuals were added to the committee in this first meeting, Abraham Thompson, who had been proving a difficult individual for the new church, and John Dungy, who by this time was being considered one of the leaders of the group.[38] By September 26th the work of the committee was well nigh completed. They had selected from the discipline of the Mother Church those portions with which they agreed. George Collins had been charged with the writing of the preamble.[39] One month later, October 25th, the official members of Zion Church adopted the work of the committee on Discipline and ordered 1200 copies to be printed under the supervision of George Collins and Christopher Rush. John C. Totten did the printing.[40]

According to plan the first yearly conference of the new group opened in New York City, June 21, 1821.[41] Preachers of the two churches, Zion and Asbury, met. It is significant that representatives of the Philadelphia Church were not present, particularly since they insisted upon definite action to such a degree that the New York Churches were forced to act when they appeared to have been willing to return to the mother church. The sessions opened at 2:30 P.M. with the Reverend Joshua Soule and Doctor William Phoebus, Methodist ministers, in attendance, having been invited by the Negro ministers. The group elected one of the Bishops of the Methodist Episcopal Church as their Superintendent, and "the Bishop not being present, they chose Doctor William Phoebus for the President of the Conference *pro a viso*." [42] After drawing up some by-laws the session adjourned until 3:00 P.M. the next day.

The next day when the conference assembled with Dr. Phoebus in the chair the Philadelphia delegation arrived, as did representatives from New Haven and Long Island.[43] Reverend Joshua Soule became

---

[37] *Ibid.*
[38] *Ibid.*
[39] Rush, *loc. cit.*, p. 48.
[40] *Ibid.*
[41] *Ibid.*, p. 69.
[42] *Ibid.*
[43] *Ibid.*, p. 70.

the Secretary of the Conference. Another personality came to lend his support, Freeborn Garretson, who encouraged the group.[44] He felt that at the next General Conference some definite arrangement could be worked out.

On the 27th the conference closed with the following appointments: Abraham Thompson was appointed to the mother church, Zion; William Miller, Asbury Church; Simon Murray, Wesley, Philadelphia; and William Carman, Long Island.[45] James Varick became District Chairman. At this time the Discipline did not provide for presiding elders, for that is essentially what James Varick was, but with the unsettled state of affairs Rush says that this was the only course open.[46]

The statistics for this conference are important for it shows the strength of the new denomination at the time. Other ministers at Zion Church were: Leven Smith, Christopher Rush, Charles Anderson, James Smith, Timothy Eatto, Samuel Bird, Peter Van Has and John Dungy who later withdrew from the church.[47] At Asbury Church, besides William Miller there were: Abraham Marks, Christopher Anderson, John Palmer. At New Haven were listed James Anderson, and on Long Island were William Carman and Elijah Jackson. Philadelphia listed Edward Johnson, Durham Stephens, Daniel Pernal and Arthur Landford. In all 22 preachers appeared on the roll.

The membership of the churches was as follows:

Zion, New York	763
Asbury, New York	150
New Haven, Conn.	24
Long Island	155
Wesleyan, Philadelphia	300
Easton, Pennsylvania	18
Total membership	1,410
Amount collected for the Conference (Zion Church)	$27.30
Amount collected for the Conference (Asbury Church)	7.78
Total amount collected	$35.08

The place for the next meeting of the conference was to be Philadelphia.

To sum up, then, it appears to this writer that the New York Conference did adopt a sort of conciliatory attitude toward the peti-

---

[44] *Ibid.*, pp. 69, 70.
[45] Rush, *loc. cit.*, p. 70.
[46] *Ibid.*, p. 70.
[47] *Ibid.*

tion. The communication was not merely *sent*, it was delivered by individuals who were known and respected by the Negro members of Zion and Asbury. Joshua Soule was likewise respected and held in high esteem in his own denomination. While the communication or reply did not state in so many words, the olive branch appears to have been offered in respect to elder's orders for Negro preachers so long as this right occasioned service to the Negro chapels. The difference of opinion appears to have come at two points, both of them of extreme importance.

The first difference had to do with ultimate membership on an annual conference level. The New York Conference certainly had legality on its side when it was declared that no conference could be established without the consent of the General Conference placing its stamp of approval on such establishment.

On the matter of control of local church property we can scarcely see how Zion and Asbury could have had a wider control of their property. They were already independent of the John Street Congregation and its Board of Trustees in-so-far as the physical property and finance was concerned—at least that part of the latter raised by the Chapels. The point, then, of major difference came on lay participation and changes to bring this about in the Methodist Discipline.

It should not be overlooked that this first Book of *Discipline* of Zion and Asbury Churches or Chapels was an instrument of a layman's mind, basically. It certainly had the influence of the Stillwell *surge* which brought into existence a short-lived denomination the essence of equality, brotherhood and democracy in church circles, at least those circles with an Episcopal form of government.

THE AGREEMENT BETWEEN ZION AND ASBURY CHURCHES

WHEREAS—The official members of the African Methodist Zion and Asbury Churches are desirous of becoming more united in their spiritual government and privileges (the two Churches being separately Incorporated, and, consequently, their temporal concerns being transacted by separate bodies of Trustees), they deem it necessary in order to have a clear understanding between them, mutually to agree upon the following Articles, viz.:

1. It is provided and declared, between the parties, that the two bodies of trustees shall not interfere with each other, relative to the transactions of the temporal concerns of their respective Churches.

2. It is provided and declared that, in every case, when persons come forward to join on probation, or bring certificates of membership from other circuits or stations, the Elder having charge of the aforesaid Churches, from time to time, shall inquire of each person in order to ascertain on which Church Register he wishes to have his name enrolled, and the said elder shall proceed according to the determination of the applicant.

3. It is provided and declared that, no person shall at any time, receive applicants on probation, or otherwise, to become members of either Church, but the aforesaid Elder, for the time being, or any Elder, deacon, or preacher he may especially request to do so.

4. It is provided and declared that sick and poor members of one Church shall have no claim on the poor fund of the other, and that each Church give relief only to her own sick and poor members, according to the state of her poor fund and former custom.

5. It is provided and declared that there shall be but one Quarterly Conference to transact the spiritual concerns of both Churches, and all business to be done at the Quarterly Conference according to the discipline of the connexion, and that the official members of both Churches, consequently, have a seat and a voice in the said Conference; but that each Church shall have separate Leaders' and Trustees' meetings, and attend to business agreeably to the rules of the aforesaid discipline.

6. It is provided and declared that, in all cases when houses are to be built, hired, or enjoyed gratis, for the purpose of Divine worship, wherein regular collections of money are to be made, in any place within the limits of the Incorporation of either Church, a fair representation of the same shall be made at the Quarterly Conference, from time to time, by the party intending so to build, hire, or enjoy gratis, for the aforesaid purpose, in order that there may be always a clear understanding between the two bodies of Trustees relative to the revenue arising from such establishments.

7. It is provided and declared, also, between the parties, that in all cases of differences between them which cannot be settled by the Quarterly Conference, it shall be the duty of the Elder having charge, to refer the case to the ensuing Yearly Conference, where it shall be finally decided.

8. It is further provided that these Articles shall not be so construed as to affect any former agreement made by the Asbury Church and its stated Minister.

The foregoing Articles were agreed to first, by the official members of the Asbury Church, and on the 30th of November 1820, they were sanctioned by the official members of Zion Church.

(Signed)   WILLIAM M. STILLWELL
President, for both parties
ABRAHAM MARKS,
Secretary for Asbury Church.
GEORGE COLLINS,
Secretary for Zion Church.

CHAPTER IX

The Zion Church in the 1820's

BETWEEN THE first and the second sessions of the newly formed conference of African Methodists, two significant things took place. The matter of ordination had not been successfully settled and the other had to do with the activities of the ministers. It will be recalled that Abraham Thompson and James Varick had been *elected* to the eldership and not ordained. In the letter to the Philadelphia and New York Yearly Conferences the writers (see letter) mentioned a third *Elder*. For some reason Rush mentions the names of the two as stated above but the third individual remains unknown. It has been noted, as well, that the Reverend Mr. Stillwell concluded that he had not sufficient elders to perform the rite. Bishop Moore, in his history, states that the matter was a vexing one for the new denomination. Many of the members, as a result, hoped that the mother church would consent to ordain their elected elders but as time went on this hope went a glimmering. John Dungy, one of the preachers, went from New York to New Haven where he applied to the Methodist Episcopal Church for a license to preach and attempted to get the New Haven congregation to join the mother church with him.[1] With this feeling of unrest prevalent a small group hoped that the new organization could get along until the meeting of the next General Conference of the Methodist Episcopal Church when a solution to the vexing problem might be expected.

A new committee was appointed by the New York group to take up the matter again following the Second Yearly Conference. Leven Smith had stated to the group that he understood Bishop McKendree was in New York.[2] Accordingly, Abraham Thompson, Christopher Rush, Leven Smith, James Varick, and James Smith were appointed to call on the Bishop.

Bishop McKendree declared that he could do nothing contrary to the wishes of the Mother Church but that he would appreciate a statement in writing which was to be drawn up by the committee.

---

[1] John Jamison Moore, *History of the A.M.E. Zion Church* (New York, 1884), p. 90.
[2] Rush, *loc. cit.*, p. 74.

'This was done and appears at the close of this chapter. In June, 1822, three of the members of the Committee called upon Bishop Mc-Kendree (Abraham Thompson, Christopher Rush and James Smith) only to find that he had left the city.[3] However, they talked with Bishops George and Roberts who informed the Zion ministers that nothing could be done unless the members agreed to return to the Mother Church and further agreed to $100 per year for the service of the white elder.[4]

That night the Negro members met to hear the result of the Committee's investigation. The group was authorized to work until a solution of the problem was reached. One can almost see the grimness of the committee as it set to work. Meanwhile, Wesley Church in Philadelphia, was insisting on a solution, raising two objections to procedure at once, one, against any further overture to the Mother Church and the second against the use of Reverend Stillwell as it was felt this would hurt the status of the Wesley congregation. The committee, mentioned above being charged with the finding of a solution, went ahead.

Finally on June 17, 1822, after a most solemn service, with a sermon delivered by Dr. James Covel, Abraham Thompson, James Varick and Leven Smith were ordained elders.[5] Dr. Covel was assisted by the Reverend Sylvester Hutchinson and Reverend William Stillwell, all at one time members and elders of the Mother Church.[6] The following month the newly ordained elders consecrated Christopher Rush, James Smith, James Anderson, William Carman, Edward Johnson and Tilman Cornish as deacons and the same afternoon ordained them elders.[7] Rush states that this was done since there was such a great need for some supervision of the new churches being formed. As we have stated above, John Dungy, one of the preachers of the church, had gone to New Haven and there had attempted to secure a re-uniting of that group with the Mother Church, looking forward to ordination himself. In order to do this he withdrew from the new group and was licensed to preach by the Methodist Episcopal Church.

The second yearly conference met in Philadelphia. Problems arose

---

[3] Rush, *loc. cit.*, p. 77.
[4] *Ibid.*
[5] *Ibid.*, p. 78.
[6] Rush, *loc. cit.*, p. 78.
[7] *Ibid.*, p. 79.

in organization when it was learned that the Bishops of the Mother Church refused to preside, and the great friend of the group, Ezekiel Cooper, a man who never allowed anything to interfere with that which he considered right, found conditions over which he had no control of such that he could not attend.[8] Bishops George and Roberts did call upon the conference in session, advising them to take little action until the General Conference.[9]

Perhaps, all the angles of the case will never be known, but it appears that the Zion and Asbury people as well as all Negro Methodists had every reason to hold the New York Yearly Conference responsible for the stand taken by the Methodist Bishops. Thinking, on their part, retarded the growth of Negro Methodism in the Mother Communion more than 100 years. The present existent unsatisfactory arrangement of the Central Jurisdiction may have developed to a step nearer common brotherhood given these added years of experimentation. Since it was impossible for either the Methodist Bishops to attend or Doctor Cooper, Abraham Thompson was appointed President of the Second Yearly Conference. Again the main item to come before the conference had to do with the relations with the Mother Church, and again, Wesley Church demanded action which would indicate the existence of a separate denomination. The local church insisted on following the discipline which had been drawn up.[10]

Meanwhile, many of the ministers had been dissatisfied with the action and attitude of Asbury Church in New York City. Evidently their action in allowing the use of the church building for services by the Allen group precipitated the difference. When questioned about this action they waited until the Second Yearly meeting was in session at Philadelphia and then dispatched an official letter to the new denomination stating that they had concluded to act independently.[11] In fairness to Asbury Church it might be said that no doubt they felt that it would be useless to have a minister appointed if they did not intend to be governed by their mutual agreement. Rush states that James Varick was appointed anyway, "provided they would receive him." [12] Asbury later made the separation final by

[8] *Ibid.*, p. 72.
[9] *Ibid.*
[10] Rush, *loc. cit.*, p. 72.
[11] *Ibid.*, pp. 23, 74.
[12] *Ibid.*, p. 74.

returning to the fold of the Mother Church, accepting the proviso of paying $100 per year for the support of the Elder.[13]

As much of the work which needed to be done was not accomplished at Philadelphia an adjourned meeting was held in New York in July. It was at that time that the deacons listed above were ordained in the morning and elders in the afternoon. The appointments were made at this adjourned session as follows: Zion Church, Abraham Thompson; Newark and other points in New Jersey, Christopher Rush; Leven Smith, Missionary, to go as far as Boston; James Smith was to assist William Carman on Long Island; Wesley Church, Philadelphia, Edward Johnson; and New Haven, James Anderson. The Newark society was incorporated Monday, April 7, 1823. Its first meeting house was a structure 40 by 30 feet.[14]

At this adjourned meeting the following number were present: eight from New York, two from Philadelphia, one from New Haven and one from Long Island. The other important action of the group was the appointing of James Varick as Superintendent.

The Third Yearly Conference was held in New York beginning on May 21, 1823. The roll included the names of James Varick, Superintendent, Abraham Thompson, Christopher Rush, James Smith, Samuel Bird, Timothy Eatto, Peter Vanhas, William Carman, George Tredwell and James Anderson. Because of differences within the Wesley Church congregation in Philadelphia no minister represented this church. A new society was listed for the first time, evidently Middletown, Conn. Abraham Thompson was retired at this session while Leven Smith became the pastor of the Mother Church, Zion. Meanwhile Asbury Church had withdrawn again from the Methodist Episcopal Church and under William Miller, had joined Bishop Allen's group.[15]

The hopes of the new organization mounted somewhat as the time for the General Conference of the Methodist Episcopal Church drew near. For that reason it was deemed advisable to postpone the Fourth Yearly Meeting until after this general session was held. Consequently when the ministers gathered on July 15, 1824 a pall of gloom hung over the sessions. In the reading of the appointments James Smith was assigned to the Mother Church, Leven Smith went

[13] Ibid., p. 77.
[14] Rush, loc. cit., p .79.
[15] Ibid., p. 80.

to Newark, James Anderson to Middletown and Christopher Rush was made a Missionary. New Haven had become disgruntled because the minister had expelled one of their number for a *gross* crime and so received no appointee at this conference.[16] Changes in the next year, 1825, were limited for the only preachers attending were from New York City. Rush states that "there was no extra preaching" for this reason and therefore they had a "flat time." Rush was appointed to the Mother Church and Peter Van Has was ordained an elder and assigned to the society in Harlem. Abraham Thompson left retirement to accept Newark and Elizabethtown in New Jersey.[17]

The Fifth Yearly Conference was to see the end of the active role played so many years by Abraham Thompson. While he was in attendance at the sessions in 1826 he was not assigned so far as the records show. This session was held in New York, May 18, 1826. The following attended: James Varick, Superintendent, Christopher Rush, Leven Smith, Peter Vanhas, Timothy Eatto, Abraham Thompson, Charles Anderson, William Carman, and George Tredwell. Charles Anderson and George Tredwell were ordained deacons and Timothy Eatto, elder.[18] Rush was assigned again to the Mother Church, William Carman and George Tredwell were assigned to Long Island, Timothy Eatto and Charles Anderson to New Jersey and Peter Vanhas to Harlem.

The Seventh Yearly Conference again met in New York, May 17, 1827. Present for the first time were: Joseph Hopkins representing Buffalo and Jacob Matthews "who," according to Rush "became a preacher while he was a member of Zion Church, and had, a few years past, withdrawn from Zion and joined Asbury Church, and had afterwards attached himself to the Allenites, previous to their having a church in this city, made application to return to the bosom of Zion Church again, and was, on the 15th day of August, 1827, received to membership as an Elder." [19] Of course, James Anderson of New Haven, William Carman and George Tredwell were also present along with the Superintendent, James Varick, Christopher Rush. This was the last session over which James Varick was to preside.

Because of the peculiar circumstances under which the Zion Church was laboring it will be remembered that it was decided to

[16] Rush, *loc. cit.*, p. 81.
[17] *Ibid.*
[18] *Ibid.*, p. 82.
[19] Rush, *loc. cit.*, p. 82.

appoint a District Elder or Superintendent in 1821. It was the Super-intendent's task to supervise the work in all the churches. While Rush states that there was no real precedent for such a move, yet the office which the chief elder held in the City of New York may have given the ministers the idea. Abraham Thompson, from all custom, should have been chosen the District Elder, but possibly because of his early actions in the chuch he was passed over and the position given to James Varick. Bishop Moore uses the term "District Chairman" instead of Elder or Superintendent. He may be right in taking this stand since ordinations to this offce had not been accom-plished. It appears, however, that seniority played a part in the election as would naturally be the custom among the group. It is this writer's opinion that background and custom would have dictated this.

The available records allow no lofty conclusions about the selection of James Varick to this position. He was one of the two original elders, having been elected first, by the members of Zion Church, so little choice was to be had. A great many of the later writers of Zion history paint Varick as the moving spirit of the early church. This writer cannot agree with this interpretation. Possibly, in time, some records may be uncovered to substantiate this viewpoint but at the present, one can only conclude that Varick was more of a follower than a great leader. From the ministerial angle certainly Abraham Thompson appeared to insist on his viewpoint more frequently than any other of this group. One cannot overlook the shadow of Peter Williams behind every action of the Negro group in New York. While we have only Rush to whom to turn (and all writers, John Jamison Moore and J. W. Hood, included, have had only his records for this early period) all other accounts which can be located have brought no other interpretation.

Little is known about Bishop Varick and all that does appear of the record is confusing. Bishop Jones states that the date of his birth has been certified as being 1781.[20] Hood and Moore declare that Varick was one of the members who first began meeting separately in 1770. Still another account states that he was licensed to preach at the age of 17,[21] in 1813. To have been a leader in 1780, makes it

---

[20] Bishop E. D. W. Jones, *Comprehensive Catechism of the A.M.E. Zion Church* (Washington, D. C., 1934), p. 16.
[21] Benjamin Franklin Wheeler, *The Varick Family* (Mobile, 1906), p. 6.

appear that something must have been wrong with this calculation as well as prevailing custom. It is not at all unreasonable to suppose that only older people were accorded the privilege of leadership. Some educational attainment may have allowed for greater participation but in no account can we find a record of this educational attainment. Comparing him with Christopher Rush, the latter was at least 38 years old before he was licensed to preach. He, Rush, served his church approximately seven years before receiving any orders, and then, as he states, only because of necessity.

It is concluded that Varick was born in Newburgh, New York, anywhere between 1750 and 1796. Somewhere between these two dates seems more reasonable. We call attention to the fact that Rush speaks of Abraham Thompson as being old, but nowhere states such of Varick. If the latter, as Hood states, was born in 1750,[22] by 1820 he would have been 70 years old, an advanced age even in these days of longevity. Certainly Thompson could not have been much older. Father Thompson was passed over because of his age and his earlier stand. Certainly Varick had to be younger.

Wheeler states that James Varick was the son of Richard Varick, a man of Dutch descent. Richard is supposed to have been born in Hackensack New Jersey. He moved, with his parents, to New York City. James Varick's mother was of Dutch-Indian-Negro lineage. He is supposed to have been born in Newburg, New York (according to Wheeler, in 1750) while his mother was in that city visiting. It is unknown whether his mother was free or slave.[23] The Varick family was very influential in New York and it may have been that James was sent to school, there being two or three available at the time.[24] James Varick became a shoemaker and maintained a shop in Orange, now Baxter Street.[25] He must have been a boy of 16 when Philip Embury and Captain Thomas Webb began their preaching mission in New York.

According to some calculations James Varick was married to a Aurelia Jones in 1798 when he was approximately 48 years of age.[26] (This again, would make him rather old by the time the first yearly

[22] Bishop J. W. Hood, *One Hundred Years of the African Methodist Episcopal Zion Church* (New York, 1895), p. 162.
[23] Wheeler, *loc. cit.*, p. 8.
[24] *Ibid.*, p. 10.
[25] *Ibid.*
[26] Wheeler, *loc. cit.*, p. 16.

conference was held.) To this union were born four children, Daniel, Andrew, Emeline and Mary.[27] No member of Varick's family ever became a member of Zion Church. While this is also true of the family of Peter Williams, yet, Peter never left the Mother Church as such and when he died he was buried in an Episcopal Church yard.[28]

In 1822, according to the Disciplinary provisions, James Varick was elected the first Superintendent of the new denomination. He was re-elected in 1826. Some writers state that he died in his second term, "shortly before the conference in 1828," "early in 1828." [29] Bishop Moore, who was very close to the period and was enough of a student to be at one time one of the secretaries for the General Conference, has him presiding in 1828.[30] Bishop Singleton T. Jones states that he was Superintendent for four years while Christopher Rush apparently associated him. Bishop E. D. W. Jones states that he had passed away by the conference of 1828.[31] The difference of opinion is too divergent to allow for a decision as many of these accounts and statements are based on reminiscences and are not wholly reliable. When the conference met in New York in 1828, Leven Smith was urged for the position of Superintendent.[32] He declined, and Christopher Rush was selected. At this conference James Anderson came from New Haven and George Tredwell from Long Island. Jacob Matthews succeeded Christopher Rush as pastor of the Mother Church.

It might be stated that from 1829 on, the name of Varick is not noted in the records. One account of Rush does not mention either Varick or Abraham Thompson after 1826.[33] Moore has him present at both the Seventh and the Eighth Yearly Conferences.[34] This leads one to believe that Varick had passed on by 1829 without a doubt, and possibly earlier. Since the 1828 session was the General Conference year, Varick should have served until that time. The 1828 Conference elected Christopher Rush as Superintendent. The writer cannot reach a conclusion as to whether this was the *regular* time for

[27] *Ibid.*, p. 17.
[28] J. B. Wakeley, *Lost Chapters* (New York, 1858), p. 446.
[29] Hood, *loc. cit.*, p. 168.
[30] Moore, *loc. cit.*, 100.
[31] Bishop E. D. W. Jones, *loc. cit.*, p. 20.
[32] Bishop E. D. W. Jones, *loc. cit.*, p. 20.
[33] Rush, *loc. cit.*, pp. 82, 83.
[34] Moore, *loc. cit.*, p. 100.

election or not. Certainly as late as 1822 no General Session could have been said to have been held for the group had conversations with Bishop McKendree at that time. However, our General Sessions, since 1828, have been held in the proverbial *Leap Year*.

Christopher Rush, the second Superintendent of the Church, was born in Cravens County, North Carolina in 1777 (February 4th). He was converted at the age of 16 (1793). While it is not known whether he was "manumitted or purchased" through his own industry or the benevolence of friends, but he himself states that he came to New York in 1798, joining the A.M.E. Zion Church in 1803. In 1815 he was licensed to preach. He was ordained deacon and elder on the same day, in 1822. In 1828 he was elected Superintendent and is supposed to have served four years "with Varick in this position." [35] It appears that he served the church twenty years following the death of Superintendent Varick. We call attention to a discrepancy here in that Varick is listed as the first Superintendent from 1822-27. Bishop Singleton T. Jones gives the information listed above in which Rush is said to have served four years with Varick. This, too, is a little amiss for Rush is said to have lost his sight in 1852,[36] which would mean that he served 26 years or 28 in all. Bishop Hood states that he served twenty-four years.[37] Whether Varick failed of re-election in 1828 or died prior to that General Conference is a mooted question. Hood states that he died shortly before that Conference while Flood carries the account that Varick and Rush shared the Superintendent's honors for four years. Again there is a difference of opinion on the death of Superintendent Rush. Flood states that he died July 6, 1873 in his 96th year while the Official Directory issued by J. Harvey Anderson puts his death a year earlier.[38] Supposing that he lost his eyesight in 1852, according to Flood the grand old man lived 21 years in darkness, part of the time confined to his room. He maintained a keen mind to the last.[39] He is buried in Cypress Hill Cemetery in Brooklyn, New York.[40]

One fact of Father Rush's life which is mainly overlooked is his efforts to further education. It was he who secured the property for

---

[35] Hamilton, Flood, *Lives of the Methodist Bishops* (New York, 1882), p. 689.
[36] *Ibid.*, p. 689.
[37] Hood, *loc. cit.*, p. 168.
[38] J. Harvey Anderson, *The Official Directory of the African Methodist Episcopal Zion Church in America* (New York, 1895), p. 35.
[39] Hood, *loc. cit.*
[40] Flood, *loc. cit.*, p. 690.

the school in Essex County, New York. While this effort failed it early showed the interest of the church leaders in higher education.[41]

Superintendent Rush will be known as one of the greatest leaders of the Church. One year after assuming the position of Superintendent, new organizations were noted in Fredericksburgh, Harrisburgh, *western country, State of Pennsylvania*.[42] After the 1829 conference had adjourned a preacher arrived from Prescott, Upper Canada, "hoping to be in time to join the conference and represent a society in that part of the country." [43]

In 1829 (April 21st) Superintendent Rush received a letter from the Wesleyan Church in Philadelphia informing him that this organization intended to join the new denomination and had appointed delegates to the forthcoming conference.[44] Thus, when the sessions opened on May 21st the following were in attendance: Superintendent Rush (the title Bishop became common a few years later. At this time this office was still called, "Superintendent."), Leven Smith, James Smith, Peter Van Has, Timothy Eatto, Jacob Matthews (all of New York), William Carman and George Tredwell of Long Island, Charles Anderson of Newark, Edward Johnson, Richard Phillips, David Stevens and David Crosby, delegates from Wesley in Philadelphia, David Smith from Fredricksburgh and Jacob Richardson from Harrisburgh.[45]

The Philadelphia Conference was set off from the New York area at this session of the Mother Conference. The new conference met for the first time, June 14, 1829.[46] The following appointments were made: Wesley, Philadelphia, Edward Johnson, Western District, Jacob Richardson, Missionaries, David Smith and Richard Phillips. William Miller, at one time minister of the Asbury Church and who had left Zion to join Bishop Allen, came back in 1830, along with Asbury Church (Hood states that only a portion of the members came back with Miller) .[47]

A significant item appears in the records for this period. For several years Zion ministers invited the elders of the Mother Church to fill the Zion Church pulpit every two weeks. Under Timothy Eatto this

[41] Flood, *loc. cit.,* p. 690.
[42] Rush, *loc. cit.,* p. 83.
[43] *Ibid.*
[44] *Ibid.*
[45] *Ibid.,* p. 83.
[46] *Ibid.*
[47] Rush, *loc. cit.,* p. 82.

arrangement was continued. Thus it is shown that relations with the Mother Church were not only cordial but, it appears, that the deep feeling of resentment was not against the ministry of John Street but rather the New York Conference.

By this time the new denomination had grown considerably. In the statistics of 1831, 1,016 members were listed in the New York Conference [48] and 673 members in Philadelphia Conference.[49]

While the writer does not wish to list the following as conclusive records it appears that by 1843 Rush was listing the following churches as Zion organizations: New York, Zion and Asbury Churches, Rochester, Ithaca, Bath, Binghamton, Lockport, Syracuse, Buffalo (one in progress), Troy, Poughkeepsie, Newburgh, New Rochelle, White Plains, Harlem (one in progress), Long Island, Sag Harbor, Lakeville, Flushing, Brooklyn, Boston, Mass., Salem, Mass., Nantucket, Providence, R. I., Hartford, Middletown, New Haven, Bridgeport, Newark, N. J., Elizabethtown, Schrewsbury (evidently near or in Red Bank, possibly Eatontown), Philadelphia (two organizations), Harrisburgh, York, Carlisle, Shippensburg (one in progress), Lewisto(w)n, Bellefonte, Williamsport, Johnstown, Pittsburgh (two organizations) Wilmington, Baltimore (two organizations), Washington.[50]

While the new church appeared to be moving steadily ahead all these years, the passions at which Rush hints from time to time did not die out with the inclusion of new members and more preachers. It will be recalled that two diversions had already taken place while another reached this serious stage.

Asbury Church, which had begun as an opposition movement to Zion, signed an agreement with the first group, and then, after some time, withdrew, first to return to the Mother Church and later to Bethel. While we cannot be certain, it appears that the opening wedge was made when Bishop Allen secured permission to hold a conference in Asbury Church. Rush and many others were extremely bitter as the Philadelphia movement invaded New York and possibly made it a bit uncomfortable for William Miller, the leader of Asbury. Miller left the church with his people, only to return some years later. The fact that he was able to gain high position on the church

---

[48] Moore, loc. cit., p. 103.
[49] Ibid., p. 122.
[50] Rush, loc. cit., pp. 88, 89.

after this secession leads one to believe that he was not at fault entirely.

Hood declares that the movement which made William Miller an associate to Rush in the Superintendency was born of selfish men, jealous and ambitious. At times the Bishop was harsh in his sayings but in this case he adds a note that bears attention. He states from 1828 to 1840 Rush "filled the office alone and filled it well." After the death of Miller in 1846, Hood states that Rush carried on as if there never had been an assistant.[51] It is stated in Flood's *Lives of the Bishops* that Miller became an associate of Rush after the death of Varick, implying that the matter of an associate was not new. Bishop E. D. W. Jones declares that this action was not entirely legal [52] but it brings into focus the determination of the sincere leaders of the church to carry on even if it meant effecting a compromise. Rush, however, makes no mention of *associates* prior to this time.

The second yearly conference of the Philadelphia area met in the Colored Wesley Church on Lombard Street, June 12th, 1830 with Bishop Rush presiding and David Stevens as Secretary. The conference met for five days after which the appointments were read.

The final session of the New York Conference of the decade met on May 17, 1830. It was during this session that William Miller made application for re-admission. The sessions closed to meet May 21, 1831.

LETTER PRESENTED AT REQUEST OF BISHOP MCKENDREE STATING THE DESIRES OF THE AFRICAN SOCIETY

We, the subscribers, composing a committee appointed by the official members of the African Methodist Episcopal Zion Church, in the City of New York, beg leave to present the following on the subject of ordaining our preachers, as instructed by our church:

First, That the said church in New York, several societies on Long Island, a society in New Jersey, one in New Haven, Conn., the Wesley Church in Philadelphia, and several societies in the state of Pennsylvania have resolved to be established in a connection according to the rules and regulations of the Discipline selected and printed in New York for the African Methodist Episcopal Connection.

Second, That the aforesaid societies or connection wishes to be in perfect union with the mother church, as respects brotherly and friendly affection, so that we may not be in opposition to each other in the course of our operations in our great religious work.

---

[51] Hood, *loc. cit.*, p. 71.
[52] Jones, *loc. cit.*, p. 21.

Third, We think the foregoing desire can be accomplished if one of the bishops of the mother church could be allowed to preside at the yearly African Methodist Conference from time to time; and in case of his absence the superintendent contemplated by the aforesaid Discipline of the African M. E. Conference shall have full power to preside and perform the duties of a bishop, so far as it shall become essentially necessary for the prosperity of the aforesaid connection, and without any opposition to the interests of the mother church.

Fourth, That in order to accomplish the object of the third item, reciprocal regulations can be adopted, to secure the bishops of the mother church the prerogative of superintending at the African Conference from time to time; also, to secure to him compensation for his extra service and expense; also, that the said African Conferences be so convened as to suit the convenience of the bishops, and not too laborious or expensive for the African preachers to attend.

Fifth, That the members, particularly of the Zion Church, regret exceedingly to see this necessary among Methodists, especially subdivisions among their African brethren. We believe this unhappy division will continue to exist, unless a permanent African Connection is formed, to meet the want of the colored people in the land.

Sixth, If the foregoing items are thought to be impracticable by the bishops and conference of the Methodist Church, we shall be under the necessity of procuring ordination otherwise, but without the least intention of opposition to the interests of our white brethren. As the unity of our societies depends upon our obtaining ordinations for our preachers, we must this summer secure this provision and become established under the Discipline we have selected and which these societies have approved.

CHAPTER X

The A. M. E. Zion Church and Slavery

THE METHODIST CHURCH, from its founding in America, can be said to have been one of the great sentiment molding organizations on the North American Continent. In another chapter we have given a brief account of her stand on slavery which continued to increase in intensity until the outbreak of the Civil War. We reiterate that often overlooked is the deep influence the Churches of America had on this conflict. In fact, one could easily state that the attitude of these evangelical churches had as much to do with the arrival at crisis as any other cause.

Not only, then, did the Negro Methodist Church have this background of antagonism to slavery but there was also the more potent reason of race. The A.M.E. Zion Church not only was formost in the carrying on of this struggle for freedom but appears to have been the leader along this line. At one time or another every great racial advocate of freedom was a member of this organization. Many of them received their impetus and great encouragement from the membership of the church and this no doubt had tremendous influence on these aggressive leaders.

At the founding of John Street Methodist Church in New York, Negro slaves and freedmen were welcomed and several made their contributions to the building of this old Church. When Mother Zion was established several of her leaders were individuals who owed their freedom to the Methodist Church and naturally that spirit of freedom became a fundamental part of the new organization. At times mass meetings were held and a general concerted effort was made to keep before the free north the wrong of human servitude.

As one turns again to the lives of these Negro men and women it is not just a matter of chance that they belonged to the A.M.E. Zion Church. Once free, it was well known that this new church of freedom would leave no stone unturned in behalf of the new man. So all along the Mason and Dixon Line, and farther west, in Ohio and Indiana, Zion Churchmen and their friends, became beacon points of hope to the escaped slave, and, no doubt out of gratitude and faith, they, likewise became Zion members. In many localities this work of leading to the more abundant life was aided and abetted by *Friends,* members of that Society, commonly called Quakers. In at least two and possibly three instances Bishops of the Church owed their very lives to this group. Among them were Bishops John J. Moore and Jermain Louguen. Such little way stations as Fishertown, Pennsylvania, Bedford in the same state, Jamestown, New York and Rochester and Auburn as well as Syracuse were whispered havens for the slave who became desperate enough to do something about his lot.

Mother Zion in New York, Wesley in Philadelphia, New Haven, New Bedford in Massachusetts, Rochester, Memorial Church, Auburn (in New York) and Jamestown in the same state, all can boast of churches, who were literally born out of this grave necessity to bring a new interpretation of Christ into the hearts of men who merely *wondered* about God interest in men of low estate. So it was that Catherine Harris, Thomas James, Frederick Douglas, Harriet Tubman, Jermain Louguen and Sojourner Truth led this Methodist crusade for human rights when it was extremely dangerous to do so. Later, to this group would be added such names as J. J. Clinton, J. W. Hood, and John Williams. To a great extent Bishop Hood has given a good account of the work from 1864. It is our thought merely to preserve for posterity those bits of history which remain to be noted.

The following account was carried by the *Jamestown* (New York) *Sun* on Sunday, September 3, 1950:

> Strong-willed Catherine Harris, who never, never would tell a lie— and had a sparing touch with the truth if need be—has ceased to be these 43 years. But her vitality is part and parcel of today's living, breathing Jamestown.
>
> Her celebrated "boxed slave" is no more. But in spite of the fact that the packaged fugitive from the pre-Civil War South was delivered elsewhere his grandson was drawn back into the orbit of high events (the grandson, in fact, is barber Manley Jefferson, of 56 West Tenth Street).
>
> And though the original homestead that once was among the hottest underground railroad stations in the country no longer sits at 12 West Seventh Street, the house that stands there now is an extension of the amazing old lady's spirit. Her great-grandson built it.
>
> Today, a marker, dedicated in 1936, tells passing motorists briefly of the site of the underground railroad. It tells of Catherine Harris' heroic work for the fugitives.

It says nothing about the fact that this was one of the few Negro-operated undergrounds in America; nor of that "extra cellar"; nor of the strange moral position forced upon a woman who felt herself obliged to evade and confuse the agents of the fugitive slave law, and at the same time never lie to a human soul.

In the case of the "boxed slave," as Mrs. Entzminger of 32 West 18th Street recalls hearing it told, it worked this way:

The pursurers were hot on the trail of Manley Jefferson's grand-father. As he made the lap between stations—from Sugar Grove to Jamestown—the agents came down with a powerful conviction that the fugitive was being harbored in the Harris homestead.

They banged on the door and when "Aunt Catherine" Harris answerd they demanded stormily:

"Is that runaway here? Don't give us any lies. Where is he?" Mrs. Harris met their bluster with a level gaze and a thin smile. "I don't plan to lie," she said. "I don't have to. He WAS here!"

"So you shipped him out, did you?"

Mrs. Harris let a histronic glint of triumph in her eye speak for itself. The man went away fuming, cutting the discussion short in the hope of catching up with the fugitive before he reached Dunkirk and the underground's "ferry" across Lake Erie to Canada, where there was no fugitive slave act.

It so happens that they were men of too few words. Or they were dense in their tense sense. If they had been able to make Mrs. Harris put a fine point out of it, it would have come out that the fugitive not only WAS on the premises, but hadn't even left.

It was after that that the people in the "homestead" at 12 West Seventh Street decided to put the fugitive up like a crate of loose castings and deliver him coffin-wise to the country across the border.

Breathing holes were bored sparingly in the box, it was loaded in a wagon—and although the countryside was being scoured by the pursurers, the crate safely reached Dunkirk and the journey's end was freedom.

Mrs. Entzminger, who recalls this episode as one of the choice memories of the Harris Clan, is a half-sister of Richard Whitfield, who built the present home on the site of the old homestead.

Whitfield, who visited Jamestown a few weeks back, put up the present two-story house about 40 years ago. The original building consisted of an "upright" facing the street, two stories in height, and an "el" which ran three stories and contained the attic which served as main dormitory for the fugitives. It was built in 1836 and at the time it was torn down its entrance was several feet below street level. It was a strong clap-board structure which had consistently been kept in paint and was considerably larger than its replacement.

As an old, old lady (she died in 1907 at the age of 98), Mrs. Harris was unable to look back on herself as a woman of guile or high dramatic doings. She seems to have thought of herself as a person whose chief aim to remembrance was built on devotion and hard work. Her outstanding memory was of the occasion in the early "50's" when she had

17 slaves in the house at one time and cooked and "did" for all of them until it was safe for them to go.

In her late years she presented something of the aspect of a down-to-earth Harriet Beecher Stowe, with something of Grandma White-oaks thrown in for good measure. Her will power reflected itself powerfully in her face, but it was not the irascible kind that seeks domination for its own sake. The depth of her resolution was suggested oddly in the story of her death as told by Mrs. Entzminger.

Mrs. Mary Hall, the youngest daughter of Mrs. Harris, began to fail as she neared the age of 77. Mrs. Harris was then pushing the age of 98. The mother had retained the keenness of mind and spirit, but she was exhausted under the weight of nearly a hundred years—many of them heavy years indeed. She hardly made it a secret that she was ready to "let go." "But it seemed as if she couldn't," Mrs. Entzminger recalled. "She felt that she had to live to take care of her daughter, even though the daughter was twenty years younger than she was.

"Finally the day came when Mrs. Hall died. The news was kept from Mrs. Harris, but somehow she sensed what had happened. I guess that was the release she'd been waiting for, for she felt that she was free to go now, and she did. She died two days after."

Born in Titusville, Pa., in 1809, she married John Harris of Erie, and in 1831 became one of the pioneers of Jamestown. She was far better known in the early community as a natural doctor, nurse, midwife, and "all-around woman" than as the presiding genius of a station on the underground railroad. In this her motive had been entirely humane, for she never had any personal connection with slavery. (Author's note: This has made Catherine Harris exceptional in the annals of Zion's active anti-slavery group for all the others had experienced slavery.)

Today a living community honors her labors by its very existence. It was about seventy-five years ago that the A.M.E. Zion Church came into being in her homestead. The church grew, the meetings moved elsewhere. But the tie that bound—still binds. For in the house at 12 West Seventh Street on the very site of the old underground railroad station, lives the pastor of the Zion Church, and before him the erstwhile pastor lived there too. The building today is the church's regular parsonage.

The present pastor is the Reverend William T. Henderson, who came to the house with his wife, Flora, and two children, from Ansonia, Conn., about a year ago. Before him, the Reverend Thomas Taylor lived there. Before him, without filling in all the details, Richard Whitfield lived there, and before him and his mother, Mrs. Harris was. And from the large thumbprints her capable hands left on the community—still is.[1]

To the north others struggled in this great pre-battle of freedom. In Rochester the Reverend Thomas James, sensing that he, along with others was engaged in a crucial and vital struggle, one which

_____
[1] *Jamestown New York Sun*, Sept. 3, 1950.

posterity should know about, sat down to write the story of his life and then decided to have copies printed. Jermain Loguen, later a Bishop of the Church, decided on writing a book of his life. Meanwhile, Frederick Douglas was engaged in furthering the struggle for freedom by editing a paper in Rochester. The fact that he was a member and closely identified with the Zion Church is verified not only in the statements he made himself but his years in Rochester, the statement of Bishop Hood and the highly significant statement of the Reverend Thomas James. Bishop Hood has this to say in his History:

> Fred Douglass, one of the most remarkable men that the race has produced, admits that he is indebted to the African Methodist Episcopal Zion Church in New Bedford, Mass., for what he is. As sexton, class leader, and local preacher in that church he got his inspiration, training and send-off, which have made him the wonder of his time.[2]

The Reverend Thomas James mentions the following in his pamphlet:

> It was at New Bedford that I first saw Fred Douglas. He was then, so to speak, right out of slavery, but had already begun to talk in public, though not before white people. He had been given authority to act as an exhorter by the church before my coming, and I some time afterwards, licensed him to preach. He was then a member of my church. On one occasion, after I had addressed a white audience on the slavery question, I called on Fred Douglass, whom I saw among the auditors, to relate his story. He did so, and in a year from that time he was in the lecture field with Parker Pillsbury and other leading abolitionist orators.[3]

Reverend James makes a significant statement in his auto-biography concerning Frederick Douglass which makes one wonder about his later affiliation with the Negro Church. Evidently, at one time, Douglass had the idea that the Christian Church was not doing all it could toward the destruction of slavery, and yet, to a man of his ability, there should have been the clear thought that no other basis could equal the Christian contention of the brotherhood of man. It certainly is inconceivable that he could live in Rochester, New York (after leaving New Bedford where he had resided nine years, with two additional years being spent abroad) without identifying

---

[2] Hood, loc. cit., p. 15.
[3] Life of Reverend Thomas James, by Himself.

himself with Memorial Church. He actually lived in Rochester around twenty-five years.[4]

Perhaps the bit of confusion concerning Douglass' church affiliation is occasioned by his subsequent removal to Washington, D.C. and his being buried from another church. The explanation usually given for this is the need for as large a church building as possible for his funeral. He certainly considered Rochester his home and it was to that place that his body was returned for burial. His wife, Anna Murray Douglass is likewise buried in Mount Hope Cemetery.[5]

The Reverend Thomas James, who has been quoted above in the matter of the church affiliation of Frederick Douglass, was born in Canajoharie, New York in 1804. One of four children, he was the property of Asa Kimball. When he was eight years old he was separated from mother, brother and elder sister when they were sold to someone in Smithtown, a village near Amsterdam, New York. He states that his mother refused to go with the new master and ran away but was captured and tied hand and foot for the journey to her new home. Reverend James never saw his mother and sister again, but did contact his brother.

At seventeen, his master having been killed by a runaway horse, James was sold to a Mr. Cromwell Bartlett who resided in the same vicinity. In a few months this owner sold or traded James to a third individual, George H. Hess. Bartlett received a yoke of steers, a colt and some additional property for the slave. Hess not only worked his slaves hard but was not too kind and the result was that James escaped into Canada. He later returned to New York state and worked on the Erie Canal as a warehouseman. Here, under his employer a Mr. Freeman, he was taught to read and write with the clerks under Mr. Freeman helping whenever they could.

James joined the A.M.E. Zion Church in 1823 (the organization later was known as the Memorial Church of Rochester, New York). In 1828 the ex-slave was teaching school on the street where the church is now located. Five years later Bishop Rush ordained Reverend James and he became a traveling minister in the Church.

One point which struck this writer was the logical way in which slaves who were practically nameless assumed their names. Thomas James was called Jim when he worked at the warehouse. When he

[4] *The A.M.E. Zion Quarterly Review*, Vol. LXIII, No. 4, pp. 193-196.
[5] *Ibid.*, Vol. LXIV, No. 1, pp. 8 ff.

was a slave they had called him Tom, so he merely put the two together and called himself Thomas James.

In 1831 a Judge Sampson turned over to Thomas James some anti-slavery literature which he read with such enthusiasm that he became one of the greatest advocates of freedom in the Nation. By 1833 he was one of the leaders in promoting a series of anti-slavery meetings in Rochester. Perhaps a noteworthy statement of James is that which allows the reader to understand that even in that section of the country promotion of this anti-slavery sentiment was a hazardous undertaking. He gives great credit to such outstanding, fearless individuals as William Bloss and a Dr. Reid, as well as a Dr. W. Smith.

In 1835 James left Rochester to found a church in Syracuse. There, as well, he took up the work of the anti-slavery movement. In 1838 he was transferred to Ithaca to pastor this congregation. He remained there two years. He was subsequently transferred to Long Island and then to New Bedford, Massachusetts, where he met Frederick Douglass. Bishop Hood states that Douglass served this church not only as exhorter but as sexton and class leader as well.[*]

The writings of Reverend James establishes the fact that Zion ministers were *expected* to take an active part in this struggle for freedom. Some of his experiences are worthy of note here since they have not appeared widely in print.

"It was soon after this that great excitement arose in New Bedford over the action of Reverend Mr. Jackson, a Baptist minister, who had just returned from a Baltimore clerical convention, which sent a petition to the Maryland Legislature in favor of the passage of a law compelling free Negroes to leave the state, under the plea that the free colored men mingling with the slaves incited the latter to insurrection. Reverend Mr. Jackson was vice president of that convention and a party to its action. Printed accounts of the proceedings were sent to me, and at a meeting called to express dissent from the course taken by the minister named and his brethren. I introduced a resolution of which the following is a copy:

Resolved that the great body of the American clergy, with all their pretensions to sanctity, stand convicted of their deadly hostility to the Anti-Slavery movement, and their support of the slave system, as a brotherhood of thieves, and should be branded as such by all honest Christians."

[*] Hood, *loc. cit.*, p. 15.

Perhaps a study which would be of vital interest is that which involves the local ministers of the American churches. There is little doubt that in both south and north the struggle was a bitter one. Certainly the few revelations which have come to our attention disclose the fact that many pulpits of the nation were occupied by individuals who cared little or were outright hostile to this new interpretation of Christianity. It throws in to richer focus those who were courageous enough to argue this larger concept of brotherhood. Perhaps Frederick Douglass had reason to be convinced that the Church was not the forceful agent it should have been in the struggle.

Another incident of the life of Thomas James is recounted here:

"On my journey homeward from a visit to New York City, I met Mr. Henry Ludlam, and his wife, two children and a slave girl from Richmond, Va., all bound for New Bedford to spend the summer with Captain Dunbar, father-in-law of the head of this party of visitors. I said that I met them, but the meeting consisted only in this, that they and I were on board the same train, but not in the same car. I was in the "Jim Crow" car, as colored persons were not permitted to enter the others with white people, and the slave girl was sent to the same car by the same rule. I talked with her, and, and as I was duty bound to do so, asked her to come to my church during the stay of the family in New Bedford. After some weeks had passed and she did not come, I took with me a colored man and another friend to call on her and learn, if we could, why she did not attend the services. Her master or owner met us at the door, and gave us the answer, "Lucy is my slave, and slaves don't receive calls." In short, he refused to let us enter the house, whereas we took advice from friends, and applied to Judge Crapo for a writ of habeas corpus. The judge sent us about our business with the advice not to annoy Mr. Ludlam, who was entitled to hospitable treatment as a visitor and guest.

Instead of taking this advice, we journeyed to Boston, and were given by Judge Wilds the writ his judicial brother in New Bedford had denied us. We had Sheriff Pratt and the writ with us when we made our next call on the slave girl's master. The latter at first refused to give even the sheriff leave to see the girl, and finally proposed to give bail for her appearance before the judge. The sheriff turned to me inquiringly when this proposal was made, and I answered: "Mr. Sheriff, you were directed to take the person of the girl Lucy and I call on you to do your duty." Thus we got possession of the girl, but not before her owner had obtained leave for a few minutes' private conversation with her. In this talk, we afterwards learned, he frightened Lucy by telling her that our purpose was an evil one, and obtained her promise to display a handkerchief from the room in which she would be confined as a signal for the rescue he promised her.

We took the girl to a chamber on the upper floor of the residence of the Rev. Joel Knight, and that evening we prepared to lie down before the door. Lucy displayed the handkerchief as she had promised, and when we questioned her about it, answered, "Master told me to do it; he is coming to take me home." At this we quietly called together twenty men from the colored district of the place, and they took seats in the church close at hand, ready for any emergency. At one o'clock in the morning Ludlam appeared on the scene, with the backing of a dozen men, carrying a ladder, to effect the rescue. The sheriff hailed them but they gave no answer, whereat our party of colored men sallied forth, and the rescuers fled in all directions. The entire town was now agog over the affair.

So many took sides against us, and such threats were made, that the sheriff was forced to call to his aid the local police, and thus escorted, the girl was placed aboard the cars for Boston. The other party, to the number of 150 men, chartered a train by another route, with the design of overpowering the sheriff's posse in the streets of Boston— Lucy was brought before Judge Wilds—she asked for her freedom, and received it the next day, when the case came up in open court. The girl afterwards married, had children, and I believe, lived happily among the people of her own color in the North.

Reverend James later was assigned to the Boston Church and in 1856 returned to take charge of the church in Rochester. This appeared to have been his last charge in the Zion Church for later he decided to take up full-time work in the cause for freedom."

To him we must give proper credit for the outlawing of *Jim Crow* cars on the railroads of the Northeast. Evidently his first appearance at Court in the matter was unsuccessful for, later, the Supreme Court of the state of Massachusetts ruled that the word "color," as it applied to persons, was unknown to the laws of the commonwealth of Massachusetts and that the youngest colored child had the same rights as the richest white citizen.[7]

While Thomas James was having his stirring experiences in Western New York state and in New England, another great soul was reaching maturity in this struggle for the rights of man. Eliza Ann Gardner, the pioneering missionary spirit of the Church was not only instrumental in making the Church mission conscious but shouldered significant responsibility in this race struggle. Her mother was a member of the Mother Church somewhere around 1796 and she herself was a moving spirit in the Boston Church. She knew well such individuals as William Lloyd Garrison, Wendell Phillips, Frederick Douglass, Harriet Tubman, Sojourner Truth and Susan B. Anthony.

While it is not our purpose to write at length here of this pioneering woman, for in a succeeding chapter we will deal with the

---

[7] *Life of Thomas James*, by Himself.

missionary movement of the denomination, but her work so over-lapped phases of history that she must be mentioned among those who made the Zion Church a giant in this struggle for opportunity. It was she who turned the Church's eyes to work in Southeastern Canada (Nova Scotia) and it was she who insisted on mission work in the West Indies and it was she, as well, who made it possible for the work to begin hard on the heels of the Northern Army in the war between the states.

It is to be hoped in this closer study of Eliza Ann Gardner that we can as well trace the work of the Daughters of New England of which she was a member.

We have already mentioned two great spirits of the Western New York area, Elizabeth Harris and Thomas James. Two others remain to be told about here, Jermain Loguen, who later became a Bishop of the Church and that noble woman, Harriet Tubman. Let us turn first to the ex-slave who later became one of the highest officers of the denomination.

BISHOP J. W. LOGUEN

Because Jermain W. Loguen was born a slave little is known of his father as is true of all slaves to a great extent. When the first accounts of his life were written, however, his mother, a pure African, was presumed to be alive and at that time about seventy years of age. The Bishop's recollection of his mother allows us to know that her skin was jet black and her hair short and curled close to her head. She had regular features, was well built, full of health and a splendid specimen of her race.

Evidently the mother of Jermain was a free child for her accounts later given to her children tell of living somewhere in Ohio on the farm of a Mr. McCoy. Here she remained until she was about seven years of age when a man with a covered wagon drove by one day and covering her mouth with his hand so that she could not scream carried her off along with several other Negro children. The story of their grief at being snatched from their mothers is pathetic to read about, here, almost one hundred years after the writing of the story. Naturally they could not understand this treatment and cried until exhausted and asleep.

The children, including Jermain's mother, were taken across the river (Ohio) and sold one after another until all were disposed of.

Jermain's mother was sold to three brothers, David, Carnes and Manasseth Logue "who lived in a small log house on Manscoe's Creek (so called) in Davidson County, about sixteen miles from Nashville, Tennessee." According to the accounts given the brothers were not only rough, poor and almost disgusting but either shiftless or unconcerned for their plantation was "miserably cultivated."

At first Jermain's mother had the idea that the three unmarried brothers were kindly men. She began telling them how she had been kidnapped from her home with all the ruthlessness involved. It was her thought that they would return her to her mother but instead she was whipped severely until she was was quite willing to give her promise "never again to repeat the offensive fact of her freedom."

There is little doubt that the brothers were well aware of the practice of stealing the children in free territory and selling them across the river for one of their first acts was to change the name of the little girl from *Jane* to *Cherry*.

To say that the days of *Cherry* were hard would be putting it mildly for she was called upon to do every type of work from working in the fields to labor in the distillery. She was strong and at the same time fearless and at times, rebelled at the harsh treatment given her. Punishment usually followed, of a severe nature but her spirit was never broken. While she seemed aware that she would have to endure some harsh treatment at the hands of her owners she never endured it from any other persons. At one time she defended herself so vigorously that the white man who pressed the attack was left for dead.

The vicious system which existed in the south where Negro women slaves were concerned finally engulfed *Cherry*. She evidently became the property of one of the three brothers, Dave. Of Bishop Loguen's father this should be stated as it appears in the record: "when a very little child he was the pet of Dave, as his father was also nicknamed, that he slept in his bed sometimes, and was caressed by him—he also received from him many little favors and kindnesses which won his young heart."

The kind of relationship which existed between father and son was to remain but a short time for David, the father finally took a wife from among his own race and his co-habiting with *Cherry* ceased. From this point on Jarm, as he was called, found that more and more he was being considered as any other slave on the plantation. Partly because of the breaking off of David's relationship with Cherry and partly because of the economics involved it was thought best to find a husband for Cherry. This was soon done and a slave from a neighboring plantation by the name of Henry was selected. It must be said that his owner insisted that Henry be considered in the matter and after the slave exacted the promise that neither he nor Cherry or any of their children would be separated by more than ten miles the marriage was agreed to. It was David, however, who broke the promise.

It appears that David soon began experiencing some reverses on the plantation thus finding it necessary to sell some of the slaves. His brother who evidently was living in Tennessee (Manasseth), agreed to take several of them and so Jarm, his mother and the other members of his family found themselves on Manasseth's plantation.

This change of owners was merely one in a series, the circumstances of which are merely the repeated patterns of the slave system in the south. However, the process was ended when Jarm and a slave friend by the name of John decided to escape. After days of frustration, danger and privation they succeeded in getting to Detroit where John remained, Jarm proceeding on to Canada. We have deemed it wise to include in this short sketch a letter which was written to Frederick Douglass, dated Syracuse, New York, May 8, 1856:

"On the western termination of Lake Ontario is the village of Hamilton. It is a large, enterprising place, amid scenery, placid, beautiful and sublime. It is in a delightful valley, which runs east and west. On the north is a beautiful lake, and on the south a perpendicular mountain towers up some two or three hundred feet, and hangs its brow over the village. Here are quite a number of our people, doing well so far as I could learn—able and willing not only to help the fugitive, but to join with able and willing white men around them to furnish him an asylum. How changed in twenty years! My dear friend, indulge me here a moment. Hamilton is sacred and memorable spot to me; and I cannot slightly pass it. I could not stand upon its soil without a flood of sad and sweet and gushing memories. It seems to me, and ever will seem to me, a paternal home. I shall never visit it without the feelings which a child feels on returning after weary years to his father's house.

Twenty-one years ago—the very winter I left my chains in Tennessee—I stood on this spot, penniless, ragged, lonely, homeless, helpless, hungry and forlorn—a pitiable wanderer, without a friend, or shelter, or place to lay my head. I had broken from the sunny South, and fought a passage through storms and tempests, which made the forests crash and the mountains moan, difficulties new, awful, and unexpected, but not so dreaded as my white enemies who were comfortably sheltered among them. There I stood, a boy twenty-one years of age (as near as I know my age) the tempests howling over my head, and my toes touching the snow beneath my worn-out shoes—with the assurance that I was at the end of my journey—knowing nobody, and nobody knowing me or noticing me, only as attracted by the then supposed mark of Cain on my sorrow-stricken face. I stood there the personification of helpless courage and finited hope. The feeling rushed upon me, "Was it for this that I left sweet skies and a mother's love?" On visiting this place now, I contrast the present and the past. No Underground Railroad took me to Hamilton. White men had not then learned to care for the far-off slave, and there were no thriving colored farmers, mechanics and laborers to welcome me. I can never forget the moment. I was in the last extremity. I had freedom but nature and man were against me. I could only look to God, and I prayed, "Pity, O my Father—help, or I perish!" and though all was frost and tempest without, within came warmth, and trust and love; and an earthly father took me to his home an angel wife who became to me a mother. He thought a body lusty and stout as mine, could have cold, could brave cold, and cut cord wood, and split rails and he was right. I agreed to earn my bread, and did much more than that; and he rewarded my labors to the extent of justice. They paid me better than I asked, and taught me many lessons of religion and life. I had a home and place for my heart to repose and had been happy but for the thought that ever torments the fugitive, that my mother, sisters and brothers were in cruel bondage, and I could never embrace them again.

My dear Douglass, you will not think it strange I speak of my case in contrast with the now state of things in Canada. Hamilton was a cold wilderness for the fugitive when I came there. It is now an Underground Railroad Depot, where he is embraced with warm sympathy. Here is where the black man is disencumbered of the support of master and mistress, and their imps, and gets used to self-ownership. Here he learns the first lessons in books, and grows into shape. Fortunately for me, I gained the favor of the best white people. My story attached them to me. They took me into the Sabbath School at Hamilton, and taught me letters the winter of my arrival; and I graduated a Bible reader at Ancaster, close by, the succeeding summer. All the country around is familiar to me, and you will not wonder I love to come here. I love it because it was my first resting place from slavery, and I love it more because it has been, and will continue to be, a city of refuge for my poor countrymen."

That first year of Jarmain's being in Canada he made a living by working for a neighborhood farmer for ten dollars a week. It was during this time that he took the name of Jarmain Wesley Loguen. Two years later he took a farm of 200 acres on shares. So long as he worked the farm alone he was successful but he decided to take a partner and lost all that he had gained. Loguen, becoming disgusted lift the area and settled at St. Catherines where he bought a house and lot. Soon thereafter he crossed into the United States and secured a job at the Rochester House in Rochester, New York.

At the end of about two years Mr. Loguen left this place of employment and proceeded to Whitesboro and there entered the Oneida Institute which at that time was headed by Beriah Green.

It is impossible to devote many pages to the life of Bishop Loguen even though his work was such that keen interest is manifested by students today in his activities.

While at school he married a Caroline Storum. This was in 1840. She was the daughter of a Mr. and Mrs. Storum who emigrated from New Hartford in the state of New York and settled at Busti in 1816. Properous and thrifty they soon were the owners of one of the best farms in that area.

It is impossible to trace in detail the activities of Bishop Loguen in the succeeding years. Some highlights should be mentioned, however. For example, the attempt on the part of the people of Cortland, New York to purchase the freedom of Cherry, the mother of Jarmain. This was unsuccessful even though an individual made the trip south in this cause. The effort failed since there was reluctance to sell slaves to a runaway. Bishop Hood states that Bishop Moore passes over Bishop Loguen in silence. It may be that Bishop Moore, drawing on his memory and the records at hand, did not recall the work of Bishop Loguen. There is the further possibility that the work of the Bishop in the field of abolition so overshadowed his church affiliation that Bishop Moore considered this his sphere rather than that of Zion Church. At any rate, he is not mentioned.

Bishop Loguen was ordained by Superintendent Rush and spent several years of service in the western New York area. The meager details of his ministerial work may have been a contributing cause to Bishop Moore's neglect for even in his own autobiography Loguen pays little attention to his work as a minister of the church. From these short references we do know that he was stationed at Syracuse in 1846-1848. In this last year he was made presiding elder and appointed to preach in Troy. He stayed in Troy but a short time when the Fugitive Slave Act was passed making it unsafe for him to remain far from Syracuse, his home.

Jarmain Loguen was an intimate friend of Frederick Douglass, his daughter later marrying Douglass' son.

Bishop Loguen was first elected to his church's highest office in 1864. Bishop Hood states that he discovered that no doubt he would be sent south to supervise the work there so resigned. We cannot blame him for this action for he was still considered a fugitive from slavery and there was great danger that he might have been seized.

In 1868 his name was presented again. Naturally he met with some opposition. Hood states that he would have been defeated but the move to have six Bishops gave him the opportunity to be successful. He was appointed to the Fifth District which included the Allegheny and Kentucky Conferences and the "adjacent mission fields." At the end of two years he was to change with Bishop Jones and go to the Second District which included the Genesee (now the Western New York) and the Philadelphia and Baltimore Conferences. In 1872 he was appointed to the work on the Pacific Coast. Bishop Hood is not certain as to whether he reached his field of labor or died before he could do so.

According to the official Directory of the Church issued in 1895, Jermain W. Loguen was licensed to preach at Syracuse in 1841 and joined the Annual Conference in June (20) 1843. The following year, in May, he was ordained a deacon and in 1845, an elder. He was consecrated a Bishop May 29, 1868, and died in 1873, the time of the year evidently not being known at the time.

The actual birth year of Harriet Tubman appears to be unknown. Some authorities place it as early as 1820 [9] and another, 1823.[10] Agreement seems to have been reached as to her birth place, Bucktown,[11] Dorchester County, Maryland, on the Eastern Shore of that state.

Her father evidently was a man by the name of Benjamin Ross who was married to Harriet Greene. One writer states that Harriet, the daughter of this union, could trace her ancestry in America as far back as 1725 or 1750. Another writer states that she may have been a member or rather a descendant of the Ashanti group. A Reverend Samuel Miles Hopkins of Auburn, New York, states that there appears to have been a relationship too, with the Fellatas.[12]

---

[9] Dorothy Sterling, *Freedom Train* (*The Story of Harriet Tubman*) (Doubleday, Garden City, L. I., 1954), p. 12.
[10] Earl Conrad, *Harriet Tubman* (Associated Publishers, Washington, D. C., 1943), p. 3.
[11] *Ibid.*, p. 3.
[12] *Ibid.*, p. 5.

Harriet was married to a freeman, John Tubman, around 1844. A few years later, impatient with the hardships of slavery, in 1849, she and her two brothers attempted escaping. In this venture, after many hardships, Harriet Tubman was successful. She returned to her old home in 1851 but found that her husband had remarried. In 1852 she married again, this time a man by the name of Davis. She died March 10, 1913.

Harriet Tubman (Davis) will long be known as the Moses of her people.[13] While it may never be known just how many slaves she was able to lead to freedom it is estimated that the number was considerable. Many of the stories of her experiences in freeing slaves are told in a little pamphlet issued by Bishop William J. Walls in the interest of the restored Harriet Tubman Home.

Harriet Tubman was a stanch Zionite. There were times when she did not see eye to eye with the leaders of the Church as when they wished to charge a fee for care in her old folks' home. As an example of this close tie the following appears:

"Sometimes Harriet and her slave collections took shelter inside a Rochester Church. That was the African Methodist Episcopal Zion Church at Spring and Favor Streets. Fugitives by the score hid in its pews. Here also was her spiritual home while in Rochester." [14]

This Negro leader was not only interested in freeing her fellow-men and women prior to the War but later busied herself in two other ventures. Conrad states that "she supported the woman suffrage movement, going to nearby meetings whenever she heard of them. She likewise took an active part in the growth of the African Methodist Episcopal (Zion) Church in Central and Western New York which fought for her pension.[15] She eventually established her cherished dream of a home for the aged and indigent.

"But it was not easy to operate an enterprise like this, and because of lack of funds the permanent incorporation of what Harriet wished to call the 'John Brown Home' was not achieved until 1903 when she deeded the 25 acres and her home to the African Methodist Episcopal Zion Church." [16]

The home was formally opened in 1908.

Harriet Tubman believed in many things for her people as we

---

[13] Bishop, W. J. Walls, *Harriet Tubman*, p. 16.
[14] Conrad, *loc. cit.*, p. 61.
[15] *Ibid.*, p. 211.
[16] Stirling, *loc. cit.*, pp. 78, 79.

have stated above. In addition she urged ownership of land, the use of the ballot and education.[17]

This chapter would not be complete without at least a mentioning of another great woman and abolition leader, Sojourner Truth. She was born around 1797, just a year after the founding of the Zion Church. She was the next to the youngest child of James and Betsey who at the time were located in Hurley, New York, Ulster County. It appears that she was at first called Isabella. She died November 26, 1883.

While Sojourner Truth is well known in American history we would like to mention one incident here as it seems to have a direct bearing on Frederick Douglas' attitude toward the church in those tragic days. It appears that he was speaking in Faneuil Hall. He had reached the point when it is recorded that he said that "no justice was to be found in all America. The only salvation for the Negro was in his own right arm." It was then that Sojourner Truth rose up in her place and asked: "Frederick, is God dead?" [18]

---

[17] *Ibid.*, p. 221.
[18] Benjamin Brawley, *Negro Builders and Heroes* (University of North Carolina, Chapel Hill, 1937), p. 76.

CHAPTER XI

The Church in the Critical Years of the Nation's History
1830-1860

IN A preceding chapter we have mentioned the first serious division in the forces of the new denomination when Asbury Church decided to go her way, later, however, to return. The second, and less serious division came in the period of indecision over ordinations. Wesley, in Philadelphia, withdrew but renewed her connection with the church the year following Rush's election to the Superintendency. Still another division came when the New Haven congregation decided to withdraw when the elder expelled a member whose morals demanded action on the part of the church. The people felt that they could ill afford to get along without the expelled member.[1] Thus the stage was set which was to see a goodly portion of the church with draw just prior to the Civil War. From our time, a little short of one hundred years after the titanic struggle, it was the best thing which could have happened for the young denomination. Once the breach was healed, the new church was definitely stronger than she would have been without the misunderstanding.

The Eleventh Yearly Conference met in New York, May 21, 1831, with Christopher Rush presiding. New names appear on the roll at this time, the list being: James Matthews, William Miller, Leven Smith, Timothy Eatto, George Tredwell, Jehiel C. Beaman, Henry Drayton, Charles A. Boyd, Charles H. Anderson and George Garnett. Statistics proved that there had been a gain of 263 members over the ten year period, a slow gain, but this may have been occasioned because of the unsettled conditions of the church. By 1833 the church had eleven elders, seven deacons, and five preachers. Four individuals remained on trial.[2]

The fourteenth New York Annual Conference met May 18, 1834 in New York City. The Church at that time was located on the corner of Church and Leonard Streets. Moore states that at this conference William Miller, Sr., Elder associated Christopher Rush so by this

---

[1] Rush, *loc. cit.*, p. 81.
[2] *Ibid.*, pp. 87, 88.

time some honor was being accorded him. William Serington was elected secretary and John A. King assistant secretary. The roll included thirty preachers from the New York Conference with three others serving as delegates from the Philadelphia Conference. Since so many of these preachers appear to be new we list them below: William H. Serington, J. A. King, Dempsey Kennedy, Henry Johnson, James Simmons, John Tappan, John Dungy, Jacob D. Richardson, Jacob Matthew, William H. Bishop, Jehiel C. Beaman, David Blake, Richard Noyee, Peter Ross, John Lyle, John P. Thompson, Leven Smith, Peter Van Hass, Timothy Eatto, James Smith, Daniel Vandevier, John Chester, Nathan Blunt, John A. Williams, John L. Mars, George Garnett, J. B. Johnson, Thomas James, Edward Bishop, Thomas Jackson, and the following delegates from the Philadelphia Conference: Edward Johnson, Solomon T. Scott, George Stevenson.[3]

Since the statistical report of 1831, the church had increased in membership from 1,689 to 2,356. While Moore does not say so it appears that this report was for the New York Conference only. This would mean that there had been an increase of 667 with the figures of the New York Conference alone. The following individuals joined the conference at this time: William Tilman, Edward Bishop, Thomas Jackson, John Lyle and Jacob B. Johnson.[4]

The 1835 conference was significant for three reasons. For the first time, evidently, delegates were in attendance at the conference, Moore listing three. Thirty-two ministers assembled and the conference reported a loss of 153 members. The third significant item had to do with finance. There was reported the first sums for the support of the superintendent, $260.00 for the year.

The sessions of 1836 showed thirty-five preachers present, three ministerial delegates from Philadelphia, an increase in membership, to 2,425 (this more than made up for the loss reported the previous year) but the superintendent's money dropped to $75.00 while the conference money appears in the reports for the first time, the sum being $117.00.[5]

In 1839, a forward step was taken by the New York Conference when it was decided to establish the Annual Conference Fund for the

---

[3] Moore, *loc. cit.*, p. 105.
[4] *Ibid.*, p. 105.
[5] Moore, *loc. cit.*, pp. 105-106.

relief of ministers in service who did not get sufficient support to take care of their families. The resolution follows:

Whereas, on account of the people's delinquency in many of our stations and circuits, our preachers fail to get means to support their families and are compelled to neglect their duties as ministers, or suffer. We have therefore agreed in our associated capacity as ministers, to establish a fund to be used in relief of our brother ministers connected with this conference, when they are in want of relief or help. We therefore adopt the following constitution:

CONSTITUTION

ARTICLE I

Section 1—The fund shall be known by the name of the New York Annual Conference Fund.

Sec. 2—The members of this fund shall consist of all the preachers belonging to the conference, who shall pay in the treasury one dollar annually, or such sum as the conference may determine.

ARTICLE II

Section 1—The officers of this fund shall consist of nine persons, who shall be members of this conference, to be elected annually (President and Vice-President excepted) ; the Superintendent shall be the President and the Senior Elder, Vice-President; a Secretary, a Treasurer, and a Board of Managers consisting of three elders and two deacons or preachers.

Sec. 2—The duty of the officers shall be as follows: The President shall preside at all meetings of business, the Vice-President shall preside in his absence; the Secretary shall keep the books and hold all correspondence as directed by the Board; the Treasurer shall hold all funds, under sufficient bonds, and report the same annually to the conference; he shall keep an account of all funds received and expended in behalf of the conference, and submit the same to the Secretary.

Sec. 3—It shall be the duty of the Board of Managers to transact all business during the recess of the conference not otherwise provided for; it shall also be their duty to use their best endeavors for the advancement of the fund, by forming auxiliaries whenever it is in their power to do so, and in conjunction with other officers of the Board, determine who are suitable applicants for aid.

ARTICLE III

Section 1—The official Board of this fund shall meet monthly, or as often as the President may deem it necessary, at which meeting the funds shall be examined.

Sec. 2—An audited report of all the proceedings of the Board, in the recess of the conference, shall be made to the conference annually.

Sec. 3—The constitution may be altered or amended by a vote of two-thirds of its members.[6]

The first session of the 1840s met in Asbury Church on Elizabeth Street, the fourth Saturday in May, 1840. By this time the membership had grown to 2,680.[7]

By 1840, William Miller had sufficient strength in the church to clamor for a position. He, by this time, was the oldest elder, which appeared to be something in his favor. The Rush group, evidently seeing the battle going against them, compromised with the Miller faction but tied the new superintendent's hands so that he could do no damage. They elected him "The Associate of Superintendent Rush," leaving no doubt as to who was the chief pastor.[8] Flood, in his *Lives of the Methodist Bishops* places his election as early as 1836.[9] And there is ground to believe that he is right, since all the accounts from 1836, and even earlier, list Superintendent Miller as Senior Elder, associating Superintendent Rush. All accounts agree with this. Superintendent William Miller was born in Queen Ann County, Maryland, August 23, 1775. He was converted March 4, 1788 and was licensed to preach in New York City in 1808. He joined the conference June 21, 1821 and was ordained deacon June 22, 1798. He received his elder's orders in 1823 and was elected a superintendent (full) in 1840. He died June 10, 1849.[10] Flood has his death listed in Philadelphia in 1846.[11] while Moore reports his death in the twenty-sixth Conference (New York, 1846).[12] We feel that the first account (June 10,1849) is therefore incorrect.

In the conference of 1844, Superintendent Rush opened the session with a message which received "happy responses." We mention this here to show that apparently the senior superintendent was in good health at this time. The following General Conference his sight must have been good for he not only presided but read the Scripture lesson.[13] However, William Miller having died, the committee decided to elect two superintendents. No question was raised as to

---

[6] Moore, *loc. cit.*, p. 106 ff.
[7] *Ibid.*, p. 110.
[8] Jones, *loc. cit.*, p. 21.
[9] Flood, *loc. cit.*, p. 692.
[10] J. Harvey Anderson, Editor, *The Official Directory, loc. cit.*, p. 35; Flood, *loc. cit.*, p. 692.
[11] *Ibid.*
[12] Moore, *loc. cit.*, p. 113.
[13] *Ibid.*, p. 208.

Father Rush's election, so we can again conclude that it was in this quadrennium that his sight failed and he was forced to forego a great part of his work. The telling blows of discord were made, therefore at a time when the beloved Father Rush was unable to stem the tide or keep abreast of the dangerous currents within the Church. For that, no doubt, we all feel a twinge of sympathy.

One writer in history has stated that the greatest good any man can do himself is to remove himself from the scene at the right moment. One of the high notes of Zion's history is that her beloved Rush was no part of the hurt she suffered.

In the General Conference of 1840 it was decided to elect two superintendents instead of one, as had been done up to this time.[14] Just where the old title of superintendent was discarded is not definitely known. Moore in his *History* uses the title in 1840 [15] but Jones states that the title of Bishop was not used until the General Conference of 1864.[16] We may assume that this latter statement is true since no doubt Moore was influenced by the prevailing custom when he published his book in 1884. Hood links the change with the efforts of unification of the A.M.E. and A.M.E. Zion Churches.[17] Rush uses it as late as 1843, beyond the date of the 1840 conference. At any rate, the Committee on Nomination of Candidates for Superintendents reported, with the above recommendation.

A strange item is noted in this general session. Yet the circumstance was evidently the rule and not the exception. A resolution was offered calling for the "Rev. Christopher Rush to preside until a further stage of business." It appears that contrary to present form in elected individuals the Superintendent was considered out of office on the opening day of the General Conference.[18] Election of Superintendents was the first order of business. Christopher Rush was duly elected for four years.[19] On motion it was resolved to elect a second superintendent. A committee of seven was appointed to make nominations. They recommended William Miller and Edward Johnson. Twenty-five votes were cast for William Miller and eight for Edward Johnson. William Miller was declared elected.

---

[14] Moore, *loc. cit.*, p. 206.
[15] *Ibid.*
[16] Jones, *loc. cit.*, p. 76.
[17] Hood, *loc. cit.*, p. 147 ff.
[18] Moore, *loc. cit.*, p. 205.
[19] *Ibid.*, p. 206.

The 1840 General Conference stands out for another action taken, that of appointing a committee to make the first revisions of the *Discipline*. The following were appointed: Jehiel C. Beaman, Leven Smith, Jacob Matthews, David Stevens, Solomon T. Scott. The Revision Committee reported on the third and concluding day of the Conference.[20]

The Sixth General Conference of the Church met in New York City, May 18, 1844. Fifty-three ministers were in attendance, most of them from the New York area. Others were listed from Pennsylvania and Baltimore. Bishop Moore, who was in attendance at the conference gives us this information. For the first time a General Book Steward reported,[21] and while we have not the report before us this fact alone establishes a trend which was in evidence in other Methodist groups who were following the instructions of their founder, John Wesley.

During the next four years the denomination increased to a noteworthy degree. It was found necessary to set aside a new conference embracing the New England points. This New England Conference was set aside in June 1845. Superintendent Rush presided at this session which met in Hartford, Connecticut, with eight ministers enrolled.[22] The first statistical report showed the following churches and membership: Nantucket, Massachusetts, 30; Middletown, Connecticut, 50; Providence, Rhode Island, 125; New Haven, 69; Stonington, 23; Bridgeport, 73; Hartford, 100. By 1847 this conference had grown to fifteen ministers and 464 members.[23] The third session as well as the fourth met in Boston where in 1849, seventy-three members were reported. Another new church appeared on the lists of that year, Worcester, Massachusetts with nine members. Two other points were listed but later disappeared, Norwalk, Connecticut, and Springfield, Massachusetts, (this later point is now one of the strong churches of this conference).

Another new conference, established in 1849, formerly designated as the Western District of Pennsylvania, became known as the Allegheny Conference. As early as 1829, according to Hood and Rush, Jacob D. Richardson, Samuel Johnson and Abraham Green were laboring in this area. The earliest statistics for this conference,

---

[20] Moore, *loc. cit.*, p. 207.
[21] *Ibid.*, p. 209.
[22] *Ibid.*, p. 140.
[23] *Ibid.*, p. 141.

those for 1854, showed 407 members.[24] The old Genesee (now the Western New York) was established in 1850.[25] The first session met in Ithaca on September 13, 1851, according to Moore. This conference reported twelve preachers, two lay delegates, three Sunday schools with ninety-five students.[26] Hood declares that this conference was established in 1849 instead of 1851.[27]

Records of the old Baltimore Conference not being available we are compelled to conclude that somewhere 1840 and 1848 this conference was organized. Moore makes little mention of it while Hood seems to think that it was the outgrowth of the old Southern Conference. However, the name Baltimore Conference appears prior to 1852, for in the General Conference of 1848 statistics for this area were reported.[28]

Evidently the Southern Conference is of a much later date and has oftentimes been confused with the name "The Southern District" which, at one time, was composed of the Philadelphia, Baltimore and Allegheny Conferences (see the Minutes of 1852). It was in this period, too, according to Jones, that the word *Zion* was inserted in the denominational title (1848).[29]

When the General Conference met in New York City, May 18, 1844, approximately fifty-five ministers were in attendance. Some of those attending later played a leading role in the history of the church. Among these were Superintendent Rush and Superintendent William Miller, Sampson Talbot, William H. Bishop, George A. Spywood, Joseph P. Thompson, Solomon T. Scott, and several of the original ministers, Peter Van Hass, Timothy Eatto, John Dungy and Leven Smith.[30] Excepting the election of the two Superintendents, Christopher Rush and William Miller the only other note of interest Moore records is the report of the Book Steward.[31] The vitally interesting thing is Moore's presence which certainly makes him an authority in his own right during this period.

The Seventh General Conference met again in New York City,

[24] Moore, *loc. cit.,* p. 150.
[25] Anderson, *loc. cit.,* p. 66.
[26] Moore, *loc. cit.,* p. 156.
[27] Hood, *loc. cit.,* p. 276.
[28] Moore, *loc. cit.,* p. 211.
[29] Jones, *loc. cit.,* p. 22.
[30] Moore, *loc. cit.,* p. 208.
[31] *Ibid.,* p. 209. According to Jones the first book steward was Jacob D. Richardson who began his term of service in 1841.

May 29, 1848, again with Christopher Rush presiding. Here it is noted that the Chairman read the Scripture lesson so his affliction must have come upon him between 1848 and 1852. Only forty-six ministers were in attendance at this session. Rev. J. J. Moore was elected Secretary *Pro tem*. After appointing a committee of seven to nominate individuals for the Superintendency the first day's session was adjourned.

The next day, May 30, Moore states that the committee reported on the election of superintendents. Those designated were: Christopher Rush, James Simmons, George Galbreath, and John P. Thompson.[32] Christopher Rush was the first elected. Voting for the second individual resulted in George Galbreath being selected. Of note is the appointment of the committee on revision of the *Discipline* and the selection of George Galbreath as President of Rush Academy.[33]

The Reverend George Galbreath, by his election, became the fourth Superintendent of the Church. Father Rush, by his election, was to serve his last term in office, as has been pointed out previously. While his name was offered in the next general session there is little doubt that he himself was well aware that it was a matter of courtesy.

The occasion of the retirement of Superintendent Rush brought the first major disagreement in the church.[34] In the Eighth General Conference, June 1852, the storm broke. For the first time sectional lines could be discerned in the denomination. Many of the church's early writers hint at friction between the East and West and South as far back as 1840 and the election of William Miller.

According to Flood, George Galbreath was born in Lancaster County, Pennsylvania, March 4, 1799. His parents, named Adam and Eve, were apparently slaves of a Dr. Galbreath. George was reared in the family of Moses Wilson in Hanover Twp., Pennsylvania, learning the carpenter's trade from a John Miller in Lancaster County. He first joined the Methodist Episcopal Church and then under Reverend J. D. Richardson, Zion. He joined the Philadelphia Conference in June 1830, was ordained a deacon in 1832, and elder in 1835.[35] His conversion had taken place, we have failed to state, in a Winsbrennarian Meeting in 1826. He served a little less than five years,

---

[32] Moore, *loc. cit.*, p. 210.
[33] *Ibid.*, p. 211.
[34] Hood, *loc. cit.*, p. 71.
[35] Flood, *loc. cit.*, p. 693.

plagued with hardships and poverty. He died in 1853 from an attack of asthma after a trip across the Alleghenies.[36]

Bishop, or rather Superintendent Galbreath having been elected as William Miller's successor, he logically expected to succeed Rush when his retirement should take place. One angle cannot be clearly understood. The Committee on Superintendency in the 1852 Conference recommended both Christopher Rush and George Galbreath. The only answer we can give to this recommendation is that the General Conference wanted to honor Rush or actually thought he could continue the work. Rush was defeated, and his friends were not too well satisfied as the activities of the succeeding days indicate. In this session the election of the second or associate superintendent saw Reverend Simmons declining the nomination after he had been presented along with William H. Bishop. The name of Solomon T. Scott was substituted by the committee. The Reverend William H. Bishop was elected.[37]

For two days the legality of the balloting for the superintendency was debated. Finally, it was decided that the whole election was illegal and was therefore thrown out. The ninth day, to clear up the matter and restore harmony Superintendent Rush took the chair and voting began again with the names of William H. Bishop and George Galbreath being offered. The former won the election.[38] On a second ballot the names of S. T. Scott and George Galbreath were offered. This time George Galbreath was elected but in his statement to the conference he declined "serving in the capacity he had in the previous term; but if a platform was made to suit the wants of the people, he would serve." [39] Reverend Galbreath was referring to the custom of the second superintendent serving as an assistant. A resolution was offered suspending the rule of the General Superintendency for the time being. The movement had such a strong minority opposition that it was finally decided to elect three superintendents. In addition to the two already elected, George A. Spywood was elected.[40] This decision was based on a resolution which prevailed stating that there would be no General Superintendent but all would be equal. The assignments of the superintendents were as follows:

---

[36] *Ibid.*, p. 695.
[37] Moore, *loc. cit.*, p. 214.
[38] *Ibid.*
[39] Moore, *loc. cit.*, p. 39.
[40] *Ibid.*, p. 215.

William H. Bishop, New York, Genesee and Canada West.

George Galbreath, The Southern District embracing Philadelphia, Allegheny and Baltimore Conferences.

G. A. Spywood, The Eastern District, embracing New England, Nova Scotia and British Guiana Conferences.

The 1852 Conference adjourned apparently on a harmonious note but this was not the case as it is to be noted later. Superintendent Galbreath evidently wished that the Associate Superintendent would automatically succeed to the General Superintendent's position. If such happened to be in his mind it was necessary to set aside Superintendent Rush. In this move success crowned determined efforts. But when the time came for the election of his successor, Reverend Bishop, and evidently, the East, was strong enough to defeat Galbreath.

As has been stated above, the Conference adjourned with little thought of a breach. Bishop Jones declares that the movement to elect three superintendents of equal rank was a violation of the constitution in that the Quarterly Conferences of the Connection did not have an opportunity to vote on the change.[41] He further states that while Superintendent Bishop was the chief pastor of the New York group he was the product of the Southern wing or the Philadelphian-Baltimore-Pittsburgh area.[42] He also makes the assertion that Spywood was likewise lined up with this group but later became a Rush follower.[43] According to this same authority Reverend Bishop said that "we elected one (Superintendent) prospectively, but not to act as such, until there should be sanction given to the revised matter by two-thirds vote of the Quarterly Conferences of the entire denomination."[44]

It is interesting to note that Bishop Jones likewise makes the following statement:

New York was endeared to Superintendent Rush and though he was blind, they still thought that he should have been continued and even Rush himself was disappointed. When he failed of election it caused at least a sympathetic protest, and at the slightest provocation, those of the East were ready for drastic action. Anyhow, the General Conference adjourned with three Superintendents, all having equal power —Rush with Mother Zion and all the Eastern wing disgruntled, Bishop

[41] Jones, loc. cit., p. 23.
[42] Ibid., p. 23.
[43] Ibid.
[44] Ibid.

Galbreath and Spywood of the Southern wing around Philadelphia jubilant.[45]

William H. Bishop was born in 1793 at Troy, New York. He was converted January 9, 1830. He was licensed to preach at Troy in 1835. He joined the Conference June 20, 1837 and was ordained deacon the following year, May 18. Two years later in 1840, May 22, he was ordained elder. He requested the retired status in 1868 [46] and died May 20, 1873.[47]

Bishop Jones' statement as to the beginning of the church's difficulties of the 1850s is given in full:

> The Southern (wing) or Bishop wing hearing the rumblings from the Rush wing in New York, issued a circular asking the word "African" be stricken out of the title and the name "Wesleyan" inserted. The conferences refused to accept the change of name but Supt. Galbreath held a conference in Pittsburgh and called it "Wesleyan." [48]

Bishop Hood states that all may have gone well if Superintendent Galbreath had lived.[49] However, he passed away in 1853. It was then that Superintendent Bishop became eager to set aside the decision of the 1852 General Conference in which the three superintendents were considered equal. Bishop Hood further states that on noting that this extreme decision could not stand Bishop issued a statement in which he stated: "I am all that the *Discipline* makes me." [50] This satisfied one party but not the other. Accordingly he was charged and ordered to appear for trial. This he refused to do and was therefore suspended.[51] This action was the immediate cause of the division with the south and west going with Bishop to form the Wesleyan Methodist Church. Hood states that the fact of the existence of a stronger minority in the east for the Episcopal form of government with fewer in the west preferring the Congregational form hastened the healing of the breach.[52] Another fact also hastened the healing of the breach, Hood states. The fact that in the civil courts of Lycoming County, Pennsylvania (Williamsport) an adverse decision was made in the Superintendent's case somewhat startled the group

---

[45] *Ibid.*
[46] Hood, *loc. cit.*, p. 184.
[47] Anderson, *loc. cit.*, p. 35.
[48] Jones, *loc. cit.*, pp. 23, 24.
[49] Hood, *loc. cit.*, p. 72.
[50] *Ibid.*
[51] Jones, *loc. cit.*, p. 24.
[52] Hood, *loc. cit.*, p. 72.

and at least made them willing to listen to the compromises of the eastern group. An account of this case is carried at the close of this chapter.

According to Hood's transcribed account of the court case the Superintendents made their own assignments in 1852. This, Rush, who appeared as a witness, declared they had no right to do. The decision of the court stated that Bishop, in changing the name of the Church had seceded and was therefore guilty to the extent that he could not hope to hold title to any church property belonging to the A.M.E. Zion Church. Bishop Hood infers that the entire matter need not have happened if Bishop had appeared for ecclesiastical trial for in his opinion he would not have been found guilty. The writer certainly agrees with this opinion.

In this entire matter it is clear that Superintendent Galbreath was equally as guilty for he was just as determined to use the term *Wesleyan* as was Bishop. He may have lent his weight to prevent the separation, however.

When Superintendent Bishop went ahead and allowed the conference, held at Ithaca, New York, to use the term "Wesleyan," the New York Conference proceeded to *try* him. It appears that Bishop, noting that he would lose the fight, adjourned the session from (evidently) New York to Williamsburg. The Conference, however, continued its business with the Reverend John C. Spence presiding until the Superintendent could be tried. Superintendent Bishop refused to submit to the decision of the Annual Conference. He continued to exercise the prerogatives of the office, in the meantime holding a conference at Baltimore and another in Philadelphia. It was at the conclusion of this latter session that the New York group refused to allow him the *chair*. In the year 1853 the conference conducted the trial and expelled Reverend Bishop.

Since Superintendent Galbreath had died prior to the trial of Superintendent Bishop, the denomination was left with but one General Elder, Superintendent Spywood. Accordingly an interim General Conference was called, July 9, 1853. At this session, Superintendent Spywood was elected General Superintendent. John Tappan was elected assistant to Superintendent Spywood and a new *Discipline* was adopted.[53] Bishop Jones says that Robert Henderson

---

[53] Jones, *loc. cit.*, p. 24.

was likewise elected as a Superintendent but Bishop Moore says nothing about him. This may have been caused by that which Jones comments on in another statement. He insists that we have heard little of this incident in Zion's history because the following were more or less involved: Joseph J. Clinton, Singleton T. Jones, J. J. Moore, J. W. Hood. Two men, he definitely states, were not involved or rather were not members of the seceding group, Bishops Thompson and Moore.[54] Bishop Jones further states that Reverend Henderson dropped out because he had no work to supervise.[55]

It appears that it is safe to state that the trial of Superintendent Bishop allowed him to take out of the denomination a major part of the church. It was conceded that no doubt the majority followed him. In this respect, however, the majority were declared violators of the laws of the church. Hood states that the whole incident was unfortunate with plenty to be said on both sides.

The regular General Conference was held June 26, 1856 in New York. Superintendent Spywood presided assisted by John Tappan. No quorum was present so the session adjourned until Monday, June 30. In the election of Superintendent which took place subsequently Reverend Spywood was defeated by James Simmons and S. T. Jones succeeded John Tappan.[56]

The Wesleyan wing of the church met at Williamsburg the same year and elected William H. Bishop as General Superintendent and Rev. Joseph J. Clinton as his assistent. Reverend Singleton T. Jones was a member of this group. He was given the task of editing the *Discipline*.

The first move for a reconciliation was made by a Rev. Leonard Collins who attended the New York General Conference of 1856, conveying the idea that the *Southern* wing as it was called, desired reunion. Nothing was done immediately, however, for he was instructed to bring the statement in writing.[57]

One fact which has not been given its proper place in our history is the stand of that which was then known as Old Zion Church (evidently the Mother Church). It appears that this organization had held itself aloof from the whole matter, leaning neither to one

[54] *Ibid.*
[55] *Ibid.*
[56] Moore, *loc. cit.*, p. 217.
[57] *Ibid.*, p. 220.

side nor the other. In other words, in this period, of five or seven years the Mother Church was actually independent of either group. Her role in the matter of reunion is perhaps the most glorious epoch in her history. It warms the heart to see the Mother Church assuming the position that is her due.[58]

According to Hood, Old Zion Church was taken into "the confidence of the movers in this matter through her pastor, and she was induced to say that she would not support either faction unless they united. Hood states that the Bishop group was desirous of securing the aid of the Old Zion Church, feeling that if the other faction decided against union, the Mother Church would cast her lot with that group. The loss of the Mother Church so stirred the Spywood faction that they were inclined to compromise.[59]

A meeting was held in historic Newburg, New York, either in 1859 or early 1860 and a platform was drawn up to be submitted to the two groups. The delegates of the Newburg Conference were seated in the Philadelphia General Conference as honorary members. This General Session was that of the Southern or Bishop wing of the Church and should be known as that of the Wesleyan Methodist Episcopal Church. The resolutions from the Newburg Conference were presented and debated without any decision being reached. On Friday, June 1, the Reverend S. T. Gray arrived with "credentials from the officers of the Old Zion Church." He presented a letter informing the conference that it could meet in New York on and after June 6. The regular group of the denomination had decided to meet in New York at the same time so the move was obvious. The memorial of the Newburg Conference was finally adopted and the Wesleyans decided to accept the invitation to meet in the Mother Church on the date selected. After routine business the session adjourned June 5 to meet in New York the following day.[60]

On Wednesday, June 6 at 4:00 P.M. the two groups met in Old Zion Church (Church and Leonard Streets). Superintendents Bishop and Clinton were present but the Superintendents of the regular group were not. Father Rush, however, arrived and explained the absence of Superintendent Simmons by stating that he had been taken ill rather suddenly. Reverend Scott never appeared.[61]

[58] Hood, loc. cit., p. 78.
[59] Hood, loc. cit., p. 78.
[60] Moore, loc. cit., p. 224 ff.
[61] Ibid., p. 226.

The crux of the Newburg agreement can be found in the first section which is given here: "Resolved: That all matters pertaining to former difficulties be laid aside forever." Thus was the breach healed. The full text, however, will be found at the end of the chapter.

It was agreed that the *Discipline* of 1858 "with such revision as the wants of the connection demanded, be adopted." Another vexing problem was taken care of when Reverend Gray moved that the words "Assistant Superintendent" be stricken.[62]

On the matter of the election of Superintendents it was agreed that Rev. Peter Ross and Rev. J. J. Clinton be selected. Upon their election the Committee on Districts reported, listing three districts instead of two. This allowed for the election of Rev. W. H. Bishop again.[63]

This period of the church's history can be concluded with a brief statement on Reverend Peter Ross. It appeared that the law allowed the Superintendent to collect back salary on any district over which they had presided. Both Clinton and Bishop being well known and claiming back salary soon gleaned Ross's field. Then, as was provided by law, when the time came for him to exchange fields after two years he found that this, too, had been well gleaned. Hood states that since he could only see traveling expenses he decided to resign.

By this time, as noted above, several conferences had been organized. The denomination now consisted of the following areas: New York, Philadelphia, New England, Allegheny, Genesee and Baltimore (Southern). One breathes a sigh of relief that the church was able to overcome the grave differences of the 1850s and bring about reunion at a time when other denominations were finding themselves in positions of uncompromising disunion. The nation, too, was experiencing major difficulties from which it was not able to extricate itself short of four years of bloody war and seventy years of violent discussion over its basic cause. The spirit existent within the denomination was not a minor item. In truth, there are those who have continuously stated that the name "African" is not compatible with the Spirit of Christ which we would emulate. We feel that this history of the church is no place to discuss these controversies but it is deemed wise to recognize their existence. The evident willingness of

---

[62] Moore, *loc. cit.*, pp. 229-230.
[63] *Ibid.*, p. 230.

all parties to *forget* the incident does bring them into greater Christian focus, however.

The clearly unjustified act of the Wesleyan group cannot be dismissed without due notice, nevertheless. The church not only provides machinery for the resolving of differences of opinion but has always held to the principle of majority rule. The ignoring of the General and the Quarterly Conferences was not only a dangerous step but could as well have destroyed the fundamental doctrine of a church primarily founded on the democratic attitudes of the eighteenth and nineteenth centuries.

It is well to call attention to one other development of this period, one, which for some reason unexplained, was not in vogue long enough to show its apparent worth—the rotation of Superintendents.

BASIS OF THE AGREEMENT OF 1852 [64]

Section 1. That all matters pertaining to the former difficulties be laid aside forever.

Sec. 2. That these parties agree to use both books of *Discipline* until the sitting of the General Conference of 1860, and at the assembling of the General Conference to proceed to organize upon the *Discipline* suitable to the wants of the people of the connection.

Sec. 3. That this connection recommend the General Conference under Rt. Rev. W. H. Bishop, which is to meet in Philadelphia on May 30, 1860, that they adjourn to meet in New York at Zion Church, on the sixth day of June, 1860, where the union will be consummated. . . . and be it further resolved that we recommend the election of the Bishop, and the revision of the *Discipline* until the union is effected. Resolved that this convention recommend the New England Conference under the Rt. Rev. James Simmons, which is to meet on the second day of June, 1860, to adjourn to meet again to complete the unfinished business of the conference, after the General Conference or reunion is consummated.

Sec. 4. *Resolved,* that we cordially invite the two superintending Bishops with their assistants to meet the adjourned General Conference which reassembles in New York the sixth day of June, at 4:00 P.M. to assist in consummating the union.

Sec. 5. *Resolved,* that nothing in the foregoing basis be construed

[64] Moore, *loc. cit.*, pp. 227, 228.

as to interfere with the privilege of any of the members of the General Conference.

Sec. 6. *Resolved,* that as a convention, we stand united on the foregoing basis.

Superintendent George A. Spywood was born January 5, 1798, in Providence, Rhode Island, where on March 7, 1818, he was converted. He was licensed to preach in the same city in 1831. He joined the traveling connection June 20, 1842, was ordained as a deacon May 18, 1843, an elder, eleven years later, in 1844 (June 22) and was consecrated a Superintendent May 24, 1852. He died March 9, 1876.

Superintendent John Tappan was born June 20, 1799, in North Carolina, later evidently moving to New York where (after his conversion, September 5, 1830) he began preaching in 1832. He joined the conference June 18, 1833, and was made a deacon May 20, 1834, and an elder May 20, 1844. The date given for his elevation to the Superintendency appears as being June 4, 1854, which evidently means that he was elected in a special General Conference of that year. He died in December, 1862.

Solomon T. Scott was born August 20, 1790, in Smyrna, Delaware. He was converted there in 1830 and was licensed to preach the following year, 1831, beginning his ministry in his birthplace. He joined the conference June 25, 1834, and was ordained a deacon evidently prior to this time, May 22, 1834. The only explanation which we can give to this strange state of affairs is that he was evidently used as a pastor prior to the convening of the annual conference and was therefore ordained a deacon so that he could be of greater service. He waited ten years, May 20, 1844, before he was given elder's orders. He was elected a bishop in 1856, May 21. He died January 4, 1862.

James Simmons was born December 3, 1792, in Accomac County, Maryland. He was converted in early life and joined the conference May 19, 1832. A year later he was ordained a deacon, May 18, 1833, and on the same day was given elder's orders. He was elected bishop May 24, 1856, and died November 25, 1873.

Joseph J. Clinton was born October 3, 1823, in Philadelphia where he was converted February 7, 1832. He was licensed to preach in Philadelphia in 1840 and joined the conference June 20, 1843. The date listed for his being made a deacon is May 18, 1838, which does not appear correct since he did not begin preaching until 1840. He was given elder's orders May 22, 1846, and was consecrated a bishop on May 24, 1856. He died May 24, 1881. To him must be given credit for the major expansion of the church under Reverend Hood into the South hard on the heels of the Civil War. While one or two of the later bishops made significant progress in expansion Bishop Clinton gave to the church its greatest impetus up to this time.[65]

Peter Ross was born November, 1821; the actual date of his birth is not known. He was born in Nova Scotia and began his ministry in that part of the continent. He joined the conference in June, 1834, and was ordained a deacon December, 1840, and an elder May 21, 1840. He was consecrated a Superintendent May 24, 1856, and died April 10, 1889.

IN THE COURT OF COMMON PLEAS

LYCOMING COUNTY, PENNA.

Hon. A. Jordan, Judge

George Johnson, Ferdinand Capes, and Anthony Stokes, Trustees of the African Methodist Episcopal Zion Church,

vs.

Isaac Coleman, Lewis Hill, David Thomas, Joseph Davis, Isaac Lloyd, James Sherman, George Roach, and Isaac Thompson.

Council for Plaintiffs: Messrs. Dietrick and Scates. Counsel for defendants: Messrs. Armstrong, Campbell and Emery.

CHARGE

"Of all the disputes that arise those which arise among the professing Christians are most to be deplored, and are the bitterest. Strange as it may appear, it is nevertheless true that these disputes are more difficult to arrange among the disputants than any other, and perhaps more difficult to adjust, rightly and justly before a court and jury. Each church has its own peculiar form of government, its Discipline and creed. They are usually governed by a constitution, each of its members either expressly or implicitly engaging to be bound by it. It is necessary for the good government of all religious organizations that there should be a form of government, without which it would not only be difficult but perhaps impossible, to keep the members together for any length of time.

---

[65] Flood has these additional notes on the life of Bishop Clinton. He married Letitia Sisco in Pittsburgh Oct. 22, 1844. In this account Bishop Clinton was called to preach in 1839. He transferred to the Baltimore Conference in 1855 and was ordained a deacon in 1845 and an elder in 1846 by Superintendent Rush. He served the following churches: Trenton, N. J.; Georgetown, D. C.; Pittsburgh, Philadelphia; Allegheny (now Avery Memorial), Baltimore.

"The parties to this action all profess to belong to the African Methodist Episcopal Zion Church in the United States. They are not disputing as to the doctrine of the Church, the form of worship, or the constitution or Discipline by which the Church is to be governed. The dispute is, who has the right to the possession of the Church in this place, or had at the time of the alleged trespass? If that right was in the plaintiffs at the time they would be entitled to your verdict. The action is not brought to recover damages so much as to determine the right of the property, which, under the pleadings in this action, may be done.

"The suit is brought in the names of George Johnson, Ferdinand Capes, and Anthony Stokes, Trustees of the African Methodist Episcopal Zion Church, Williamsport. Their election as Trustees was proven by the Minute Book of the Church.

"The property in dispute was conveyed by Abraham Updegraff and wife to George Johnson, Ferdinand Capes, and David Thomas, Trustees of the Colored Methodist Episcopal Zion Church in Williamsport, by deed, dated on June 21, 1854. Both parties claim under this deed. To determine which of these parties is entitled to hold the property it will be necessary to examine the proceedings of their conferences with a view ascertaining whether Mr. Coleman, the preacher recognized by the defendants and other members of the church, was properly and duly elected and appointed to take charge and oversight of this Church. He, as well as his predecessors from the first organization of the church in this place, was appointed by the Philadelphia Conference. The right of this Conference to appoint was not disputed for some time, but the acts of that body were recognized as binding and were submitted to. In June, 1852, a General Conference met in Philadelphia. At that conference a question arose whether a General Superintendent should be elected in Committee of the Whole or General Conference. At that Conference it was concluded to elect a General Superintendent and an Assistant Superintendent in Committee of the Whole, which, it is said, was contrary to the Discipline and Constitution which had been adopted for the government of the Church.

"At that time Christopher Rush, the old gentleman who appeared on the stand as a witness, was General Superintendent, and had been for some years before, and George Galbreth, the Assistant Superintendent. Mr. Rush was at that time nearly blind, and wished to resign his position, that another might be elected in his place. A committee was appointed to name Superintendents. They reported the names of Rush and Galbreth, and Galbreth was elected over Rush. A question arose then as to the proper mode of electing these officers. The provision in the Book of Discipline is that the Superintendents were to be elected in a General Conference, not in Committee of the Whole. It was concluded that he must be elected according to the Book of Discipline. A General Conference was then entered into, a committee was appointed, who named James Simmons and William H. Bishop. Simmons resigned or declined an election, and Mr. Scott was named as the opposing candidate to Bishop. Bishop was elected over Scott for four years. Galbreth was elected Assistant Superintendent. Galbreth

142

became dissatisfied, and a motion was made to have three Superintendents on equal footing. The Book of Discipline provides for the election of two Superintendents—one of them a General Superintendent and one, Assistant Superintendent. Bishop then put a motion, and a third Superintendent was elected, namely, Spywood. Subsequently Bishop, Galbreth, and Spywood made an agreement among themselves, splitting up the connection, which the witness states they had no right to do.

"Also, after the election of these three Superintendents the Philadelphia Conference issued a circular to change the word 'African' and insert the word 'Wesleyan.' The Quarterly Conference refused to receive the circulars, because they thought the General Conference had taken away the rights of the people. The conferences would not receive the change at all. Bishop was recognized as the General Superintendent, and Galbreth, assistant.

"Bishop went on and held a conference at Ithaca. Galbreth held one in Pittsburgh, and called it the Wesleyan Conference. A charge was preferred against Bishop for permitting it to be called by that name. A copy of the charges was given to him. In the meantime Galbreth died. Bishop appeared at the conference, but refused to submit to the trial. While Bishop was under censure he held a conference at Baltimore, came to Philadelphia and held one there. When he got through at Philadelphia he came to New York Conference. He then wished to hold that conference without submitting to be tried for his misconduct. He was then informed that he could not take the chair until he was tried. The conference proceeded to appoint a chairman *pro tem,* to act till Bishop was tried. Bishop refused to be tried, and denied their right to try him, holding that he could only be tried by a General Conference. Whether his position was correct or not can only be determined by referring to the Constitution or Book of Discipline. He was tried in 1853 and expelled. Before he was expelled Bishop made a motion to go to Williamsburg; a few members of the New York Conference went with him, and some of the Genesee Conference went with him, and four of the Philadelphia Conference.

"When Bishop was expelled a convention was called to supply the vacancy. This convention met on July 9, 1853. All the elders were warned to attend. A General Conference was organized, the Book of Discipline adopted, and George A. Spywood elected General Superintendent, and John Tappan, Assistant. It is stated by one of the witnesses examined that the General Conference had never before 1852 elected three Superintendents.

"The Philadelphia Church is still attached to the General Conference. Simmons and Scott succeed Spywood and Tappan.

"Mr. Thompson says Bishop was never Superintendent since 1853. From the state of facts which the court submits to you, with all the other facts in the case, was Bishop, after his expulsion in 1853, a general superintendent, having the right to act as such? This involves an inquiry into the regularity of the proceedings in the Philadelphia Conference when three superintendents were elected, and the subsequent conduct of Bishop in permitting Galbreth to change the name

143

of the Conference, the charges preferred against him, his refusal to submit to a trial before the New York Conference, his right to occupy the chair, the right of the members of the Conference, while charges were pending against him, to prevent him sitting as the presiding officer, and his right to call a convention or Conference at Williamsburg. If this Conference at Williamsburg was held without authority, and in violation of the Constitution or Discipline of the Church, the members of that convention departed from the form of government of the Church, and cannot, by virtue of such act, claim to be the Church, no matter whether they were a majority or minority. The same remarks apply to other acts enumerated by the court.

"Which of these parties, the plaintiffs or the defendants, adhere to the doctrines of the Church, the form of worship practiced in the Church, and the government in the Church, must be submitted to you, with instruction that your decision should be in favor of the party so adhering, and having in those respects the regular succession, no difference whether that party be in the majority or minority.

"Here read from Book of Discipline and Doctrine, Section 4, Art. IV, pp. 35, 36; Art. V, p. 36; Section 11, p. 53, of General Conference; p. 56, General Superintendent; p. 57, Assistant; p. 65, Yearly Conference.

"Mr. Rush was the General Superintendent of the Church for twenty-four years. He appointed elders for Williamsport Church. The Philadelphia church formed part of his charge, which he visited. He, wishing to resign, being superintendent in 1852, Bishop came in after him. The Church in this place was attached to the Philadelphia Conference.

"It is to be hoped that your verdict will repair the troubles that exist in this breach of the African Methodist Episcopal Zion Church in the United States, and restore peace and harmony among the members. This appears to be the desire of the court. We are sure it is your wish as it is that of the Court. If Bishop, when he seceded or called a Conference at Williamsburg, should be considered as acting in violation of the government of the Church, and was properly expelled, then, his power as general superintendent having ceased, he could not confer power upon others to officiate in the Church."

The Court found Superintendent Bishop acting illegally in this matter.

The General Conference of 1864 is important in our history for several reasons among them being the reaffirmation of the equality of the elected Superintendents, the presence of several recognized lay delegates, the movement for organic union and the Committee investigation of the resignation of Superintendent Ross.

Of the lay delegates registered the names of the following appeared: Philip Buchanan of Wesley Church, Philadelphia, William Wilson of John Wesley, Washington, D. C., George Brooks of Zion Wesley, Washington, D. C., Edward Hill of New Bern, N. C., Plato Gale of Oyster Bay, Long Island, N. Y., James T. Butler of Baltimore Md., John J. Smith of Boston, Mass., and a Mr. Pulpress of Alleghany (now North Side Pittsburgh, Pa.).

The movement for organic union between the A.M.E. and the A.M.E. Zion Churches evidently had been thoroughly discussed prior to 1864 for the Superintendents in their quadrennial message strongly urged action. It appears that the subject was not brought to the floor, however, until Thursday, May 26, 1864 when Reverends A. McIntosh, M. Stuby and a Dr. Watts of the A.M.E. Church were presented. The delegation from the sister church, given an opportunity to present the matter, suggested that a Committee of Nine be appointed in addition to two Bishops (Superintendents in our case). The two committees were to meet and lay plans for a convention (at a time and place selected) of duly elected individuals providing the combined committee thought this fesible. The Convention would determine the conditions under which unification could be arranged and then the plan was to be submitted to the annual conferences for ratification.

As a result of this proposal the General Conference passed the following resolution:

"That we cordially receive the representation made to this Conference by the sub-committee from the Committee on Church Union appointed by the A.M.E. General Conference and that we promise to give the subject a Christian and fraternal consideration which its importance so justly demands at the earliest opportunity."

After debate it was resolved that a Committee of three should be appointed to present "the Christian greetings and resolution" of the A.M.E. Zion Church to the A.M.E. General Conference. The Committee selected consisted of Reverends Singleton T. Jones, J. B. Trusty and S. M. Giles.

The Committee returned reporting a "cordial reception" from the sister denomination but stressed this one difference in the initial report: "that the entire Bench of Bishops were to be united with nine from that body and the same from us or an equivalent number."

From this point the Minutes are somewhat confusing but it appears that on Friday, May 27th "after roll call" resolutions calling for agreement with the A.M.E. suggestions were adopted. Reverends J. W. Hood (his appointment or election on the committee is significant because of his violent bitterness and opposition to organic union years later), J. H. Smith, and J. P. Hamer were delegated to so inform the A.M.E. General Conference. It appears that a meeting was held at Bethel Church on 6th Street the same day (5:30 P.M.). Those representing the A.M.E. Zion Church (ministers) were: Reverends S. T. Jones, J. W. Loguen, P. H. Laws, J. W. Hood, Samson Talbot, H. H. Washington, J. Coleman, J. D. Brooks, J. P. Hamer. The reserves were: S. M. Giles, W. F. Butler and J. Williams.

Evidently this meeting was held with the A.M.E. delegation and agreement reached on further procedure. Since Bishop Moore was evidently close to the facts we turn to his history for a clearer interpretation than the Minutes appears, at first hand, to give.

At the meeting at Bethel Church (May 27, 1864) "the meeting was organized by Bishop Clinton with singing and prayer; Bishop J. D. Brooks was called to the chair; Revs. J. M. Brown and J. P. Hamer were chosen Secretaries. After deliberation it was decided that this should be a formal meeting. The object of the meeting was stated, whereupon the proceedings of the committee who originated the matter in the A.M.E. General Conference were read, but the resolutions in those proceedings not being sufficiently full, they were laid upon the table, and the matter referred to the following committee: Revs. Birch, S. T. Jones, J. H. Williams, J. W. Loguen, S. M. Giles; these persons were instructed to draw up resolutions expressing the sentiments of the joint committee on the subject. The committee withdrew and after an absence of half an hour returned and reported as follows:

REPORT OF THE SUB-COMMITTEE

WHEREAS, the committee of the A.M.E. Zion and the A.M.E. General Conferences met in joint committee, and having interchanged sentiments on the great question of union between the bodies represented by them; therefore,

Resolved, that it is the opinion of this meeting that the great question of consolidation may be safely committed to a convention to consummate a union upon the basis which will be satisfactory to all concerned.

Resolved, that it is the sense of this joint committee that such a convention be held in the city of Philadelphia, commencing on the second Tuesday in June, 1864, in Wesley Church on Lombard Street, at 10 o'clock A.M., and that twenty-five delegates from each connection shall compose said convention; and the result of said convention shall be submitted to the Annual Conferences of both Churches, and if agreed to by a majority of each, shall be final; all of which is respectfully submitted.

Reverend J. W. Hood offered the following preamble to the resolution:

WHEREAS, it is indispensably necessary that the minds of the people of both organizations be prepared for this important event contemplated; therefore,

Resolved, that a committee of three be appointed to issue an address to the churches through the columns of the Christian Recorder and the Anglo-African, setting forth clearly the object for which the convention is called.

According to the Minutes of the General Conference and the statement of Moore the suggestion of J. W. Hood prevailed and the following were appointed to make such a statement to the two papers noted: J. W. Hood, S. T. Jones and E. Weaver. According to Bishop Moore a discussion followed as to just how the delegates to the convention were to be selected in the respective denominations and finally an agreement was reached to refer this election to the two General Conferences.

The Zion section of the Committee returned to the General Conference and made their report. While the debate was *spirited* (states Moore) the mere fact that it was not a long drawn out affair indicated general agreement to the idea from the first. Both Moore and the Minutes of 1864 agree that the following were elected delegates:

New York Conference: Reverends William H. Pitts, Jeptha Bancroft, Isaac Coleman and Jacob Thomas.
New England Conference: Reverends S. M. Giles, G. H. Washington, W. F. Butler and J. W. Hood.
Philadelphia Conference: Reverends Sampson Talbot, S. T. Jones, Charles J. Carter and J. B. Trusty.

Southern Conference: Reverends J. D. Brooks, J. P. Hamer, R. H. Dyson and J. A. Williams.

Alleghany Conference: Reverends Abraham Cole, James A. Jones, and J. B. Cox.

Genesee Conference: Reverends J. W. Loguen, William Sanford, James H. Smith and Basil MacKall (last not named by Moore).

Reserves: Reverends J. P. Thompson (New York); Jacob Anderson, Philadelphia; George A. Spywood, New England; R. A. Gibson, Southern; P. C. Laws, Alleghany and John Thomas, Genesee.

While no word is stated concerning the lay position on this union it appears that the few present must have reflected some dissatisfaction at no lay representation for great bitterness developed in a fight to force *instruction* of the delegates. This move was led by the laymen in the Conference and became so intense that only a telegram telling of the severe illness of Dr. S. T. Gray (father of the movement to heal the breach between the factions in 1856) was seriously ill. A second telegram informing the conference of his death caused an immediate adjournment. While somewhere they may exist the full minutes of the meeting held at Wesley Church, so far we have mainly conjectured as to that which transpired. We do know that the keen enthusiasm of J. W. Hood for organic Union must have received a rude jolt in the weeks following the rise of the 1864 General Conference. How justified he was in his bitterness remains to be a conclusion drawn by those who read his history and glean the over-all viewpoint. Suffice it to say that four years saw the Zion Church with waning faith in union with Bethel. The seeds of the *oneness of the church* were so alive that the best opportunity of again entering the folds of the Mother Church presented themselves in the immediate years ahead. This failure can only be attributed to the fresh circumstances surrounding the division of North and South in the Mother Church. And so again the point at which the Methodist Church was to find itself less than 100 years later could have come to pass in 1868, or certainly by 1870.

The A.M.E. Church requested that certain changes be made in our discipline that would make it conform with their system. The major point involved the election of bishops for life. At the time we were still electing Superintendents every four years. In this the Zion Church agreed. On the matter of the rights of the laity the Zion Church appeared to be unwilling to comply. As has been stated, from the beginning of the Church lay activity and authority had been a characteristic and it is certainly true that the denomination would have been taking a backward step had it agreed to a restriction of these rights. The Committee rightly felt that to do so would defeat the union so far as Zion was concerned.

The convention evidently found no difficulty in agreeing on the name—United African Methodist Episcopal Church. Both churches had a privilege to this title. But the major concern was that of the episcopacy—and actually the great question of ordination. This being the stumbling block it was suggested by the Reverend Jermain Loguen that "we begin at the other end and work up." To this everyone agreed. No difficulty was encountered until the matter of the episcopacy was reached again. Bishop Hood states in detail the circumstances which followed. He states:

> The first question voted on was that we adopt the superintendency as it exists in the Zion Church. As it had been agreed that just enough of our men were to vote with them to defeat this proposition it was defeated by a close vote.

> Editor's Note: We must keep in mind that each church had an equal number of representatives.

Bishop Hood continues:

> The next proposition was that we adopt the lifetime bishopric. This was adopted by a close vote. The last proposition to be considered was a proviso that before the final consummation of the union the General Conference of the Zion Church should be called into extraordinary session and the bishops elected for life and ordained. On this question the convention was a tie; but according to the rules of the convention in case of a tie the chairman had the casting vote. Bishop Clinton was in the chair and voted for the proposition, and it was then adopted.
> They (the A.M.E. members) then asked that we have another session.—Notwithstanding it was our day to have the chairman— (they) had Bishop Campbell in the chair before the hour to which we had adjourned. When we assembled—one of their delegates—had a long preamble and resolution—The substance of the resolution was that we put off the final consummation of the union for four years, each doing all it could during that time. For this all their delegates voted. All our delegates voted against it, but Bishop Campbell gave the casting vote in its favor. . . . There would have been no harm in these resolutions if they had honestly intended to take the four years in preparing their people for the change as they stated.[1]

The A.M.E. Zion Church went ahead with the idea of union

---

[1] Hood, loc. cit., pp. 88-92.

having printed several thousand copies of the proposition but the deep interest in organic union was never to reach the imminent point of 1864. As we have stated, by 1868 the Church was looking forward to some agreement with the Methodist Episcopal Church North.

Perhaps the second great subject which came before the General Conference of 1864 was the matter of the resignation of Superintendent Peter Ross. Superintendent Ross had been elected first in 1856.

Bishop (then Superintendent) Clinton introduced the matter of the resignation of Superintendent Ross on Saturday, May 28, 1864. The matter was placed in the hands of a special committee composed of Abraham Cole, John W. Hood, Charles J. Carter and Samson Talbot. After deliberation, the committee reported that they felt the case should have been settled in the annual conference but concluded that Superintendent Ross had no seat in the General Conference. When a vote on the committee's report was taken an adverse ballot resulted and again the matter was before the General Conference. Superintendent Ross then asked for a select committee before whom he could go and give his reasons for resigning. The Conference agreed and the following were selected: Reverends J. D. Brooks, J. W. Loguen, G. H. Washington, J. Ricks and J. Bancroft.

The committee reported Tuesday, May 31, 1864. It appeared that Superintendnet Ross had stated to the committee that the reason for his resignation was the lack of funds on which to live. "The field had been so gleaned" under the rotation system that he barely secured $200 excluding traveling expenses. It being impossible for him and his family to exist on this sum he caused a statement to be published in the *Anglo-African* of August 17, 1863, that the would resign. He purchased a set of shoemaker's tools and returned to his trade.

A Col. Nelson Viele requested him to serve as Chaplain of the 14th Rhode Island Heavy Artillery while it remained in the vicinity and he accepted.

The report of the Committee recommending that Superintendent Ross be received as a member of the General Conference was adopted and the matter was closed.

A petition from North Carolina requesting that an annual conference be set up was referred to the Committee on Boundaries, which, when it reported, provided for such a conference taking in territory of that state and that section of Virginia, south of the city of Richmond or the James River and including Tennessee. California also received attention when Upper and Lower (that part which belonged to the United States) became an annual conference while the Louisiana Conference (also new) was to take in all that part of the South below North Carolina and Tennessee.

Two other matters of interest came up in this conference, that of Rush University and the Publication House. On the matter of Rush University, considerable difficulty was noted in its affairs, since, for some reason, a faulty deed was held to the property. It appears that the educational situation was somewhat unsettled and for a time, the conference entertained the ideas of sponsoring other institutions, among them being Avery College (presumably in Allegheny (Pittsburgh)). On the matter of the Publication House a printing press was ordered for the *Anglo-African* (June 6, 1864).

Elections resulted in the following being elected Bishops of the Church: Joseph J. Clinton, J. D. Brooks, Samson Talbot and Jermain W. Lougen (Loguen).[2]

The General Conference of 1864 also makes mention of General Officers. For example: the General Book Steward elected was Isaac Coleman. Trustees of the Book Operations were S. T. Jones, William H. Decker, William H. Pitts, Jeptha Bancroft, and Jacob Thomas. Rush Academy officers selected were: S. Talbot, J. P. Thompson, Samuel M. Giles with the treasurer, Christopher Rush. Trustees selected were Joseph P. Thompson, John Tappan, J. W. Loguen, J. H. Smith, William Sanford, John Thomas, Edward V. Clark, John Durnel, Henry Travis, Samuel J. Howard, Christopher Brown, James Stockley. A Sabbath School Union was formed with the following officers: President, Samuel M. Giles, Vice-Presidents: William H. Bishop, S. Talbot, J. J. Clinton and J. D. Brooks. The Secretary was to be William H. Butler while the Treasurer was to be Peter Ross. To aid this group the following were designated a *standing committee:* G. H. Washington, J. Thomas and G. A. Spywood.[3]

---

[2] Minutes of the General Conference of 1864 listed as the *General Conference of the A.M.E. Zion Church of 1864 With Appendix*, published by S. M. Giles, Hartford, Conn. (Press of Case, Lockwood and Co., 1864).

[3] Minutes of General Conference, 1864, *loc. cit.*

The Twelfth General Conference met at Wesley Zion Church, Washington, D. C., May 6, 1868. In this session two matters of importance came up on the matter of unification and two other items were at least brought to the point of clarification. As the reader will note the union with the A.M.E. Church was practically laid aside indefinitely. While in a subsequent writing it will be stated that union with the sister denomination reached the stage of ratification by local congregations the high tide seemed never as hopeful as in 1864. Certainly in the developments of 1868 Hood appeared justified in his change of attitude. The second matter had to do with the union with the Mother M. E. Church. Other vital items concerned the official change of the title of Superintendent to Bishop and the election of Bishops for either 12 years or life.

Hardly had Bishop (for with this conference we can safely use this term) Bishop opened the General sessions when the members turned to the consideration of the following resolution:

> Resolved, that there be a committee of three appointed, consisting of Reverends S. T. Jones, George H. Washington and William F. Butler, to prepare an address to be forwarded to the M.E. General Conference now in session in Chicago, Ill.

The next day the Committee on the address to the M. E. General Conference reported. Evidently, the report was adopted for Reverend Jones was sent to Chicago to appear before the Methodist Episcopal General where he was received with great cordiality and given ample time to speak before that body. The writer is not sure that Reverend Jones had departed for Chicago by the time the A.M.E. Zion General Conference got around to drawing up the following but it appears that there is a possibility that he did carry the document with him.

> To The Bishops and Members of the M.E. General Conference: We are ready to enter into arrangements by which to affiliate on the basis of equality, and to become one and inseparable now and forever. On the condition of full equality with the most favored of the church, we desire the further stipulation, that a sufficient number of those whom we may select to exercise the episcopal oversight of the colored element of the body may be set apart to that office, on the basis of perfect equality with all other Bishops of the M.E. Church; as we have practically demonstrated that a lay representation, especially in the law making department of the church, is at once sound, safe and productive of harmony among the people. We hope if at all compatible with views

of religious progress that you will adopt the same as the rule of the church.

If Reverend Jones carried this document with him to the Methodist Episcopal General Conference he did so prior to the ratification of the same by our own body. Our only support to such a belief is that he was so closely associated with this movement that he possessed it as a member of that committee. The fact that he was elected a Bishop after leaving Washington on his way to Chicago and this resolution occupied the attention of the Zion General Conference just prior to these elections states that officially the document appeared only after Jones' departure.

Of added significance is the alluding to the determination of the Zion General Conference to preserve its 1820 stand on lay privileges and rights in the church "especially in the law making" conferences. It appears here that the A.M.E. Zion Church has never pushed her right to a pioneering championing of the lay representative idea and its co-equal thought of lay responsibility. If no other thought resulted than this the conversations with both Bethel and Mother Methodist Churches were worth while.

Bishop-elect Jones made his report to the Zion General Conference on Friday, May 29, 1868, and following his statements the following was adopted:

> *Resolved* That while we gratefully acknowledge our thanks to Almighty God for the safe return of our beloved Bishop Singleton T. Jones from his mission to the M.E. General Conference, in session at Chicago, Ill., we return our thanks for the manner in which he expressed the sentiments of this conference to that body, and the prospective success attained by his mission.

As far as Zion Church was concerned the matter of union with Mother Methodism now rested with that body.

Prior to the taking up of unification with the M. E. Church at this General Conference the action on a like move involving the A.M.E. Church remained to be attended to. On May 14, a committee from the A.M.E. Church appeared and read a message from that body. We have neglected to say, that we feel it is important, that just after the reading of this communication, and the acting upon of the same, it was David Stevens who presented a resolution that the Zion Conference communicate with the M. E. General Conference in Chicago.

155

John Jamison Moore offered the following resolution Saturday, May 16th: (This was presented before an executive session of the Church.)

> *Whereas*, this General Conference has been officially informed by a committee from the African Methodist Episcopal Bethel Church that they are not prepared to unite with us on the plan agreed upon by the convention of the two connections held at Philadelphia in 1864, and submitted to the Annual Conferences of each connection for ratification; and
>
> *Whereas*, They decline uniting on the basis agreed upon, but now ask us to meet with them to unite on some other basis or plan; and
>
> *Whereas*, Our people in adopting the plan proposed by the said convention did it in good faith and did not authorize us to offer or accept any other plan; therefore
>
> *Resolved*, That we deem it inexpedient to meet with them according to their proposal.

It does not appear what final action was taken on these resolutions for the session stood adjourned and the matter was taken up again on May 19th. A new set of resolutions were introduced by a committee consisting of Reverends Cain, Johnson, Young, Walker and Warner. The plan, while not as harsh as the Moore Resolution nevertheless set forth the same thoughts but suggested that a new meeting be held. The General Conference was not satisfied with this approach either for at the end of debate the following action was taken:

> *Whereas*, The A.M.E. Bethel General Conference say in their communication or document that while they are willing for a union, they are not ready to unite upon the platform agreed upon by the convention in Philadelphia in 1864; therefore
>
> *Resolved*, That the whole matter lay on the table until 1872.

It was this action which J. P. Hamer, W. F. Butler, J. J. Moore, J. Holliday and M. B. Coss delivered to the A.M.E. General Conference.

In the matter of the changing of the name of Superintendents to Bishops, Jones states that this was done in 1864 while tenure, which came up in this session (1868) was not settled until much later, 1880.[4] Elections resulted in the selection of the following: John J. Moore (78 votes, necessary for choice 38, votes received, 59) ; Singleton T. Jones (75 votes cast, needed, 38, received, 62) ; Joseph Jackson Clinton (78 votes cast, needed, 40, received, 66) ; J. D. Brooks (votes

---

[4] Jones, *loc. cit.*, p. 76.

cast 80, needed, 41); S. D. Talbot and J. W. Loguen were also elected.

At this session the church paper *Zion Standard* and *Weekly Review* came in for careful attention. J. N. Gloucester was elected the editor after a committee report. His salary was to be $1,200. The Bishops were to receive $1,500 per year while action concluded that ministers should receive a minimum salary of $700.

There was still the desire for rotation of Bishops and again this was provided for. Bishop Brooks did not agree and tried to resign but the Conference would not permit his resignation.

At this time there were 21 conferences organized and provision was made for the formation of five more. Some of these listed as in evidence have since disappeared or were not in evidence when mentioned. For example: North-Western (Minnesota and Dakota Territory), and the Illinois Conference which was to embrace Illinois, Iowa and Nebraska.[5]

The Conference adjourned, Friday, May 29, 1868.

---

[5] *Minutes of the General Conference of 1868.*

CHAPTER XIII

The Church and the Opening Years of Reconstruction

OF interest to many readers will be the *estimated* statistics for the A.M.E. Zion Church over the period from the organization of the first church in 1796 to the crucial days of Methodism in 1860. In the organizational year J. Harvey Anderson stated that we had one organization, one deacon, one preacher and 60 members. By the end of the century this membership had grown to 150. In the next ten years the church acquired property valued at $25,300, had two church buildings and three organizations. Two deacons and three preachers cared for the needs of the 360 members. We call attention to the fact that it was the policy of the Methodist Episcopal Church to ordain Negroes to the office of deacon but to withhold that of the eldership.

By 1820 the number of organizations had grown to five but only one church building was owned and this was valued at $45,900. The church then had two elders, three deacons and three preachers caring for a membership of 500.

Twenty years later there were 38 organizations, 29 buildings valued at $157,000. There were two annual conferences, 37 elders, 10 deacons and three preachers caring for a membership of 3,020 scattered over nine states. Three Superintendents supervised the work. By 1860 there were 85 organizations, 64 church buildings valued at $248,000, five annual conferences, 82 elders, 15 deacons, eight preachers, 4,600 members in 11 states.[1]

Growth was slow in the South prior to this year simply because of the early stand of the church against slavery. In the Book of Discipline of 1820 appear these words: "*Of Slavery:* We will not receive any person into our societies who is a slave holder. Anyone who is now a member and holds slaves, and refuses to emancipate them after notice is given to such member by the pastor in charge, shall be excluded."

It may seem strange that such a statement was made in that early Book of Discipline, but, it must be recalled that it was not unusual

---

[1] Anderson, *loc. cit.*, pp. 41, 42.

for Negroes to own other Negroes as slaves. The statement not only clarified the church's position but likewise took care of any such instance. It was not until 1862 that any real gains were made in the South. As the Union armies forged ahead the Church followed, being well received by freedom everywhere. Just how news of the organization and its stand on slavery ever came to these people ten and twenty years prior to any contact may be forever a secret but Zion's work appears to have been well known to many a slave. Bishop Hood states that the work of the Church was known even in New Orleans.

This hostility to slavery is said to have held up the establishment of a church in Baltimore for several years.[2] In some instances open hostility to the new denomination was so pronounced that violence flared up.[3] In Alexandria, Virginia, Bishop Clinton and several others were sent to jail and the local organization broken up. In Richmond the Zion Church was lost for the same reasons.[4]

The battle against slavery appears to have been waged more bitterly in the Methodist Churches than in any other. Perhaps the reason is that the organizational systems as well as the idea of majority decisions allowed for the ruling out of local sentiment on a given proposition. The Congregational type of government of course, allowed local churches to formulate many of its own policies.

As early as 1856 the General Conference saw the need for very vigorous action on the slavery question for in that session the following is recorded:

> WHEREAS, the whole nation is now agitated upon the great sin of American slavery, which is regarded as the sum of all villainies, it is time for every honest hearted man to define his position, before the world either for or against this great moral evil. Upon this subject no neutral ground can be taken, for Christ says: "He that is not for me is against me." Therefore, the minister who evades or does not come on the side of liberty and the Gospel is not on the side of God. Therefore,
> *Resolved,* That it is the duty of the members of this General Conference to take a Gospel stand against the sin of slavery, as against all other sins, in teaching, preaching, praying and voting; and to let the world know that so long as this sin remains, and we live, we will, through God's help, be found on the side of the slaves, whether they

[2] Anderson, *loc. cit.,* p. 44.
[3] *Ibid.*
[4] *Ibid.*

may be white or black; and, that our motto is and ever shall be, "Liberty, and Freedom forever." [5]

Credit for the beginning of the Southern work evidently goes to the Church in New Haven, Conn. Bishop Hood states that "quite a number of our members" came from the church at New Bern, North Carolina. While there they were members of Andrew Chapel, evidently a Methodist Church connected with the Methodist Episcopal Church, South. Bishop Clinton was urged to send a minister into the South by these people. However, mission money had been raised in the New England conference as early as 1858 when $18.25 was reported at the Conference as *Mission Money*.[6] The writer believes that there is a reference dated earlier than this. At any rate, the Reverend John Williams was appointed and given $50 by the New England Mission Board to cover expenses.[7] When a year had passed and Reverend Williams had not gone, the Bishop being impatient, appointed Reverend J. W. Hood (in 1863) to proceed into the South. He, likewise, was given $50 by the same Board. Reverend Hood started at once and moved his family as far as Washington.[8]

Honor must be paid, as well, to a Miss Melvina Fletcher of Washington, D. C., who was instrumental in aiding in the financing of this Southern Mission work. Jones states of her: "When he (Bishop J. J. Clinton) arrived in Washington, D. C., Miss Melvina Fletcher of Zion Church, who was the trusted and beloved maid of the family of the Postmaster General, Hon. Montgomery Blair, became deeply interested in his mission. She gave him a contribution in gold and at her solicitation Mr. Blair secured from Secretary Stanton the Pass and Permit to follow in the wake of the army for religious purposes.[9]

Arriving at Washington, Rev. Hood found the Chesapeake Bay frozen over and was delayed until the middle of January, 1864.[10] He finally arrived in New Bern January 20th. Here he found about 400 members who agreed to unite with Zion Church. A few weeks later, he states, the church at Beaufort was added to the connec-

[5] Moore, *loc. cit.*, p. 218, 219.
[6] Moore, *loc. cit.*, p. 144.
[7] Hood, *loc. cit.*, p. 85.
[8] *Ibid.*, p. 86.
[9] Jones, *loc. cit.*, p. 26.
[10] Hood, *loc. cit.*, p. 86.

tion. While there is no record, Hood makes mention of several other organizations in the country surrounding New Bern which later became a part of the Zion Church.[11]

The dispute regarding the place of Manteo or Roanoke Island Church in Zion Connection comes up at this point. It is necessary to point out that at least in part Bishop Hood appears to lay no claim to New Bern being the oldest church but does seem to place its entry into the Zion Connection as the Mother Church of the South. He declares that Reverend Williams, who had been appointed earlier as a missionary arrived about the "first of March" and "finding the field at New Bern and vicinity occupied, he went to Roanoke Island and Washington, North Carolina, and was received by the churches at those points." [12]

There is little doubt that Rev. John Williams has not been accorded the place he should occupy in the history of our church. He may have been two months behind Hood but the fact that he did arrive and that he did organize several groups ought not to be overlooked. Bishop Hood states that he established two or three churches near New Bern, across the Trent River.[13] It may be stated here that the Manteo Church which closed several years ago is now restored and no doubt will be brought to her rightful position.

Bishop J. J. Clinton ranks with Father Rush in his pioneering efforts. He braved many dangers to follow up his workers in the South. This can be understood when it is realized that by May, 1864, he was in New Bern where he ordained William Ryle and Ellis Lavender as deacons and then went on to Beaufort where he ordained Enoch Wallace. He started to visit Washington but was forced to flee as the Confederate army launched a drive and re-captured this point.[14]

In July, Bishop Clinton sent out another missionary from New England, Deacon David Hill, who took charge of the church at Beaufort. In 1864 (December) the Old North Carolina Conference was organized as Hood puts it "around a stove on a cold winter day." [15] Eleven men along with the Bishop made up this mother conference of Southern Zion Methodism. The list is in itself historic: Joseph J.

---

[11] Hood, loc. cit., p. 86.
[12] Ibid., p. 87.
[13] Ibid.
[14] Hood, loc. cit., p. 86.
[15] Ibid., p. 87.

Clinton, John Williams, Ellis Lavender, J. W. Hood, E. H. Hill, all elders (Hill and Lavender were ordained at this conference) and W. J. Moore, H. W. Jones, David Gray, Joseph Green, Sampson Cooper and Abel Ferribee.[16]

On the matter of the history of these earlier churches the lack of accounts forces us to accept statements of Hood as the only authority. Bishop Jones says that Evans Metropolitan at Fayetteville, North Carolina, stands as one of the oldest Negro churches in America.[17]

Efforts throughout the South were not confined to North Carolina for, following J. W. Hood's and John Williams' work in that state, Wilbur Strong went into Alabama and later, Singleton T. Jones went into the Southwest.[18] To these four men, along with Bishop J. J. Clinton, goes the credit for the major Zion work in this area. As early as 1864 Bishop Clinton was establishing missions in Louisiana and Florida.[19]

Work began in South Carolina when Negroes of that State heard of the work going on in North Carolina. Jones states: "The Negroes of that State heard of a distinct colored denomination holding conference in North Carolina, and Rev. Horace Clinton and Titus Hogan walked through the country from Lancaster, S. C., to New Bern, N. C., a distance of 300 miles, to meet the North Carolina Conference and learn of this Negro Church in 1866.[20] As a result of this pioneering spirit the South Carolina Conference was formed by Bishop J. J. Clinton March 24, 1867.[21]

For the first time, in 1864, when the General Conference met in Philadelphia representation from the South was noted. Bishop Hood states that the first delegate was Edward H. Hill, who later was licensed to preach.[22]

Meanwhile, expansion of the Church was going on throughout the Northern areas primarily at the hands of such men as Bishop J. J. Moore, Singleton T. Jones, etc. Bishop Samson D. Talbot organized the Kentucky Conference in 1866 while Bishop Clinton was organizing the Virginia Conference (the same year). California had earlier received a visit from Bishop Moore and finally saw its first

[16] Ibid.
[17] Jones, loc. cit.
[18] Hood, loc. cit., pp. 87, 88.
[19] Ibid.
[20] Jones, loc. cit., p. 26.
[21] Ibid.
[22] Hood, loc. cit., p. 88.

Conference established in 1868. In 1867 Bishop Clinton had organized the Georgia and Alabama Conferences. Louisiana had come earlier, in 1865. The same Bishop Clinton called together the first Tennessee Conference October 6, 1868, and followed it with the organization of the conferences in Florida and West Tennessee and Mississippi in 1869.

Thus at the close of the decade the conferences totaled 17 with 840 churches, 795 buildings, with an estimated valuation of $1,271,-000, pastored by 760 elders, 142 deacons, 143 preachers, with 125,000 members. These members were located in 20 states and were supervised by an efficient group of pioneering bishops.[23]

It is not the purpose of this writer to include brief biographical accounts of all the Superintendents and Bishops in this work. It would make too long a story. However, whenever possible, we have included short sketches of their lives when it was felt that their activities warranted more than a mere mentioning of their names. To make up for a possible omission we have felt it wise to add the following that the History may be more complete and useful. This account will cover the period to 1872, however, leaving to a later time those listed after 1872.

Bishop Samson D. Talbot was born in West Bridgewater, Mass., in 1819. He married Sarah De Groat of Onondaga, New York, in 1844. Following her death he married Sarah Gassaway in December, 1865. He was converted and called to preach in 1841, joining the New York Conference in 1844, at which time he was ordained a deacon by Superintendent Rush. The following year he was ordained an elder. His pastorates included New York, Boston, Newark, N. J., Rochester, Syracuse, Washington, Troy. For some time he was treasurer of the Book Concern. He was elected to the Bishopric in 1864. He died in 1872. [24]

Bishop Singleton T. Jones was born March 8, 1825, at Wrightsville, York County, Pennsylvania. He married Miss Mary J. Talbot of Allegheny, Pennsylvania, November 29, 1846. He was converted February 8, 1842, and called to preach in September, 1844. He joined the Allegheny Conference August 23, 1849, transferring to the Baltimore Conference in May, 1853. In succession he served in the New York Conference (1857), the Philadelphia Conference in

[23] Anderson, loc. cit., p. 42.
[24] Flood, loc. cit., p. 788.

1859, the New York Conference in 1864, returning to the Baltimore Conference in June, 1866. He was ordained deacon in August, 1850 and elder, by Bishop Galbreath, in 1857. He served the following churches: Brownsville, Blairsville, Bedford, all in Pennsylvania, South Howard Street, Baltimore, Washington, Newark, New Jersey, Wesley in Philadelphia, Harrisburg, Chambersburg, all in Pennsylvania, Zion Church in New Jersey, Washington. He was the Editor of *Zion's Standard* and *Weekly Review*. He was ordained Bishop in May, 1868.[25] In *Jones's Sermons and Addresses,* edited by the Reverend J. W. Smith, the following additional notes on the life of Bishop Jones are noted. His mother and father were Marylanders, coming from the Eastern Shore region. His father, William H., marrying Catherine who was born in the town of Liberty.

At the age of ten Singleton (who was the second child of this marriage) was apprenticed to a lawyer at York, Pennsylvania, by the name of Thomas Kelley. Here he served as house, farm and cart boy. In 1839 he was legally released from service and proceeded to Philadelphia to look for work. Finding none, he left that city in midwinter, traveling on foot. At the time he had only 31 cents in his pocket. Disappointed and with his entire wardrobe in an ordinary pocket handkerchief, he started westward. One evening in January he approached the door of an inn seeking permission to sleep by the stove that night since it was bitter cold with snow falling heavily. There for the offer of 25 cents he was allowed to sleep by the stove covered with a buffalo robe. Seeing that he was in poor economic circumstances, the innkeeper not only gave him a warm breakfast but refused the 25 cents, saying: "No, as you are seeking employment I will not charge you anything. And I hope you may meet with success."

Singleton did meet with success for he arrived in Harrisburg with three times the money he had when he left Philadelphia. This addition to his funds was given by a sailor simply because he saw the need. In Harrisburg Singleton secured a job at that which was then known as Temperance House where he took care of the dining room. The inn was kept by a Mr. Reece at the time and the place of business was located near the capitol. Singleton attended church at Wesley Union where he recalls that George Galbreath preached the sermon

---

[25] *Ibid.*, p. 788.

from Malachi 4:1. Singleton was very much attached to Reverend Galbreath since he had baptized him when the lad was only two years of age.

These additional notes may likewise be of interest. When Singleton married Mary Jane Talbot or Talbert (her parents being Edward and Jane Talbert) in 1846 the ceremony was performed by the Reverend George Galbreath. To this union were born the following children: George Galbreath, Chester Stevens, Ann Catherine, David Eddie, Elizabeth Jane, Mary Ann, Singleton Thomas, William Haywood Bishop, Alice Williamson, Joll Robinson, Jennie Catherine and Edward Derussa William (later a Bishop of the Church). These last two children were graduates of Livingstone College.

For several years Singleton worked with the Reverend John E. Price as a hod carrier in Harrisburg. Later he worked on a boat on the Ohio River.

Singleton T. Jones attended his first General Conference in 1852. In 1868 he was Zion's representative to the Methodist Episcopal General Conference in Chicago. Here he attempted to negotiate affiliation and union with the mother church. It was while in attendance at this conference that he was elected a Bishop of his church. The following account from the *Daily Christian Advocate* (June 1, 1868) is of interest:

> "Dr. A. M. Obsen announced that the delegate from the African M.E. Zion Church had arrived with his papers, and, if necessary, desired that the conference should take action so that the desires of the body and that of the A.M.E. Zion Church should be furthered. W. Reddy moved that the delegate from that body be immediately introduced to the conference. The motion was carried.
> "W. H. Ferris moved that the time be extended. This, too, was carried. A. M. Obsen, the chairman of the Committee of Reception, then came upon the platform in company with Bishop Singleton T. Jones of the African M.E. Zion Church, amid loud cheers of the conference and congregation. Quick witted, ready, earnest, sarcastic at times, graceful, accomplished, the Bishop spoke with such fluency, power and magnetism that he swept everything before him."

In 1881 Bishop Jones was selected as a delegate to the Ecumenical Conference in London, England, but because of the status of his health he was unable to attend. Three years later, in 1884, he was selected as a delegate to the Centennial Methodist Conference in Baltimore, Maryland.

Bishop Jones passed away April 19, 1891, at 1019 19th Street, N.W., Washington, D.C. His funeral was conducted on Tuesday, April 21, at 2:00 P.M., in John Wesley Church (now the National Church of Zion Methodism). Present were Bishops John J. Moore, J. W. Hood, T. H. Lomax, C. C. Petty and C. R. Harris.

It would be interesting if we had at hand all the accounts of all the Bishops of the church for theirs is an intriguing story. Many were ex-slaves or individuals born of the few free men living in the nation. Theirs, likewise, is a story of suffering and sacrifice, the like of which few groups can tell.

Bishop John J. Moore was born in Berkley County, West Virginia, of slave parents, about the year 1818. His mother was born, free, but at the age fifteen years was kidnapped in Maryland and sold into slavery in West Virginia, where she married the Bishop's father, a slave. Her maiden name was Riedoubt and her husband's name was Hodge, but a change of owners caused him to adopt the name of Moore. When the Bishop was six years old his parents, by the advice and assistance of friendly Quakers, attempted a flight from slavery with their six children, of whom the Bishop was the youngest. They were recaptured, however, and the oldest four children sold South. A second attempt to gain their liberty was successful, and the Bishop's parents with their remaining two children, after many hardships and sufferings, reached Bedford County, Pennsylvania. Here a friendly farmer gave them employment and the two boys, William and John, were bound out for a term to his son, also a farmer. Owing to the pursuit of their former owner, the Bishop's parents were obliged to leave the settlement, but the Bishop remained secure on the farm. He was taught to read and write by his employer, and acquired a knowledge of farming. The last part of his apprenticeship was served to a brother-in-law of his former master, who exacted six months over the proper time and did not furnish the schooling or clothes and the cash as required by law after the expiration of the term.

After leaving his ungenerous master, he worked for six months for a farmer in the settlement at seven dollars per month. Having saved about fifteen dollars, he concluded to visit Harrisburg, and walked the sixty (should be 106 miles) miles to that place in two days. . . . In 1833, he became religiously impressed and experienced a change of heart. Leaving Harrisburg he visited his old home in the mountains where he remained some time, having obtained employment as a porter in a store. . . . He was licensed as an exhorter on returning to Harrisburg in 1834 and a year later received his license to preach. He joined the Philadelphia Conference in 1839. John Jamison Moore was one of the great pioneering circuit riders of his denomination, serving not only in Pennsylvania and Ohio but going as far west as San Francisco where he established a Zion Church. He was elevated to the bishopric in 1868 and died in 1883.[26]

Name of Bishop	Probable Date of Birth	When elected	Died
James Varick	1768	1821	1827
Christopher Rush	1777	1828	1872
William Miller	1775	1840	1849
George Galbraith	1799	1848	1853
William H. Bishop	1783	1852	1873
George H. Spywood	1798	1852	1876
John Tappan	1799	1854	1862
Solomon T. Scott	1790	1856	1862
James Simmons	1792	1856	1873
Joseph J. Clinton	1823	1856	1881
Peter Ross	1821	1856	1889
John D. Brooks	1803	1864	1874
Samson D. Talbot	1819	1864	1872
John J. Moore	1818	1868	1883
Singleton T. Jones	1825	1868	1891
Jeremiah Loguen	....	1868	1873

[26] Moore, *loc. cit.*, p. 367 ff.; Flood., *loc. cit.*

BIBLIOGRAPHY

PRIMARY SOURCES

A. M. E. Zion Quarterly Review, Vols. LXIII, LXIV.
Anderson, J. Harvey, ed. *The Official Directory of the African Methodist Episcopal Zion Church in America* (New York, 1895).
Anderson, William K., *Methodist Review, Vol. 46,* A Source Book of Early Methodist History.
Annals of the New York Conference (M.E.).
Asbury, Francis, *Journal of* in three vols. (New York, 1821).
De vinne, Daniel, *The Methodist Episcopal Church and Slavery* (New York, 1857).
Dolliver, Robert H. *The Story of the Mother Church in American Methodism,* (New York, Oct. 1943).
Embury, Philip, *Diary of.*
Godwyn, *The Negroes' Advocate* (1680).
James, Thomas, *Life of, by Himself.*
Jamestown (New York) *Sun,* Sept. 3, 1950.
Loguen, Jermain W., *The Rev. J. W. Loguen As a Slave and as a Freeman* (Syracuse, 1859).
Minutes of the Methodist Annual Conference, 1773-1813.
Minutes of the Methodist Episcopal General Conference, 1796, 1800, 1804.
Minutes of the Common Council of the City of New York, 1784-1831.
Minutes of the General Conference (A. M. E. Zion) *of 1864 with appendix* (Hartford Conn., 1864).
Minutes of the General Conference (A. M. E. Zion) *of 1868.*
Moore, John Jamison, *History of the A. M. E. Zion Church* (New York, 1884).
Rush, Christopher, *A Short Account of the Rise and Progress of the African Methodist Episcopal Church in America* (New York, 1843).
Rush, Christopher, *A Short Account of the Rise and Progress of the African Methodist Episcopal Church in America* (New York, 1866).
Watson, Richard, *Religious Instruction of the Slaves in the West India Colonies Advocated and Defended.* A sermon preached before the Wesleyan Missionary Society in Nw Chapel, City Road, London, April 28, 1824.

SPECIAL SECONDARY SOURCES

Conrad, Earl, *Harriet Tubman,* (Associated Publishers, Washington, 1943).
Du Bose, Horace M., *Life of Joshua Soule,* ed. by Bishop Warren A. Candler (Nashville, 1857).
Dunshee, Kenneth Holcomb, *As You Pass By* (Hastings House, 1952).
Flood, Theodore and Hamilton, John W. ed., *Lives of Methodist Bishops* (New York, 1882).
Greenleaf, *History of the Churches of New York* (New York, 1846).
Harris, Bishop C. R., *Historical Catechism* (Charlotte, 1916).
Hood, Bishop James Walker, *One Hundred Years of the African Methodist Episcopal Zion Church* (New York, 1895).
Janes, Edwin L., *The Character and Career of Francis Asbury* (New York, 1872).
Jones, Bishop E. D. W., *Comprehensive Catechism of the A. M. E. Zion Church* (Washington, 1934).
Lee, Jesse, *History of the Methodists* (Baltimore, 1810).
Meacham, Albert Gallitin, *A Compendious History of the Rise and Progress of the Methodist Church in Europe and America* (New York, 1832).
Paine, Bishop Robert, *Life and Times of William M'Kendree,* in two vols. (Nashville, 1874).

168

BIBLIOGRAPHY

Seaman, Samuel A. *Rise of the Methodist Society in the City of New York* (New York, 1821).

Smith, Rev. J. W. *Sermons and Addresses of the Late Rev. Bishop Singleton T. Jones, D.D. of the A. M. E. Zion Church, with a Memoir of His Life and Character* (New York, 1892).

Stillwell, Samuel, *Rise of the Methodist Society in the City of New York* (New York, 1821).

Stirling, Dorothy, *Freedom Train* (The Story of Harriet Tubman) (Garden City, L. I., N. Y., 1954).

Wakley, Rev. J. B., *Lost Chapters Recovered from Early American Methodism* (New York, 1858).

Walls, Bishop W. J., *Harriet Tubman.*

Wheeler, Benj. F., *The Varick Family* (Mobile, 1906).

GENERAL WORKS

Atkinson, John, *The Beginnings of the Wesleyan Movement in America* (New York, 1896).

Bangs, Nathan, *The Pioneer Bishop or Life and Times of Francis Asbury* (New York, 1858).

Brawley, Benjamin, *Negro Builders and Heroes* (Chapel Hill, 1937).

Gardner, Samuel Rawson, *The First Two Stewarts and the Puritan Revolution* (New York, 1891).

Green, John Richard, *A Short History of the English People,* in four vols. (New York, 1900).

Hurst, John Fletcher, *The History of Methodism,* in seven vols., (New York, 1902).

Lodge, Henry Cabot, ed., *The History of the Nations,* Vol. 23-24 (New York, 1936).

Mowat, R. B., *England in the Eighteenth Century* (New York, 1932).

Raybold, Rev. G. A. *Reminiscences of Methodism in New Jersey* (New York, 1849).

Telford, John, ed., *Letters of John Wesley,* in 8 vols. (London, 1931).

Trevelyan, George M., *English Social History* (New York, 1942).

Trevelyan, George M., *England Under Queen Anne* (New York, 1930).

APPENDIX I

We are indebted to Bishop William J. Walls for the following material:

It is said that the great growth of the A.M.E. Zion Church in the South is due to the work of one woman who has been mentioned previously, Mrs. Malvina Fletcher of Washington, D. C. Bishop Walls states that not only did Mrs. Fletcher give money for the beginning of the work in the South but persuaded a reluctant and a discouraged J. J. Clinton to undertake the work of bringing Zion to the South. It is stated by him that she, Mrs. Fletcher, had a feeling that Clinton, who had been elected Superintendent, might resign and went to him requesting this resignation in return for financial support, etc., she might be able to secure. Bishop Walls states that she tore up the resignation in Superintendent Clinton's presence.

Superintendent Clinton not only became interested in this work in the South but appears to have been responsible for the sending of J. W. Hood to Nova Scotia where Hood appears to have spent three years and established at least one church.

* * * * *

These additional facts on the Life of Peter Williams are recorded in Bishop E. D. W. Jones's Catechism:

"Peter felt a deep interest for the welfare of those of his own color. He knew religion had made him all he was on earth and all he hoped to be in heaven. He did all he could to elevate his race. Peter thought a House of Worship expressly for the people of his own color might be exceedingly beneficial. He aided in circulating a subscription and raised money to build a church at the corner of Leonard and Church Streets, which is called 'Zion Church.' It was built in 1801. This was the first church edifice built expressly for the people of color in New York. Mr. Williams laid with his own hands the cornerstone of this building and was one of the original trustees."—*Wakeley* (Lost Chapters).

According to the same source Peter Williams died in Liberty Street in February, 1823. His funeral sermon was delivered by Dr. William Phoebus, an eminent Methodist preacher, in Old John Street Church and was interred in the St. John's Episcopal Church burial ground, records of which can now be obtained in New York City.

Because he never consented with his co-founders to completely withdraw from the spiritual administration of the Methodist Episcopal Church and when our fathers and founders decided to sever all connec-

171

tion with that body and refused longer to receive their preachers as pastors, he remained out of gratitude to them under their ministrations.

One child was born to Peter and Mollie Williams, Peter Williams, Jr., who became a Protestant Episcopal minister, was ordained by Bishop Hobert in 1820 and was pastor of St. Phillip's Church when it was in Center Street. Mistakenly, Dr. William Howard Day confused Peter Williams, Jr., the Episcopalian, with Peter Williams, Sr., the Methodist.

Bishop Jones also carries the following stories concerning Peter Williams:

During the Revolutionary War the wicked soldiers annoyed the Methodists in John Street very much, during their hours of worship and after divine service closed. They crowded around the doors, and as the congregation came out the soldiers would secretly cut the ladies dresses into ribbons.

At a certain time, while the love-feast was held in the evening in the old cradle of Methodism, and the Methodists were enjoying a good time within, the wicked soldiers were busy without digging very silently a deep pit in front of the steps before the door. The benediction being pronounced the people left for home. They went down the steps, and then supposed they were going to tread on solid ground, one disappeared suddenly, and then another, tumbling one upon another into the pit until they lay in heaps in one heterogeneous mass. The soldiers were laughing in their sleeve at the mischief they had caused, and the confusion into which they had thrown the Methodists.

"But," added Peter, "the mischievous soldiers dug a far worse pit for themselves, for when their officers were informed of their conduct the perpetrators were severely punished; so they dug no more pits for Methodists to fall into."

Another story is told by Jones concerning a deserter.

At a certain time Bishop Asbury and a number of the preachers came to Peter's house to dine with him. Peter went bowing into the parlor, paying his very best respects to the dignitaries who had honored him with a visit, and who were to take dinner with him.

Peter began to count his guests, pointing with his finger. He commenced with Bishop Asbury and counted eleven, and then he made a long pause before a minister who had deserted the Methodists and gone over to another church; then he said, "Eleven—and you—" another pause. "A Judas, I suppose you would say," replied the minister who had deserted his mother (Church). "As you please, Mr. L——" said Peter; "I did not say it. But you had better return to your mother, the Methodist Episcopal Church."

This shows Peter's love for Methodism, his abhorrence for deserters, his characteristic honesty amounting almost to bluntness, though he left the minister to make the application himself. The deserter never returned to his mother, though he always professed great love for her till the day of his death.

I might as well give the name of the minister: the Reverend Thomas Lyell, successor of Mr. Pilmoor as Pastor of the Protestant Episcopal Church in Ann Street. It was certainly very appropriate that one deserter should fill the place of another.

During a part of the Revolutionary War, Peter lived near New Brunswick, New Jersey, with the Durham family. Molly was a servant in this family, and came with them from St. Christopher's Island. She remained with them until her time was out. When they separated there was a time of weeping with Molly and her mistress, for they highly esteemed each other, and separated reluctantly.

The Rev. Mr. Chapman boarded with this family. He was full of patriotism, full of courage, especially when there was no danger. He often expressed a desire for the British to come there, how he would like to face, fight and conquer them. At length the red coats made their appearance and Mr. Chapman was like the Dutch general, who was full of courage when there was no danger, and when the enemy hove in view he made an address to his soldiers and told them: "Go forward and conquer the enemies of your country; and for fear you will get out of ammunition, I will go back and run a few bullets."

Mr. Chapman fled as they approached, and was hid in a safe place. When the British arrived the commanding officer inquired for the reverend gentleman. H had made himself particularly obnoxious, and they wished to secure his person. Peter informd him he was not there. The British officer drew his sword and waved it over Peter's head, threatening to kill him, and told him he would run his sword through him if he did not tell where his master was. Peter told him he did not know. In relating it in after years, he said the perspiration ran down his back as the sword was waving over his head, and the disappointed and enraged officer threatening to kill him.

Then the officer took out a purse of gold, threw it at Peter's feet and said: "That gold is yours if you will tell me where your master is." Peter said he did not know, and the British officer soon left, and Mr. Chapman came home from his hiding place. Peter could not be frightened by the sword, nor corrupted by British gold, to tell where Mr. Chapman was, and thus endanger his life. He refused to tell and in this way saved it; though Peter in after years admitted he came very nearly telling a story in order to save Mr. Chapman from death.

Bishop Jones gives credit for the following story to G. P. Disosawy

173

Esq., who received them from a Hannah Baldwin, who was present when the events took place. They occurred while Peter was sexton.

"Religious meetings at night were then generally forbidden, but allowed in the Methodist Church, as the British imagined, or rather desired, that the followers of Wesley should favor their cause. Still the services were sometimes interrupted and disturbed by the rude conduct of men belonging to the army. They would stand in the aisle with their caps on during the divine worship, careless and inattentive. On one occasion, before the congregation was dismissed, they sang the national song, 'God Save the King.' At its conclusion the society immediately began, and sang to the same air, those beautiful lines of Charles Wesley: 'Come Thou Almighty King.'

"Upon a Christmas even, when the members had assembled to celebrate the Advent of the World's Redeemer, a party of British officers, masked, marched into the House of God. One, very properly personifying their master, was dressed with cloven feet, and a long forked tail. The devotions, of course, soon ceased, and the chief devil, proceeding up the aisle, entered the altar. As he was ascending the stairs of the pulpit, a gentleman present with his cane knocked off his Satanic majesty's mask, when, lo, there stood a well-known British colonel. He was immediately seized, and detained until the city guard was sent to take charge of the bold offender. The congregation retired, and the entrances of the church were locked upon the prisoner for additional security. His companions outside then commenced an attack upon the doors and windows, but the arrival of the guard put an end to the disgraceful proceedings, and the prisoner was delivered into their custody."

THE MANUMISSION PAPERS OF PETER WILLIAMS

To all to whom These Presents Shall Come or May Concern:

Whereas, by a bill of sale made by James Aymar, of the City of New York, tobacconist, and duly executed by him on the tenth day of June in the year of our Lord one thousand and eighty-three, he, the said James Aymar, did, for and in consideration of the sum of forty pounds current money of the province of New York, to him in hand paid at and before the encealing and delivery of the said bill of sale, by the trustees of the Methodist Meeting in the city of New York, fully, clearly and absolutely grant, bargain, sell and release unto said trustees his Negro man, named Peter, now called Peter Williams hereby

Now know ye that we, John Staples, Abraham Russel, Henry Newton, John Sproson and William Cooper, trustees for the time being of the said Methodist Meeting, for and in consideration of services rendered and payments in money made to our predecessors, trustees of the said

Methodist meeting, amounting to forty pounds have manumitted, liberated, and set free, and by these present do manumit, liberate and set free said Negro man, named Peter, now called Peter Williams hereby giving and granting unto him, the said Peter Williams all such sum or sums of money and property of what nature or kind whatsoever, which he, the said Peter Williams may, by his industry have acquired or which he may have purchased since the eighteenth day of November one thousand seven hundred and eighty-five. And we do also give and grant unto him, the said Peter Williams,. full power and lawful authority to sue for and recover in his own name and for his own use all money and property which is now due or may hereafter become due."

APPENDIX II
RECORD OF GENERAL CONFERENCES AND ANNUAL CONFERENCES TO 1872

Number of Superintendents or Bishops in Attendance	Place and Date of Meeting	Delegates	Length of Session
1	New York, July 15, 1824	12	6 days
1	New York, May 15, 1828	20	6 days
1	New York, May 19, 1832	25	6 days
2	New York, May 14, 1836	35	6 days
2	New York, May 28, 1840	28	3 days
2	New York, May 18, 1844	54	6 days
2	New York, May 29, 1848	46	6 days
3	Philadelphia, June 26, 1852	60	20 days
2	New York, June 26, 1856	25	15 days
2	Philadelphia, May 30, 1860	97	12 days
3	Philadelphia, May 25, 1864	100	25 days
4	Washington, May 6, 1868	105	20 days
6	Charlotte, N. C., June 19, 1872	140	14 days

ANNUAL CONFERENCES

Conference	Set Apart	Superintendent or Bishop
New York	June 21, 1821	
Philadelphia	1829	
New England	June 21, 1845	Superintendent Rush
Allegheny	1849	Superintendent Rush
Genesee (Now West N. Y.)	Sept. 13, 1859	Superintendent Rush
Southern (later Baltimore)	May 2, 1829	
North Carolina	Dec. 17, 1864	Supt. J. J. Clinton
Louisiana	March 13, 1865	Supt. J. J. Clinton
Kentucky	June 6, 1866	Supt. Samson D. Talbot

Conference	Set Apart	Superintendent or Bishop
Virginia	October, 1866	Supt. J. J. Clinton
South Carolina	March 24, 1867	Supt. J. J. Clinton
Alabama	April 3, 1867	Supt. J. J. Clinton
Georgia	June 15, 1867	Supt. J. J. Clinton
California	Jan. 10, 1868	Supt. J. J. Clinton
Tennessee	Oct. 6, 1868	Supt. J. J. Clinton
Florida	April 22, 1869	Supt. J. J. Clinton
W. Tennessee and Mississippi	October, 1869	Supt. J. J. Clinton

APPENDIX III

DENOMINATIONAL DEPARTMENTS AND OFFICERS TO 1872

* General Secretaries:

> 1799, George Collins
> 1868, Reverend William F. Butler
> 1872, Reverend J. A. Jones
> 1876, Dr. William Howard Day
>   Rev. C. R. Harris
> 1880, Rev. C. R. Harris

** Agent of Book Concern:

> 1841, Reverend Jacob D. Richardson
> 1864, Reverend Isaac Coleman

---

* This list does not include General Conference Secretaries.
** The Book Concern became our first official department in 1844.

INDEX

Francis Asbury
and The Development of
African Churches in America

By David H. Bradley

Reprinted from "Methodist History" Volume X No. 1, October, 1971

FRANCIS ASBURY AND THE DEVELOPMENT OF AFRICAN CHURCHES IN AMERICA

by David H. Bradley

The selection of an expressionate title for this paper has been a most difficult one, and at best leaves much to be desired. However, it is the writer's hope that the current interest in all phases of black history will allow a deeper study of the paper's intent on the part of students who may be interested in the early development of African Methodist churches.

A great amount of time has been spent in order that full justice can be given to the American bishop, Francis Asbury. To show, for example, his basic intent and convictions and carry these principles through to change and compromise, has not been elementary. Asbury knew that he was writing for posterity, so he infrequently revealed his underlying attitudes. Time after time he receded from some important stand, but only because he was reluctant to lose sight of a long-range benefit. It is my belief, for instance, that preservation and growth of American Methodism was a paramount goal. Many of his convictions stood aside in the light of this ultimate aim.

With an awareness of ultra-sensitiveness on the part of many, it has been necessary to trace several key beliefs of the bishop from unrelenting position to compromise, that all may know that no one issue alone was to suffer this fate. Where Africans were concerned, Asbury had to settle for freedom of the soul instead of freedom of the body.

It cannot be said that the Bishop had a plan of action for the use of black preachers, but his understanding that the best results came when meeting with these people "to themselves" certainly must have led to this conclusion. The organization of classes and societies could have preceded or followed this decision. Another difficult thesis to prove is whether Asbury would have sanctioned African Methodism as a distinct and separate organization or organizations. Bethel African's denominational meeting was called in April, 1816, while Zion African came some four years later. Francis Asbury died in March, 1816.

It is necessary to understand several peculiar features of American Methodism which existed in the time period of this presentation. These, I feel, must be clear if the intent and purpose of this paper is to be known.

The influence of Christian controversy around the world where the institution of slavery was concerned had its bearing upon conversations and writings as well as the total missionary effort beyond Protestantism. In this connection it is my own belief that one of the most important debates of modern civilization was involved

3

here. In truth, this is a vast subject and in itself, merely can be mentioned.

As a new livelihood was being hewn out of the American wilderness, a new type of spiritual interpretation was developing. The fertile ground of personal and national independence both at home and abroad, broke down many initial objections and provided for questioning approaches. The criteria of John Wesley with the attendant re-examination of man's spiritual relationship and knowledge of God made such approaches necessary. In a sense, the American version of Wesley's Methodism may have been more stringent in application since the atmosphere in which it was placed was so different. This was true not only of the institution of slavery but of every problem American Methodism faced.

It could be reasoned that the founder of Methodism assumed a well-nigh impossible task as he endeavored to regulate and govern the American society by information gleaned through infrequent letters carried by slow sailing ships, and these letters oftentimes written by persons of limited discerning vision. Of course, John Wesley did have communication through the returning ministers visiting England or those ending permanently their own tour of duty. However, a far more adequate assessment could have been made through a personal visit, no doubt planned, but one which he was never privileged to make.

And, finally, there is the matter of expressionate titles. Most people of color were styled Africans or descendants of Africans. The title African was generally used, just as later in succession came *Colored, Afro-American,* and at the present time, *Black.* I presume none of these designations has ever really expressed adequatedly the subject. However, the designation *African* was used in all the colonies. It referred to black churches everywhere, so the title *African Methodist Episcopal* was not peculiar to any black Methodist society, North or South. Efforts at the elimination of the confusion eventually took place when the extension of the two major groups brought them in contact with each other. The New York group then added the name of their first society *Zion* to the corporate title and thereby became the African Methodist Episcopal Zion Church.

Perhaps it would be well to suggest one other guideline in this paper, the definition of *society.* Societies were formed many times with no thought of a permanent meeting place. In truth, if there is one idea which the Methodists brought to America it was the thought that buildings were not essential to Methodist organization. Later the matter of location became more important. It appears that societies met where they could.

On October 27, 1771, Francis Asbury and his traveling companion, Richard Wright, landed in Philadelphia. Asbury arrived with certain definite ideas in mind. There was no deviation from that which he understood to be the Wesleyan mode; but it appears that changes were to come. Perhaps it was the erasing of all preconceived notions, or the understanding that circumstances alter situations. At any rate Asbury saw many of his early goals changed greatly, and this is not to say that he was weak or vacillating.

In speaking of himself, Asbury wrote, "However, I am fixed to the Methodist plan, and do what I do faithfully as to God." [1] He continued: "I expect trouble is at hand. This I expected when I left England, and I am willing to suffer, yea, to die, sooner than betray so good a cause by any means. It will be a hard matter to stand against all opposition, as an iron pillar strong, and steadfast as a wall of brass: but through Christ strengthening me I can do all things." [2] Almost a year later he himself maintained that he was a strict interpreter of Wesley's rules, so he insisted that society meetings and love feasts should be limited to the membership and not open to the general public.

> While I stay, the rules must be attended to; and I cannot suffer myself to be guided by half-hearted Methodists. An elderly Friend told me very gravely, that "the opinion of the people was much changed, within a few days, about Methodism: and that the Quakers and other dissenters had laxed their discipline, . . ." but these things do not move me. [3]

Later he added: "My business is through the grace of God, to go straight forward, acting with honesty, prudence, and caution, and then leave the event to Him." [4]

G. G. Smith states, "Mr. Asbury was afraid of no man; he seems never to have known what fear was; but he was afraid of reckless daring, and of refusing to heed the direction of Providence. . . ." [5]

Francis Asbury was not easily moved from his fixed notions of principle or program, but ultimately some of his earlier convictions were put aside temporarily or even given up. The effect of his rigidity to Methodist rule and principle may be seen in a statement of Pilmore appearing May 17, 1772:

> After preaching hastened back to the city to preach in the evening. But O, what a change. When I was here before, the great Church would hardly hold the congregation; now it is not nearly full! Such is the fatal consequence of contending about *opinions* and the minute

---

[1] *The Journal of Francis Asbury*, ed. by Elmer T. Clark (Epworth Press, London and Abingdon Press, Nashville, 1958), 10.
[2] *Ibid.*
[3] *Ibid.*, 28.
[4] *Ibid.*, 39.
[5] George Gilman Smith, *Life and Labors of Francis Asbury* (Nashville, 1898), 54.

6   METHODIST HISTORY

[details] of discipline—It grieves me to the heart to see the people scattered that we have taken pains to gather. . . .*

However many of these people later returned.

I have gone into some detail with the hope that my evaluation of Francis Asbury may not be misunderstood. From these examples it may be noted that his experience influenced future actions along other lines. Asbury's convictions may not have been changed, but time schedules and ultimate results evidently did.

On January 1, 1772, Asbury noted that Pilmore and the local clergy were not much disturbed by the ideas that the ministers should become responsible for people in the outlying districts. He stated that they were unmoved by the Methodist plan.[7] Of course, I am not so sure that Asbury thought too highly of Pilmore. Of him he wrote, "My heart was enlarged towards God. I saw a letter from Mr. Pilmoor, filled with his usual softness. Poor man! he seems blind to his own conduct."[8] At one time Asbury declared, "I find that the preachers have their friends in the cities, and care not to leave them."[9] Pilmore wrote in his journal, "Mr. Asbury set off for the Country, and I resolved to lay myself out for the salvation of the Citizens."[10] He evidently meant townspeople.

In this venture of widening the responsibility area of the city ministry, Asbury finally succeeded where a partial defeat had to be acknowledged on the doctrine, rules and discipline matter. Asbury's travels had actually formed an "extensive circuit around" New York, Philadelphia and Baltimore. "Preaching places had been opened, homes for the preachers had been procured, and people of all classes had been prepared to come together under approved guidance, as stated congregations and Societies."[11] Above all else, Pilmore was now writing: "As we have now got preachers to take care of the people that God has graciously raised up by us in New York and Philadelphia and all the adjacent places, Mr. Boardman and I have agreed to go forth in the name of the Lord, and preach the Gospel in the waste places of the wilderness, and seek after those who have no shepherd."[12]

Briefly, I would like to touch upon some of the other areas of Francis Asbury's ideas for America. His plan of organization largely succeeded. One item failed of acceptance and that was the matter of the *Council*. The plan was originally endorsed by both Coke

* Frederick Maser and Howard Maag, *The Journal of Joseph Pilmore, Methodist Itinerant* (Philadelphia, 1969), 134.
[7] Frederick W. Briggs, *Bishop Asbury: A Biographical Study for Christian Workers* (2nd ed., London, 1879), 63.
[8] Asbury's *Journal, op. cit.,* I, 133.
[9] *Ibid.,* 16.
[10] Pilmore *Journal,* 118.
[11] Briggs, *op. cit.,* 65.
[12] Pilmore *Journal,* 129.

and Asbury, but later Bishop Coke changed his mind. Its purpose was: "(1) To preserve the general union ; (2) to render and preserve the external form of worship similar in all our Societies through the continent; . . . (4) to correct all abuses and disorders; . . . improving our colleges and plan of education." [13]

Briggs writes that "so intense was the Bishop's anxiety to keep the unity of the Spirit in the bond of peace that, to use again his own words, he wrote to O'Kelly to declare his willingness to take his seat in the Council as (any other) another member, and, on that point, at least, to waive the claims of Episcopacy; 'Yea,' said he, 'I would lie down and be trodden on rather than knowingly injure one soul'." [14] The Council in question was made up of bishops and presiding elders. To calm this controversy with O'Kelly and others, which involved the perogatives of the episcopacy, a General Conference was agreed to (Nov. 1, 1792), before which date Asbury announced his intention of remaining away so that the group could legislate unhampered and uninfluenced by his presence. He wrote:

> My Dear Brethren: Let my absence give you no pain—Dr. Coke presides. I am happily excused from assisting to make laws by which myself am to governed; I have only to obey and execute. [15]

Francis Asbury, too, was subjected to criticism behind his back. He probably never learned of all that transpired between Thomas Rankin and John Wesley, although the back lash of Rankin's unfriendliness did not go unnoticed. John Wesley had seen fit to reduce Asbury in rank and even urged his return to England. He wrote the following to Rankin on March 1, 1775:

> As soon as possible, you must come to a full and clear explanation both with brother Asbury (if he is recovered) and with Jemmy Dempster. But I advise Brother Asbury to return to England by the first opportunity. [16]

Wesley was more direct in the following letter, written to Rankin from London, August 13, 1775:

> I am not sorry that Brother Asbury stays with you another year. In that time it will be seen what God will do with North America, and you will easily judge whether our preachers are called to remain any longer therein. [17]

---

[13] Briggs, op. cit., 253.
[14] Ibid., 254.
[15] Asbury's Journal, III, 112.
[16] Briggs, op. cit., 102.
[17] Frederick C. Gill, Selected Letters of John Wesley (New York: Philosophical Library, 1956), 167.

Asbury made this entry in his journal September 23, 1774:

> I set off for New York, and met some of my good friends at
> Kingsbridge. They brought me a letter from Thomas Rankin, who
> thought himself injured; but I am determined to drop all disputes
> as far as possible.[18]

Probably as a result of this difference of opinion, Asbury began
entertaining the thought of going to Gibralter when a letter came
from a Miss Gilbert in which she requested him to come to Antigua.
He recorded:

> I received a letter from Miss Gilbert of Antigua; in which she
> informed me that Mr. Nathaniel Gilbert was going away; and as there
> are about three hundred members in the society, she entreats me to
> go and labor amongst them. And as Mr. Wesley has given his consent,
> I feel inclined to go, ...[19]

The editor of Asbury's *Journal* further elaborated on this work
in Antigua for it is explained that Nathaniel Gilbert was a half
brother of Sir Walter Raleigh. He and three of his servants had
been converted by Wesley in 1758 and began preaching to the Negroes of Antigua in 1760, thereby firmly establishing Methodism
in the West Indies. At the time of Gilbert's death, there were 300
members in the society, and a great many of these people were
probably Negroes. The fact that Asbury even considered transferring his missionary endeavors to a black area such as Antigua
is interesting. He gave up the thought of going to Antigua at that
time because of the controversy over the Sacraments which was
going on within the Methodist societies.[20]

It should be emphasized again that Asbury came to America convinced of the efficacy of the Wesleyan doctrines and methods, and
this conviction carried over into the matter of the Sacrament. The
question was put in a quarterly meeting (December 24, 1772):
"5. Will the people be contented without our administering the
sacrament?" [21] Asbury insisted that administering the Sacraments
was contrary to the Methodist plan, so he could not agree, but later
he softened his attitude. In the first regular conference in America
(Philadelphia, Wednesday, July 14, 1773), conducted for three
days evidently by Thomas Rankin, Rule One stated:

> Every preacher who acts in connection with Mr. Wesley and the
> brethren who labour in America, is strictly to avoid administering
> the ordinance of Baptism and the Lord's Supper.[22]

[18] Asbury's *Journal*, I, 132.
[19] *Ibid.*, 149.
[20] *Ibid.*
[21] *Ibid.*, I, 60.
[22] Briggs, *op. cit.*, 90.

It was supposed that this prohibition was aimed at the Maryland and Virginia people.

By 1778, the still unsettled question remained. In that year many of the ministers of the Church of England had left their parishes because of the American Revolution, and the conference in that year was made up of "native preachers" only. Asbury was at his retreat at Judge White's for safety reasons, since he was one of the very few who had refused to take the oath as required by many colonial legislatures. Out of deference to Asbury, the conference decided to "let the question stand over for a year longer." [23] The war itself had caused the calling of two conferences, one at Judge White's for the convenience of Asbury, the other at Fluvanna County, Virginia.

Perhaps the reason for no decided action was occasioned by the fear of a permanent rupture in the church, no doubt partially over this issue and partially over the slave question. Asbury wrote to several of the preachers in Virginia and North Carolina, "urging them, if possible, to prevent a separation among the preachers in the south." [24] The Conference at Fluvanna meanwhile decided that "henceforth the two Sacraments should be administered generally 'to those who are under our care and discipline'." [25]

Conferences were called for Baltimore and Manakintown in the spring of 1780, and Asbury was determined to attend both. When the Baltimore Conference met, a letter was received from Virginia regarding the matter of sacraments. It appears that the Northern wing concluded to renounce the intentions of the radicals. Asbury offered the following compromise: (1) That they (the Southern wing) should ordain no more; (2) that they should come no farther than Hanover circuit; (3) we would have our delegates in their conference; (4) that they should not presume to administer the ordinances where there is a decent Episcopal minister; (5) to have a union conference. According to the account in the Journal these compromises were not accepted, but it was agreed to suspend the ordinances for one year.[26] When the Baltimore Conference met in 1781, all but one of the forty preachers present agreed to give up the ordinances.[27]

If Asbury actually retreated from his original stand on the principles mentioned, it can be concluded that he did so for one simple reason—to preserve the unity of the American societies. At what point he began to shift his several positions it is impossible to say. Certainly by 1774 this trend is to be noted. By then he must have

[23] *Ibid.*, 132.
[24] Asbury's *Journal*, I, 300.
[25] Briggs, *op. cit.*, 133, 134.
[26] Asbury's *Journal*, I, 347, 349, 350.
[27] *Ibid.*, 402.

sensed the futility of full accomplishment. If this is true, he turned
abruptly to reason and compromise. There is a tinge of bitterness,
especially in the matter of the slave issue. In 1798, for example, he
wrote:

> My mind is much pained. O! to be dependent on slave holders is
> in part to be a slave, and I was free born. I am brought to conclude
> that slavery will exist in Virginia perhaps for ages; there is not a
> sufficient sense of religion nor of liberty to destroy it. . . . I judge
> in after ages it will be so that poor men and free men will not live
> among slaveholders, but will go to new lands; they only who are
> concerned in, and dependent on them will stay in old Virginia.[28]

When he first came to America and landed in Philadelphia, Asbury was confronted by a significant number of the Society who
were Africans or of African descent. Tarrying only briefly in that
city, he went on to New York. Philip Embury, the erstwhile local
preacher and school teacher, together with his assistant, Captain
Thomas Webb, had wrought well. In the first meeting of that little
group in Embury's house there was present "Betty," evidently
the slave or servant of Barbara Heck. At least two Africans made
contributions to the building of the first John Street structure.
Tradition credits Thomas Webb with the *saving* of Peter Williams
and his wife, Mollie, a black couple who joined the Society.

According to John Street Church records, no less than twenty-
five Africans belonged to the society in 1786. When the several
annual conferences of the newly organized Methodist Episcopal
Church in America reported in 1786, there were fifty-one areas
reporting. Of this number all but fifteen listed African members.
Ten of these fifteen churches were located in the North where it
was presumed no Africans lived.[29] Later, it was reported that there
were 1,890 Negroes in the Church. By 1794, Methodist statistics
showed 65,505 whites and 13,813 Africans in the membership.

From the outset of his American ministry Asbury preached to
congregations of blacks and whites meeting together and showed
deep concern for the spiritual life of the Negro. He wrote in his
Journal for November 17, 1771:

> . . . . and to see the poor Negroes so affected is pleasing, to see
> their sable countenances in our solemn assemblies, and to hear them
> sing with cheerful melody their dear Redeemer's praise, affected me
> much, and made me ready to say, "Of a truth I perceive God is no
> respecter of persons."[30]

---

[28] *Ibid.*, II, 151.
[29] Minutes of the Annual Conference of the M. E. Church, 1773-1813, 60, 61.
[30] Asbury's *Journal*, I, 9, 10.

On Thursday, August 12, 1773, he wrote:

> In public worship, at Mr. Gibbs's, a serious Negro was powerfully struck; and though he made but little noise, yet he trembled so exceedingly that the very house shook.[31]

Joint worship of blacks and whites continued indefinitely. Methodist societies were not large so that it was normal for both races to worship together. Asbury wrote for February 14, 1797:

> I met the stewards on the subject of the new house. We have adjourned on the question. If materials fall in their price, and if we can secure £400 shall we begin? . . . The Society has been rent in twain and yet we have wrought out of debt, and paid £100 for two new lots, and we can spare £100 from the stock, make a subscription of £150, and the Africans will collect £100.[32]

The significance of this account is that Africans were considered a part of the contributing family.

On June 23, 1776, Asbury wrote:

> After preaching at the Point, I met the class, and then met the black people, some of whose unhappy masters forbid their coming for religious instruction. How will the sons of oppression answer for their conduct, when the great Proprietor of all shall call them to account! [33]

Although some critics of Methodism have tried to show that in the beginning only a small minority within the Church held emancipation views, the writer contends that this was not accurate. Methodism had become a forerunner during the eighteenth century in the field of abolition of slavery. Francis Asbury upon his arrival espoused strong abolitionist views.

Lucius C. Matlack in his *History of American Slavery and Methodism* tells of a legislative act passed by the South Carolina legislature which authorized any individual to go to Methodist meetings to disperse Negroes who assembled with or without permission of their owners. This act was "based upon the fact that Methodism at that period, whether at the North or South, was identified with the most deadly opposition to slavery." [34]

Thomas Coke, who also held strong views toward emancipation of the slaves, indicated in his journal some of the dilemmas that Methodists faced in trying to live up to the Wesleyan vows.

---

[31] *Ibid.,* 89.
[32] *Ibid.,* II, 119.
[33] *Asbury's Journal,* I, 190.
[34] *Op. cit.,* 27.

Preached to a most polite congregation at New-Glasgow, and lodged at Colonel M———'s. They gave me great attention. Colonel M——— acknowledged the force of my arguments concerning slavery, but, I saw, did not choose to take any active part, for fear of losing his popularity.[35]

Three days later he wrote:

Preached to a quiet congregation at brother Key's. He told me, as we rode together, that he was determined to emancipate his slaves, about twenty; though his miserable father, I suppose, will never give him any further assistance if he does. . . . I pushed on in the evening, with the intention of reaching his father's; but at nine o'clock at night was glad to take up my lodgings at a tavern, as I had a dangerous river to cross before I could get to Mr. Key's. Nor am I sorry that I did not go thither; for, when I called the next morning, I found that he had shut his door against the preachers, because he has eighty slaves. . . .[36]

And on another occasion:

I had now a very little persecution. The testimony I bore against slave-holding provoked many to retire out of the barn, and to combine to flog me, as they expressed it, as soon as I came out. A high-headed lady also went out, and told the rioters that she would give fifty pounds if they would give that little Doctor one hundred lashes. When I came out, they surrounded me, but had only power to talk.[37]

There were good results from Coke's stand as may be seen from the following notation in his journal:

Our Brother Martin has done gloriously; for he has fully and immediately emancipated fifteen slaves.[38]

In the minutes of that year, the following question and answer appeared:

Ques. Does this conference acknowledge that slavery is contrary to the laws of God, man, and nature, and hurtful to society, contrary to the dictates of conscience and religion, and doing that which we would not others should do to us and ours?—Do we pass our disapprobation on all our friends who keep slaves and advise their freedom?

Ans. Yes.[39]

---
[35] J. W. Etheridge, The Life of the Rev. Thomas Coke (London, 1860), 146, 147.
[36] Ibid.
[37] Ibid.
[38] Ibid., 148.
[39] Minutes of the Methodist Conferences, 1773-1813, 25, 26.

Three years later the slavery question and answer was revised in the conference minutes:

> Ques. What shall be done with our local Preachers who hold slaves contrary to the laws which authorize their freedom in any of the United States?

> Ans. We will try them another year. In the meantime let every Assistant deal faithfully and plainly with everyone, and report to the next conference. It may then be necessary to suspend them.[40]

Just how effective this move was is not known, but the conference felt compelled to say in 1784:

> Ques. What shall we do with our local Preachers who will not emancipate their slaves in the states where the laws admit it? [41]

It appears from this statement that there were Methodists, not too poor to hold slaves, who were resisting the movement towards emancipation. The following answer did take into consideration the fact that slaveholding existed in certain areas:

> Ans. Try those in Virginia another year, and suspend the preachers in Maryland, Delaware, Pennsylvania, and New-Jersey.[42]

Just a few months prior to the formation of the Methodist Episcopal Church, the conference of 1784 took this additional action on the slavery question:

> Ques. What shall be done with our travelling Preachers that now are or hereafter shall be possessed of slaves, and refuse to manumit them where the law permits?

> Ans. Employ them no more.[43]

With the institution of the Methodist Episcopal Church in late 1784, the Discipline recorded on slavery in general:

> Ques. What Methods can we take to extirpate Slavery?

> Ans. We are deeply conscious of the Impropriety of making new Terms of Communion for a religious Society already established, excepting on the most pressing Occasion; and such we esteem the Practice of holding our Fellow-Creatures in Slavery. We view it as contrary to the Golden Law of God on which hang all the Law

---

[40] *Ibid.,* 41.
[41] *Ibid.,* 47.
[42] *Ibid.,* 47.
[43] *Ibid.,* 48.

and the Prophets, and [to] the inalienable Rights of Mankind, as well-as every Principle of the Revolution, to hold in the deepest Debasement, in a more abject Slavery than is perhaps to be found in any part of the World except America, so many Souls that are all capable of the Image of God."

Whereupon it was enacted by the Christmas Conference that:

1. Every member emancipate his slaves between the ages of forty and forty-five within twelve months; and every other slave in a corresponding graduation of time.
2. A register of such manumissions shall be kept in each circuit.
3. Those refusing to obey the rules to be excluded from the church.
4. No person henceforth to be admissible who is unwilling to comply with the condition. Buyers and sellers of slaves to be expelled."

The Virginia Conference of May 7, 1783 met in Ellis' Preaching House, Sussex County. DuBose records the following appraisal:

The question of African slavery, often referred to by Asbury and more than once brought before the Conference, came up in a more pronounced form than it had hitherto assumed. The recently published peace and the settled nationality of the Colonies gave to the subject a new significance."

Francis Asbury wrote, "We all agreed in the spirit of African liberty, and strong testimonies were borne in its favour in our love feast ..." [47]
There is no denial that the Methodist stand on slavery was at first accepted by the majority of its membership and that later this stand ran into increasing opposition. Asbury could not have overlooked this trend. His activities in Maryland and southward brought him into close contact with this growing sentiment and he certainly knew that much of the Methodist strength lay in these areas. He was aware of Coke's experiences and he was clearly concerned with the results. Etheridge, for example, states: "But it is to be lamented that the Methodists of the Southern States have not permitted the action of these (anti-slavery) principles among them...." [48]
Speaking of Coke, Etheridge wrote:

---

[44] *Minutes of Several Conversations between the Rev. Thomas Coke and the Rev. Francis Asbury and others, at a Conference ... 1784. Composing a Form of Discipline* (Philadelphia, 1785), 14.
[45] See *Ibid.,* 14, 15 for complete statements.
[46] Horace M. DuBose, *Francis Asbury, A Biographical Study* (Nashville, 1916), 110.
[47] Asbury's *Journal,* I, 441.
[48] Etheridge, op. cit., 145.

It required then some amount of moral and physical courage to stand forth as the public opponent of this gigantic oppression; not on the carpets of drawing-rooms, or the floor of the House of Commons in London, but in the presence of the evil itself. . . ."[49]

One has to conclude that Bishop Coke was a determined man where the subject of slavery was concerned. He himself states:

Friday, May 13 (1785). Preached at Bent chapel belonging to the Church of England. At night lodged at the house of Captain Dillard, a most hospitable man, and as kind to his Negroes as if they were white servants. . . . And yet I could not beat into the head of that poor man the evil of keeping them in slavery, though he has read Mr. Wesley's "Thoughts on Slavery" three times over. But his good wife is strongly on our side.

Sunday, 15th. Preached in a handsome church. A very large congregation. But when I enlarged to the Society on Negro slavery, the principal leader raged like a lion, and desired to withdraw from the Society. I took him at his word, and appointed that excellent man, Brother Skelton, leader in his stead. When the Society came out of the church, they surrounded Skelton. "And will you," said they, "set your slaves at liberty?" "Yes," says he, "I believe that I shall." [50]

By 1785 it was *Resolved: to suspend the execution of the rule* (of 1783) *for the present.* This followed the 1783 action when the Methodists were saying it was their "most bounden duty to take immediately some effectual method to exterminate this abomination." In 1784, all legislation on the subject failed of acceptance, and the best the anti-slavery group could do was to persuade the conference to declare that it still held slavery in the deepest abhorrence and would not cease to seek its destruction by all wise and prudent means.[51]

In 1796 the *Discipline* of the Church was saying much milder things about slavery:

1. . . . And we do fully authorize all the yearly conferences to make whatever regulations they judge proper in the present case, respecting the admission of persons to official stations in our church.
2. No slave-holder shall be received into society till the preacher who has the oversight of the circuit has spoken to him freely and faithfully on the subject of slavery.[52]

By 1800, traveling preachers who became the owners of slaves by any means were to *forfeit their ministerial character,* and by

---

[49] *Ibid.*, 146.
[50] *Ibid.*, 146.
[51] Briggs, *op. cit.*, 295, 296.
[52] *Discipline*, 1796.

1816, slave holders were being barred from its order of elders. However, in 1800, when the General Conference had acted on the question, it found that it had aroused great hostility from the Methodists in South Carolina. Smith states:

> Asbury indorsed the utterance fully, but felt the embarrassment under which it placed him and his brethren. He advised that by increasing effort and faithful preaching they should live down the prejudice against them.[53]

How deeply Asbury felt the currents of this controversy may be noted in his entry in his journal:

> The rich among the people never thought us worthy to preach to them: they did indeed give their slaves liberty to hear and join our church; but now it appears the poor Africans will no longer have this indulgence.[54]

One known writer stated that the Methodist Bishop "often doubted the wisdom of a course which produced such a result."

On the whole, this change in attitude was slow in making itself evident. However, the Bishop must have foreseen its ultimate arrival. He was turning repeatedly to the task of ministering to these people. He wrote:

> Poor Africans brought their blessings and wishes and prayers. Dear souls, may the Lord provide them pastors after His own heart.[55]

The first general retreat of Asbury on the slave question appears to have occurred in the concluding years of the eighteenth century. A discerning student can clearly note the presence of a new decision on Asbury's part around this time. The occasion may have been brought about by many contributing forces. American Methodism was in itself changing from the society concept to permanent and stabilized organization. Along with this it faced an intensified struggle where the issue was concerned, particularly south of Maryland. In its overall membership it was taking on an interracial hue, a situation not conducive to rapid growth. The procuring of church buildings may have contributed as well. We should hasten to state that the Church's evangelistic and missionary zeal among Negroes appears not to have lessened. The resolution appearing in connection with the conference meeting two years after the crucial conversations with George Washington is a case in point and one which we will mention later.

---

[53] Smith, op. cit., 198.
[54] Asbury's Journal, II, 281.
[55] Ibid., 79.

One cannot deny that the Methodist system was more easily geared to slave unrest than that of any other denomination as membership carried contacts outside that which I would call the "contained community," so local and traveling ministers had access to a wider forum on vital subjects than those of the strictly *ordinance* churches. Slave holders evidently saw this and reacted unfavorably. What to do with early Methodist concepts was not easily answered.

It was at this juncture that the germ of the strictly African Society could have appeared. Asbury, for example, wrote in April, 1795::

> I had some talk with a few blacks, and was comfortable and happy. We lose much by not meeting these people alone . . . I met the poor blacks by themselves, and was greatly blessed.[56]

About a week earlier Asbury reported, "I spent an hour with the blacks in their quarters, and it was well received by them." [57] Still another entry declares:

> I was happy last evening with the poor slaves in Brother Wells's kitchen, whilst our white brother held a sacramental love feast in the front parlour upstairs.[58]

The Bishop's interest in the slaves and freed people naturally had its result. On one occasion he wrote:

> . . . a poor black, sixty years of age, who supports herself by picking oakum, and the charity of her friends, brought me a French crown and said she had been distressed on my account, and I must have her money.[59]

Asbury refused the money even though he records that he had only three dollars in his pocket and some 2,000 miles travel before him.

Methodist preachers in many instances were still wrestling with the subject even as their bishop was seeking new thrusts to deal with the matter. One can find grounds for believing that he was actually trying to settle a great question in his own mind—is it not more important to free a man's soul when the efforts to bring liberty to his body are being thwarted? At this point, however, Asbury was unwilling to concede total defeat where physical freedom was concerned. Attending the Virginia Conference, Tuesday, November 25, 1794, he wrote:

---

[56] *Ibid.,* 46, 47.
[57] *Ibid.*
[58] *Ibid.,* 77.
[59] Briggs, *op. cit.,* 297.

> We . . . had great siftings and searchings especially on the subject of slavery. The preachers, almost unanimously, entered into an agreement and resolution not to hold slaves in any State where the law will allow them to manumit them, on pain of forfeiture of their honour and their place in the itinerant connexion; and in any State where the law will not admit of manumission, they agree to pay them the worth of their labour, and when they die to leave them to some person or persons, or society, in trust, to bring about their liberty.[60]

One of the historic occasions of American Methodism was the meeting of Coke and Asbury with George Washington at Mt. Vernon, Virginia. It is presumed that the following is actually the background of this meeting:

> The question of slavery was uppermost with Methodists at this time, the occasion being a petition which the conference was to send to the Virginia State Assembly, asking for the immediate or gradual emancipation of the slaves. It was agreed at the Virginia session that Coke and Asbury should visit General Washington and solicit his aid in presenting this document. On May 26 [1785] they were courteously received and dined at Mount Vernon. Washington readily gave them his opinion on slavery, which was deprecatory; but he declined to sign the petition. This appears to have been the end of the scheme . . .[61]

One week later the Baltimore Conference temporarily "suspended the minute on slavery." It is supposed that the temperate judgment of Washington on this question, expressed at this crucial hour, proved of immense advantage to Methodism. Profiting by his views which were practically those of the Methodists of the South, the church retreated from its adamant position. DuBose continues to say that so long as slavery continued to be an institution, the church entered upon an era of soberer legislation than had been in contemplation and thus was left unhampered in its ministry to both master and slave.[62]

Two years after the historic meeting with Washington, conferences meeting in Salisbury, North Carolina; Petersburg, Virginia, and Abingdon, Maryland, made no reference to slavery, but did urge "spiritual care of colored people." [63]

> Question 17: What directions shall we give for the promotion of the spiritual welfare of the coloured people?

---

[60] Asbury's *Journal*, II, 33.
[61] DuBose, *op. cit.*, 134.
[62] *Ibid.*, 134, 135.
[63] W. D. Weatherford, *American Churches and the Negro* (Boston: Christopher, 1957), 87.

Answer: We conjure all our Ministers and Preachers, by the love of God, and the salvation of souls, and do require them, by all the authority that is invested in us, to leave nothing undone for the spiritual benefit and salvation of them, within their respective circuits or districts; and for this purpose to embrace every opportunity of inquiring into the state of their souls, and to unite in society those who appear to have a real desire of fleeing from the wrath to come, to meet such in class, and to exercise the whole Methodist discipline among them.[64]

I would call attention to the phrase *to unite in society*. This and the several references to meeting with blacks appear to set a pattern for the development of black classes and societies.

As one reviews the life of Bishop Asbury, the question poses itself as to the influence of these changes in his views and his ability to keep going at an incredible rate. From his first recorded opinion on the eradication of slavery to 1813, the Bishop was slowly moving to a position of reluctant acceptance of the slavery evil. Bishop Robert Paine states that "two subjects gave trouble" in the Tennessee Conference, which was in session October 1, 1813—slavery and the war. He asserts that the conference was *stringent* in its application of the rules against the buying and selling of slaves. He declares that several local preachers had been arrested and tried, but in most cases the respective quarterly conferences had suspended the individuals. An appeal was made, therefore, to the annual conference where the case was considered. The defense declared that a great deal of harm was being done by the rule against slavery because of this intermeddling with legal and private rights, and it was the concensus of opinion of some "that they could not or would not conform to their views of the rule." Bishop Asbury sat in the session saying nothing until Bishop McKendree reminded him that "he ought to keep the rule or change it." The rule was upheld.[65]

One of the great decisions Asbury made concerned the use of black preachers. In a letter to his parents, January 24, 1773, he wrote:

Poor Negroes have been deeply affected with the power of God. We have got one that will be fit to send to England soon, to preach. Here are Negroes who have astonished master of families, understanding men, when they have heard them pray; and if they were in England, they would shame their thousands.[66]

We do not know who this black preacher was. The earliest record

---

[64] *Minutes of the Annual Conferences, 1773-1828,* 67, 68.
[65] Robert Paine, *The Life and Times of William McKendree* (Nashville, 1874).
[66] Asbury's *Journal,* III, 15.

on "Black Harry," Asbury's faithful companion, is Asbury's own reference in 1780.

> I have thought if I had two horses, and Harry (a coloured man) to go with, and drive one, and meet the black people, and to spend about six months in Virginia and the Carolinas, it would be attended with a blessing.[67]

This occurred twelve years before *Bethel* Society was organized in Philadelphia and sixteen years before the official date of *Zion* in New York. On Monday, May 21, 1781, Asbury wrote:

> I preached in the afternoon at P. Hite's, and had liberty in urging purity of heart. Harry Hosier (Black Harry) spoke to the Negroes, some of whom came a great distance to hear him; certain sectarians are greatly displeased with him, because he tells them they may fall from grace, and that they must be holy.[68]

In his autobiography, Richard Allen records that he was licensed to preach in 1782, after having been converted by Freeborn Garrettson. He was ordained a deacon on June 11, 1799, the first African to receive ordination from the Methodist Episcopal Church. He had begun his traveling ministry as early as 1783 and according to his words was present at the famous Christmas Conference of 1784, along with Harry Hosier.

In 1785, while a traveling companion of Richard Whatcoat, Allen was requested to meet Bishop Asbury at Henry Gough's, where the Bishop made the suggestion that Allen become his own traveling companion. Allen wrote that the bishop told him that

> . . . in slave countries, Carolina and other places, I must not intermix with the slaves, and I would frequently have to sleep in his carriage, and he would allow me vituals and clothes. I told him I would not travel with him on these conditions. He asked me my reason. I told him if I was taken sick, who was to support me? and that I thought people ought to lay up something while they were able, to support themselves in time of sickness or old age. He said that was as much as he got, his vituals and his clothes. I told him he would be taken care of, let his afflictions be as they were, or let him be taken sick where he would, he would be taken care of; but I doubted whether it would be the case with myself. He smiled, and told me he would give me from then until he returned from the eastward to make up my mind, which would be about three months. But I made up my mind that I would not accept his proposals.[69]

According to the accounts, the Bishop was accompanied through

———————
[67] *Ibid.*, I, 362.
[68] *Ibid.*, I, 403.
[69] Richard Allen, *The Life Experience and Gospel Labors of* (Abingdon), 22, 23.

New Jersey and into New York by "Black Harry" Hosier, whose preaching was commented upon in the *New York Packet* on September 11, 1786, one of the first references to Methodist preaching in any New York paper. An added statement says that John Street Church paid two pounds for Harry's traveling expenses.[70]

Another account states that

> This man whose name was Harry Hosier had now been doing valuable service for about ten years. Asbury first took him as early as 1782 when travelling in the South, to preach to the coloured people, and he afterwards attended Dr. Coke in one or two of his excursions occasionally preaching to white as well as coloured congregations. Though very illiterate, he was popular in New England as he had been elsewhere, and contributed to rouse among staid and stately inhabitants of those States an unwonted interest in the Methodist movement. "The different denominations," said Mr. Garrettson, "heard him with much admiration; and the Quakers thought, as he was unlearned, he must speak by immediate inspiration." But though they heard the eloquent African Methodist with interest and "much applause" they made no attempt to disguise their strong antipathy to Methodist doctrine.[71]

Harry Hosier was a traveling companion to many of the leaders of early Methodism, including Francis Asbury, Thomas Coke, Freeborn Garrettson, and Richard Whatcoat. In 1790, he was traveling with Garrettson as far as Nova Scotia. It is noted that on at least one occasion he preached to more than 1,000 persons.[72] At another time Thomas Coke stated that, "He (Asbury) has given me his black (Harry, by name) and borrowed an excellent horse for me." [73] Coke continued to relate an incident involving "Black Harry."

> I had this morning a great escape in crossing a broad ferry. After setting off, Harry persuaded me to turn back and leave our horses behind us, to be sent after me the next day, on account of the violence of the wind. I have hardly a doubt but that we should have drowned if we had not taken that step. We were in great danger as it was.[74]

It is said that Hosier got the "big head" because of his successes and was relegated to work in New Jersey. Later he became a drunkard, but was reclaimed. He died in Philadelphia in 1810 and was buried in Kensington.[75]

---

[70] John Street Church Records, Book I.
[71] Briggs, op. cit., 234, 235.
[72] Asbury's *Journal*, I, 681, 682.
[73] Etheridge, op. cit., 111.
[74] *Ibid.*, 112.
[75] Asbury's *Journal*, I, 413n.

Saturday, Oct. 27, 1781: My soul is drawn out to God to know whether I ought to go to Virginia this winter in order, if possible, to prevent the spreading of the fire of division: I do not look for impulses or revelations—the voice of my brethren and concurrent circumstances will determine me in this matter. Harry seems to be unwilling to go with me: I fear his speaking so much to white people in the city has been, or will be, injurious; he has been flattered and may be ruined.[76]

However, Harry did go with him. As early as 1781, Asbury was convinced of a ministry to blacks, using, if possible, black preachers.

Slavery and cruelty still disturbed the Bishop to the extent that on one occasion he recorded for June 8, 1783:

I went to John Worthington's; but I beheld such cruelty to a Negro that I could not feel free to stay; I called for my horse, delivered my own soul, and departed.[77]

With the use of black preachers by the church, evidently the second step in the plan of Asbury was accomplished. However, we also find Asbury turning away from his goal of emancipation. He wearily wrote on February 5, 1809:

Would not an *amelioration* in the condition and treatment of the slaves have produced more practical good to the poor Africans, than any attempt at their emancipation?[78]

Three years earlier, according to Smith, the Conference had desired that he should assist in forming a charter on slavery to suit Northern and Southern sections. "Asbury knew the absurdity of the proposition, and decided to have no part in it. A committee attempted it, and egregiously failed."[79] This is the first evidence of Asbury's silence on a slavery matter.

According to the same writer, by 1806, Asbury

... had long since ceased to antagonize slaveholding as much as he disliked it, and realizing the fact that it might be an evil for which the proposed remedy of immediate emancipation was no cure, he contented himself with preaching the gospel to master and slave. The idea that Dr. Coke has so pressed—the sinfulness of slaveholding under all circumstances—he never entertained; as he grew older, and realized more and more the difficulties in the way of emancipation, he was still less disposed to speak positively as to what should be done. Gough, Rembert, Grant, Tait, and many others of his most valued friends, were large slave owners. In their homes he rested, and in their

[76] *Ibid.*
[77] *Ibid.,* 442.
[78] *Ibid.,* II, 591.
[79] Smith, *op. cit.,* 220.

piety he had perfect confidence, but he never became reconciled to slavery, and had it been in his power he would have ended it speedily.[80]

I suggest that Asbury saw the hopelessness of the struggle and determined that it was best to settle for the slaves' soul rather than lose everything. No doubt he reasoned that the worst kind of bondage was that of sin. Physical labor was desirable, but in lieu of this, the soul's salvation should claim his attention. To pursue this new course, he encouraged the societies to include Negroes to permit spiritual training, and finally he encouraged the establishment of black societies.

The Conference itself seemed to have recognized this shift to separate worship and organization when in 1780 it raised the question:

Question: Ought not the Assistant [Mr. Asbury] to meet the coloured people himself, and appoint as helpers in his absence proper white persons and not suffer them to stay so late and meet by themselves?

Answer: Yes.[81]

Briggs indicated that as early as 1795, Asbury was using "every opportunity available to him, of ministering to coloured congregations." [82] Asbury in his journal, May 30, 1795, while in Maryland, wrote: "I met the Africans, to consult about building a house, and forming a distinct African, yet Methodist Church." [83] Two years later, June 25, 1797, while in Baltimore, he pursued his intent of organizing the Africans:

I obtained the liberty of the managers of the African academy [school for black children] to congregate the fathers as well as to teach the children. We had nearly five hundred coloured people . . . I am trying to organize the African church.[84]

Around this same time the Africans who were worshipping in St. George's Church, Philadelphia, and who had helped in the purchase of that church building, were refused admittance to seats on the main floor and relegated to the balcony. In addition they were not allowed to receive the communion sacrament until after

[80] Smith, op. cit., 237.
[81] Minutes of the Annual Conferences, 1773-1813, 26.
[82] Briggs, op. cit., 297.
[83] Asbury's Journal, II, 51.
[84] Ibid., II, 128, 129. Because of white opposition, the academy was changed to a church.

the whites had been served. This brought about dissension.[85]

After an incident at St. George's in which Absalom Jones was involved, the Africans in Philadelphia withdrew and began holding prayer meetings and meetings of "exhortation." The group had the sympathy of a good many citizens, among them Dr. Benjamin Rush and a Mr. Ralston, who became treasurer of a special fund the Africans raised through a "subscription paper." The elder in Philadelphia, who appeared to be John McClaskey, objected both to the organization and to the collection of funds. He ordered the names to be erased and the subscription paper turned over. Unless this were done, the group would be read out of the Methodist society. They persisted, whereupon McClaskey called for them to meet with him, at which time he wished them well. He declared that he was their friend and was only trying to prove that they were wrong in building a separate building.[86]

The Africans appointed a committee to purchase a church lot. After the purchase had been made, the committee found what seemed to be a more suitable lot. They wished to abrogate their former agreement. Richard Allen kept the original lot for himself, while the committee took possession of the second one and built a church. At this point, without any encouragement from the Methodist elder, who had nothing to do with them even though he was still expected to preach to them, the Society met to determine their denominational affiliation. Jones and Allen alone voted to remain with Methodism. The majority approved joining the Church of England, later known as the Protestant Episcopal Church.[87]

Richard Allen remained a Methodist, but he protested that too frequently the elders in Philadelphia acted "without discipline." In instances members were turned out of the Society without the benefit of trial. He conceded that the Methodists "were the first people who brought glad tidings to the colored people," so they should receive the Africans' loyalty.[88]

In 1793, the African Protestant Episcopal Church sent a committee to Allen inviting him to become their minister. At the time there was no other colored minister in Philadelphia, but he rejected the offer. He still held title to the lot at Sixth and Lombard Streets, so he bought a blacksmith shop and moved it to the location. On June 29, 1794, Bishop Asbury opened the African Church, called Bethel.

[85] Although Francis Asbury was not closely related to the St. George Church problem, it is essential that we relate this dispute from which ultimately Bethel African, the mother society of the African Methodist Episcopal Church, was formed. Asbury was evidently not consulted in the formation of this congregation, but he did give his blessing as will be indicated in the developing story.
[86] Allen, op. cit., 26.
[87] Ibid., 29.
[88] Ibid., 30.

"I preached at the new African Church. Our coloured brethren are to be governed by the doctrine and discipline of the Methodists." [89] Only Negroes were to be admitted to membership.

Relations between St. George's and the Bethel African societies were strained from time to time, but Asbury continued to visit this congregation with apparent regularity:

Oct. 11, 1795: I preached in the morning at the African Church . . .

June 8, 1800: I preached at the African Church . . .

March 19, 1808: I preached at St. George's twice, at the Academy, at Ebenezer, and at Bethel, African. [90]

Samuel Royal was appointed to Philadelphia and demanded the repeal of the "Supplement" which was not agreed to. [91] Subsequently Richard Allen evidently was requested to minister to Bethel African. While the sequel of events is not clear, it is reasonable to suppose that the action of the elder may have produced the following paper:

The Memorial of the Trustees of the African Methodist Episcopal Church called Bethel, to the Philadelphia Conference of the Methodist Episcopal Church, ministers assembled.

Greeting.

To prevent any misconstruction and to guard against a wrong understanding of our motions and designs in the late strife we have taken in procuring a Supplement to our act of incorporation.

We judge it prudent to declare to you in your official capacity in the most explicit manner as follows Viz.

1. We have no purpose or intention whatever of separating ourselves from or making ourselves independent of the Methodist Conference and the Disciplines of the Methodist Episcopal Church.

2. Our only design is to secure to our selves our rights and privileges, to regulate our affairs, temporal and spiritual, the same as if we were white people, and to guard against any opposition which might possibly arise from the improper prejudice or administration of any individual having the exercise of discipline over us.

3. We wish and expect that the minister having the charge over us should preach and exercise discipline among us as formerly they have been accustomed to do, in conformity to the Discipline

---

[89] Asbury's *Journal*, II, 18.
[90] *Ibid.*, II, 64, 235, 567.
[91] The Supplement was a protective document to place full property and congregational control in the hands of the African Society. See Allen, op. cit., 31-33.

and the act and supplement of our incorporation, and it is our purpose to contribute toward the support of the ministers.

4. We do advise you of our cordial attachment to the Methodist Connection and of our full and entire purpose to continue Methodists in the future as heretofore.

Signed in behalf of the Board of Trustees
Philadelphia, April 8, 1807

Richard Allen, Pastor[92]

The Philadelphia Conference answered this communication the following day, April 9, 1807:

To the Trustees of the African Methodist Episcopal Church:

Your memorial of the 8th instant was laid before the Philadelphia Conference and provided the supplement to your act of Incorporation which you allude to, be not contrary to the allowed usages, customs, and privileges of the Methodist Episcopal Church according to the established principles and government of the said church, admitted of in case of incorporation among our white brethren for the protection and security of their rights and privileges, the Conference accepts your memorial and entertains a confidence that our African brethren will evince their unshaken stability and firmness as Methodists according to our Discipline from time to time. And we cordially wish you prosperity, unity, holiness and happiness.

Signed in behalf of the Philadelphia Conference.

Francis Asbury[93]

As we have stated before the title *African Methodist* was given to all these racial churches. The work of Asbury, Garrettson and Harry Hosier bore fruit in New England, New York and New Jersey as well. The same motivating spirit of opposition to slavery was a special invitation to Africans everywhere. Speaking of the New York group, Joseph Pilmore in his *Journal* writes the following for January 27, 1771:

After preaching, I met the Negroes apart, and found many of them very happy. God has wrought a most glorious work on many of their souls, and made them witnesses that he is no respecter of persons.[94]

While it is an assumption to state that the establishment of the African Zion Chapel was a less difficult undertaking in New York than that of Bethel African in Philadelphia, the course of events appears to substantiate this. The difference may have existed for

---

[92] Asbury's *Journal*, III, 367.
[93] Asbury's *Journal*, III, 367.
[94] Pilmore's *Journal*, 74.

several reasons. The twenty-five years (1771-1796) of intermittent meetings may have contributed to this relationship. John Street Church had an integrated membership from its beginning. That membership had known depression and oppression. The action of the Board of Trustees of the church in purchasing the freedom of Peter Williams early demonstrated the Methodist tradition of opposition to slavery. Perhaps it should be said that African Zion had a unique relationship between the groups which appears not to have been available to the Africans in Philadelphia. Peter Williams and Mollie (Mary) took care of the elder and the visiting ministers of John Street Church and, at times, entertained these ministers' guests. So the growth from class to society was not only smooth but logical.

Little is actually known of the beginning of African Zion. The periodic flight of the owner class to estates up the Hudson River appears to have given rise to prayer and praise services both on these estates and in New York and well could have formed a background for the establishment of the society.[95]

Christopher Rush stated that a small group decided to approach all who might be interested in the venture of an African society and "for this purpose they called a meeting of some of the most respectable and intelligent religious colored men of the city in order to consult upon the best method to proceed in this great undertaking for colored people of the city of New York." [96]

Conversations with Bishop Asbury concerning the permanent establishment of the African Chapel in New York may have taken place as early as August 1796. According to his *Journal*, Asbury was in New York in September as well. An early church writer states that one such meeting occurred in that year. At this meeting with the Bishop the following Africans represented the proposed chapel: Francis Jacobs, William Brown, Peter Williams, Abraham Thompson, June Scott, Samuel Portier, Thomas Miller, James Varick, and William Hamilton.[97] There evidently were others present, but Rush could not recall them.

The African class appeared to have had little difficulty in securing approval to meet as a society. Rush states that they were to meet "in the interval of the services at John Street" and were then "to conduct their services in the best manner they could." According to early writers only three local African preachers—Abraham

---

[95] In times of epidemic the white owner class would flee to their estates along the Hudson River, taking a portion of their servants. The help that remained looked after the property, the ill, the dead, as well as the continuation of the class.

[96] Christopher Rush, *A Short Account of the Rise and Progress of the African Methodist Church in America* (New York, 1843), 10.

[97] *Ibid.*

Thompson, June Scott, and Thomas Miller—and one exhorter, William Miller, were residents of the New York area.

Two significant matters should claim our attention in the establishment of Zion Africans: the activity of its laymen (this has carried through the entire history of the denomination) and the relationship with John Street Church.

In a matter of three years the society had so grown that the suggestion of a church building was made. No opposition to this plan from the membership of John Street Church appeared to have arisen. This seems strange in view of the interchange in the appointment of elders to St. George's and John Street Churches. John McClaskey, who appeared so opposed to Bethel African in Philadelphia, was appointed by the General Conference to work out an agreement with Zion African in New York. The approved agreement gave to the Zion African trustees a congregational authority which many of the Methodist Episcopal chapels of the city desired for themselves, a matter which led to the Stillwell Secession. This agreement was mutually desired in order to keep the two societies in union with each other.

Two years before the agreement with the Methodist Episcopal Church, the board of trustees of Zion African had moved to secure a more permanent place of worship. The old cabinet maker's shop which had been used for society meetings had been outgrown. The board authorized Thomas Miller to secure a plot of ground. Following their direction and utilizing money raised for the project, a deed for the land was drawn in Miller's name. The ruling elder advised the trustees against securing this property, so deeded. They then proceeded to purchase land at Church and Leonard Streets and build thereon.

In a letter from Charleston, South Carolina, February 11, 1797, Bishop Asbury wrote to George Roberts, the elder in New York at the time: ". . . I am pleased to hear that the house is about [completed] at the 2 mile stone [one of the churches in the New York area]; more so to hear that the Africans are about building one; help them all you can. . . ." [98]

The Bishop again referred to Zion African Society when he arrived in New York City and wrote in his *Journal*, May 25, 1802: "My first public appearance in the city was in the African church, . . . a very neat wooden house, but by far too small: my text was Ephes. ii, 11-14." [99] Encouraged and advised by McClaskey, the group proceeded to raise funds for their additional new building and purchased more land.

McClaskey was succeeded by John Wilson, who went ahead

---

[98] Asbury's *Journal*, III, 160.
[99] Asbury's *Journal*, II, 341.

according to Rush "with the progressive program of the group." The elder was a very busy man, but his schedule called for his preaching in Zion African Church every Sunday afternoon and on every Wednesday night, except, as Rush puts it, "on the days of the administration of the Lord's Supper, then his appointment was on Sunday morning, and was agreed upon to be the second Sunday of every month, because the first Sunday of the month was the time for the administering the Sacrament in his own church." [100]

Jesse Lee in 1801 offered additional comment concerning the Zion African Church:

> The churches of New York consisted of John Street, old church, Bowery, North River, Two Mile Stone and the African Church, erected by people of colour for themselves to worship in; yet they are to be governed by the Methodists in all their spiritual matters but they, themselves are to settle their temporal affairs. [101]

At the time of this notation there were said to be 645 white members of the Methodist Episcopal Church in the area and 131 colored.

For some years Zion African continued to be the only black society in New York. In 1813 a second African Chapel was founded and took the name "Asbury." Phineas Cook, then the ruling elder, and Thomas Ware met with the Zion African trustees, who, after a long discussion, agreed to the continued existence of the new chapel. This chapel and Zion African became a separate charge in the New York Conference in 1818, when William Stillwell was assigned as pastor. [102] On his last journey to New York City, June 20, 1815, Asbury referred to a visit to the African Chapel (Zion). "I spoke a few words at the African Chapel, both colours being present." [103] Even in his last year he did not forget his friends of the African societies.

As one examines the extant records of these two branches of Methodism, one is struck by the relationships of these churches to the mother organization. While at present there are no known documents to undergird the belief, all indications point to a definite right-about-face in these intra-church approaches. Could it be said that the principle of compromise prevailed where Zion African was concerned? If this is true one can perhaps see the hand of the great bishop of American Methodism, Francis Asbury. This contribution to the church may have been his final supreme gift to American Christianity—the birth of African Methodism in the new world, which gave rise to the African Methodist Episcopal, African Methodist Episcopal Zion, and those African churches that remained with the Methodist Episcopal Church.

---

[100] Rush, op. cit.
[101] *Memoirs of the Reverend Jesse Lee*, 282.
[102] *Minutes* of the New York Conference, 1818.
[103] *Asbury's Journal*, II, 782.

APPENDIX

According to the Journal of Joseph Pilmore, an early itinerant Methodist preacher, the first meetings of African Methodists, separately held, in New York City took place as early as January 27, 1771, five years after the founding of the Methodist Society in that city. Pilmore writes:

> January 27, 1771: After preaching I met the Negroes apart, and found many of them very happy. God has wrought a most glorious work on many of their souls, and made them witnesses that he is no respecter of persons.

Intermittent meetings were held for the next twenty-five years until the separate society was officially sanctioned and the formal organization of the African Chapel took place. Incorporation followed in 1801 when property was acquired and a building constructed. Of this building Francis Asbury wrote to George Roberts the elder in New York:

> Charleston, South Carolina, February 11, 1797: I am pleased to hear that the house is about (completed) at the 2 mile stone (one of the churches in the New York area); more so to hear that the Africans are about building one; help them all you can.
> . . . .

Five years later Asbury wrote:

> May 25, 1802: My first public appearance in the city was in the African Church . . . a very neat wooden house, but by far too small: my text was Ephes. II, 11-14.

Twenty-six years after the formation of the denomination, partially as a result of the Stillwell Secession the title of the first chapel, Zion was added to the corporate name to prevent confusion with the African Methodist movement originating in Philadelphia.

Printed in the USA
CPSIA information can be obtained
at www.ICGtesting.com
LVHW021827251123
764904LV00049B/1676